How to Study Religion

How to Study Religion

A Guide for the Curious

First Edition

Stephen Werner, Ph.D.

cognella®
SAN DIEGO

Bassim Hamadeh, CEO and Publisher
David Miano, Acquisitions Editor
Michelle Piehl, Senior Project Editor
Berenice Quirino, Associate Production Editor
Emely Villavicencio, Senior Graphic Designer
Stephanie Kohl, Licensing Associate
Natalie Piccotti, Director of Marketing
Kassie Graves, Vice President of Editorial
Jamie Giganti, Director of Academic Publishing

Cover image copyright © 2015 iStockphoto LP/shaunl.

Printed in the United States of America.

cognella® | ACADEMIC PUBLISHING
3970 Sorrento Valley Blvd., Ste. 500, San Diego, CA 9212

Brief Contents

Detailed Contents

Appendix: More interesting Topics in Religion 223

How to Study Religion: Bibliography

Index

INTRODUCTION

WELCOME TO THE study of religion! This book provides a foundation to get you started. Anyone wanting to learn the basics of religion will find it helpful. It is also designed for use in a college or high school *Introduction to Religion* or *World Religions* course. After reading this book, it is hoped you will continue learning about religion.

All readers should keep in mind that religion is very complicated. Religions are diverse and complex. Many religions exist around the world, and often within each religion there are many groups, sometimes with very different beliefs. Just driving down the road looking at church buildings offers a sample of the many groups that exist.

This book tries to keep things simple. After reading it the reader can go on to learn more of the detail and complexity of religion. If the book is used in class the teacher will expand upon the concepts. Also, this text can be used in class along with other books or primary readings of religious texts. This book is a foundation on which the reader can build a more complete understanding of religion. Just remember that all the complexity is still out there.

FIGURE 0.1 The Buddha

Written with an American audience in mind, this book does not treat all topics with the same level of detail. For example, more detail is given about the Bible than Buddhist writings. This text does not perfectly balance the amount of information about each religion. Rather, it is based on two principles that guide good teaching: 1) take readers and students where they are, and 2) build on their existing knowledge.

If successful, this book will provide readers with the basics for studying religion. It is hoped you will want to learn more beyond this book about the religions of the world. Be curious!

This book has three goals: 1) teach the basics of the religions of the world, 2) teach how to study religion, and 3) encourage readers to think about religion. Many people in their religious upbringing were not encouraged to think. Often in religious training people are told what they should believe and how they should act without much reasoning as to why. Have you ever been to a religious service where a minister, priest, a rabbi asked for questions? Some religions discourage people from thinking. This book wants you to question and think.

Credit

- Fig. 0.1: Copyright © Bernard Gagnon (CC BY-SA 3.0) at https://commons. wikimedia.org/wiki/File:Buddha_Statue,_Sanchi_01.jpg.

DEFINING RELIGION

A. THE DEFINITION OF RELIGION

No one has come up with a perfect definition of the word "religion." No definition covers all the groups we consider to be religions. If religion is defined as "belief in God," then religions that believe in more than one god do not fit the definition. If religion is "belief in God or many gods" then religions that see a world full of spirits and certain kinds of Buddhism do not fit.

Many things, however, are hard to define. Can you define "sport"? If "sport" is playing with a ball, then hockey is left out. If "sport" requires a team, then golf is left out. If "sport" is about enjoyment and recreation then why do professional athletes have to get paid so much to play?

This problem of how to define "religion" is solved by listing the typical elements in religion, but realizing that not every religion has all these elements. (The same strategy would work for "sport.")

Religions typically have—but not always—these elements: belief in God or multiple gods or divine beings, belief in spirits, belief in an afterlife, a belief in heaven or hell, a belief in revealed truth, a set of beliefs sometimes known as doctrine or dogma, religious beliefs sometimes set down as a written creed, a moral code—sometimes this moral code is given to humans by a divine being, sacred places and buildings, a founder, saints or holy figures or as examples to follow, religious ceremonies and rituals, holy days and holy seasons, prayer or meditation, religious music, sacred writings, ministers, priests, and leaders.

FIGURE 1.1 Guru Nanak, founder of the Sikh religion.

"Religion" is a noun. "Religious" is an adjective such as "She is a religious person." The word "secular" is used for something that is nonreligious. A private college might be part of a religious tradition. A public university is secular, since it has no religious connection.

B. MAJOR RELIGIONS AND MAJOR TRADITIONS

Of the more than seven billion people on the planet, more than five billion are religious. A huge range exists among religious people as to how seriously they take religion. Some are nominally religious ("nominal" means "in name only"). Others are causally or occasionally religious. For example, some Christians only go to church on Christmas and Easter. Many people are very consistent in their religious devotion such as going to services weekly and belonging to a local community. Devout Muslims pray every day and go to a mosque on Fridays.

Many others are so devoted to their religion that it becomes the most important thing in their lives. But there are also religious fanatics who take their religion too seriously. Some fanatics hurt others who do not believe the way they do or who do not display the same level of intense religious belief.

Studying religion is difficult because religion has a very long history and because there are thousands of religions and religious groups. Some are tiny, some are huge. There are more than two billion Christians, more than 1.8 billion Muslims, and more than one billion Hindus in the world. There are also many groups that contain a handful of people. And there are religious groups of every size in between. So how can all this complexity be organized and studied?

The first step is to look at the major religions of the world: (in alphabetical order) Buddhism, Christianity, Hinduism, Islam, Judaism, and Sikhism. Each of these religions has more than ten million people and has either a founder or agreed-upon set of core beliefs.[1]

The second step is to be aware of three major religious categories that include many people: Chinese traditional religion (400 million), ethnic religions (more than 300 million), and African traditional religions (100 million). Within each of these categories there is such great diversity of beliefs and practices that it is impossible to describe them beyond noting common themes. This book includes a description of Chinese traditional religion. Ethnic religions and African tribal religions will not be covered.

---

[1] Admittedly this definition is arbitrary and people could argue over the extent of "agreed-upon core beliefs" in these religions.

The third step is be aware of the many smaller religions that will only be touched on briefly in this book such as Native American religion, Bahá'í, Cao Dai, Jainism, Neo-Paganism, Shinto, Tenrikyo, Unitarian Universalism, and Zoroastrianism.

C. INACTIVE RELIGIONS

There are also ancient religions that are not practiced anymore such as the Greek, Roman, Egyptian, and Aztec religions. These religions have had great influence on our culture. Many people know about the Greek gods such as Zeus and Apollo or know the story of Hercules. A tourist in Greece will see the ruins of many temples to the gods. Most people know something about ancient Egyptian religion and why the pyramids were built.

Sometimes these religions are called "dead religions" or "extinct religions." Long ago these religions were very active with many participants. But these religions are not exactly dead; they still influence people, even if most people do not believe in them. Also, small groups of people still hold to the beliefs and some of the practices of these religions.

For example, there are people who still pray to the Egyptian goddess Isis. In Central America, the Mayan religion reached its peak about a thousand years ago. Mayan civilization is long gone, yet many beliefs and practices still go on. There still are Mayan timekeepers who use the ancient Mayan calendar and count out time using beans!

D. DIFFERENT TYPES OF RELIGION

Religions can be divided by type. To study religion a person needs a basic vocabulary on the various types of religion. The starting point is the word "theism." It comes from the Greek word "theos," which means "god." So, theism is the belief that God exists. But it can also mean the belief in more than one god.

To help sort out the various types of religion, the word "theism" is changed by adding prefixes for the various religions to create words such as "monotheism" and "polytheism."

A little review of word construction might be helpful for some readers. In English a basic word such as "do" can be changed into the words "undo" and "redo." The word "hope" can be changed into "hopeful" and "hopeless." In these examples, "do" and "hope" are called the root word.

A "prefix" is something put before the root to change the meaning. So "un" and "re" are prefixes that go before the root "do" and create the words "undo" and "redo." A suffix is placed after the word. "Ful" and "less" are suffixes placed after the root "hope" to create the words "hopeful" and "hopeless."

Even the word "prefix" has a prefix in it! "Pre" means to "come before." In sports, the time before the season is called the preseason. The *Pregame Show* is, of course, before the game.

1. Monotheism

"Mono" mean "one." The prefix "mono" is added to "theism" to create the word "monotheism," which is the belief in God and only one God. Three major religions are labeled as monotheism: Christianity, Islam, and Judaism.

The word "monotheism" can be turned into an adjective: "monotheistic." A person who believes in monotheism is a monotheist.

2. Polytheism

"Poly" means "many." In geometry a "polygon" is a many-sided figure. Polytheism is the belief in many gods. Each god is a separate being. Inactive religions such as ancient Greek religion, ancient Roman religion, and Aztec religion provide the best examples of polytheism.

The Greeks believed in gods such as Zeus, Apollo, and Aphrodite. The Romans believed in gods such as Jupiter, Apollo, Venus, and Pluto. The Aztec god names are long and hard to pronounce such as the plumed serpent god *Quetzalcoatl*.

The word "polytheism" can be turned into an adjective: "polytheistic." And a person who believes in polytheism is a polytheist.

An important word to know when discussing polytheism is "pantheon." The Greek word for god, "theos," also gives the root "theon." "Pan" is the Greek word for "all." So "pantheon" means "all the gods." (In sports there are the Pan American Games for athletes from all the countries in North America, Central America, and South America. Many colleges have Greek fraternities. Sometimes they form a group to work together called the Panhellenic Council for all the Greek fraternities. "Hellenic" means "Greek.")

A pantheon is a list of all the gods in a polytheistic religion. The Greek Pantheon includes Zeus, Hera, Apollo, Aphrodite, and dozens more.

FIGURE 1.2 The Pantheon in Rome, Italy

FIGURE 1.3 The Parthenon in Athens, Greece.

In Rome there is an ancient temple called the Pantheon. It was built as the Temple to "All the Gods."

But do not get your ancient temples confused. There is another famous temple in Athens, Greece, called the Parthenon. It was dedicated to the goddess Athena, and the city of Athens is named after her. In mythology Athena was a virgin. The Greek word for virgin is "parthenos." That is why her temple is called the Parthenon.

3. Pantheism

Pantheism is an important type of religion, although it is hard to explain. (Also, it is easy to mix up the word pantheism with the word pantheon.) Pantheism is the belief that "All is God" or "God is All." God and the universe are the same thing. God is the universe. A number of famous people, such as the Dutch philosopher Baruch Spinoza (1632–1677), and American writers Ralph Waldo Emerson (1803–1882) and Henry David Thoreau (1817–1862), were pantheists. Some forms of what is called New Age Religion are pantheistic.

For monotheists the universe is something made by God. For pantheists, God is the universe. Monotheists often believe that when a person dies he or she goes to heaven to be with God. In heaven a person would still have self-awareness and memory of one's life before death. A pantheist on the other hand might believe that on death one's energy is absorbed into the universe which is God and there is no self-awareness after death.

4. Monism

Now, what do we do about Hinduism, the religion of India? Is it polytheism? Hinduism has hundreds of gods such as Shiva, Vishnu, and Ganesha. It resembles polytheism. This gets a little difficult. In Hinduism each god is not a separate being. Each god is an aspect or a part of a something greater called Brahman.

In Hinduism all the gods are part of Brahman, so there is only one reality. In fact, not only are all the gods part of Brahman but everything in the universe is part of Brahman. Everything is part of Brahman. And everything is Brahman. Therefore, Hinduism is in its own category: monism. "Monism" comes from "mono," which means one. Monism is the belief that everything is one.

If you are confused about Hinduism, do not worry. You will read more about it later.

5. Animism

Another category of religions is "animism." This word comes from the Latin word *anima*, which means "soul" or "spirit." The word animism is used for religions that see the world filled with spirits. Animals have spirits and humans have spirits. Even streams, clouds, and mountains can have spirits. Many traditional religions such as Native American religion, African tribal religion, and the Japanese religion of Shinto are examples of animism.

6. Buddhism

What about Buddhism? Well, Buddhism is complicated. There are different forms of Buddhism. Some types of Buddhism would fit under monotheism, some types of Buddhism fit under polytheism, and some types of Buddhism do not believe in gods at all. Buddhism will be covered later.

E. TERMS FOR NONBELIEVERS

1. Atheism

This is a list of types of religion. But it is important to know the terms for those who are not religious: atheism and agnosticism.

In English, an "a" before a word sometimes means "not." (So "a" can be used as a prefix.) In biology there are two types of reproduction: sexual and asexual. "Asexual" means "no sex." When a cell divides it reproduces without sex. This is asexual reproduction.

Theism is belief in God or gods. If an "a" is placed before "theism," the word "atheism" is created, which means "no god." Atheism is the belief that there is no God.

Atheists do not believe in God or gods. Typically, atheists do not believe in a life after death. Atheists typically believe that when we die everything comes to an end: our identity, our sense of self, and even our memory.

The many types of atheists will be discussed in Chapter 16.

2. Agnosticism

Another word to learn is "agnosticism," Agnosticism is the view of people who say they do not know if God exists. It comes from the Greek word "gnosis," which means "knowledge." Again, an "a" in front of the root means "not." Therefore, agnosticism is to "not know" if God exists. A person who holds to agnosticism is an agnostic.

There are several types of agnostics: personal, theoretical, and militant. What is the difference? The personal agnostic describes his or her own doubts without needing to pass judgment on other people's beliefs. A personal agnostic might say, "I don't know if God exists. If you believe in God, that is fine. That is your business. But I just don't know if God exists."

The next type of agnostic goes further and believes that no one can know if God exists. This is the theoretical agnostic who believes that knowledge of God is impossible and those people who believe in God are deceiving themselves. "I can't prove that God exists, and you can't either. At least I am honest with myself. There is no way anyone can know if God exists."

There is a third category: the militant agnostic whose mission is to get religious people to admit they do not know if God exists.

Agnosticism is a common attitude in today's world, especially personal agnosticism. It is hard to know for sure how many people are agnostics since there are very few organizations for agnostics. Also, there are many people who start by saying they believe in God, but after a few moments of honest talk will admit they really do not know whether God exists or not. Such people might be agnostics despite the fact they do not call themselves agnostics.

3. Humanism

Humanism is concerned with human beings. It strives to make humans better and promote ethical values. It encourages people to treat themselves, one another, and the physical world in better ways. A humanist is one who believes in humanism.

There are various kinds of humanists. Many humanists do not believe in God. Yet they believe that humans need to follow moral rules. Religious people sometimes criticize humanists, claiming you have to have God to give moral rules such as "Do not kill" and to enforce them, even with punishments after one dies. Humanists would answer that moral rules should make sense on their own. They do not have to be revealed by God. Also, humanists often say that humans need to follow moral rules because they are good things to do, not because we are afraid of punishment in a next life.

Since many humanists do not believe in God they can be called "secular humanists." Remember that "secular" means "nonreligious." But since the term "secular humanism" has sometimes been used as a criticism of humanists by religious

FIGURE 1.4 Humanist—Desiderius Erasmus (1466–1536)

people, most humanists just call themselves "humanists." Many humanists call themselves "ethical humanists."

There are several organizations that promote humanism and trying to create a better world such as the Ethical Society. There are also religious humanists. Some people call themselves "Jewish humanists" or "Christian humanists." They believe in God but emphasize the importance of having concern for the human condition.

DISCUSSION QUESTIONS

1. Do you know anything about inactive religions such as ancient Greek and Roman religion? Do you know any Greek or Roman myths?

2. Which major religions do you know something about? Which religions do you know little about?

3. What do you think about the ideas of atheism, agnosticism, and humanism?

4. What do you want to learn about religion? What questions do you have about religion?

5. What recent news ideas items deal with religion?

Credits

CHAPTER 2

IMPORTANT VOCABULARY FOR UNDERSTANDING RELIGION

CHAPTER 1 INTRODUCED KEY vocabulary for classifying different religions and for identifying nonbelievers. This chapter explains more vocabulary for understanding the various religions.

A. THEOLOGY

The word "theology" needs to be defined since theology is a key part of many religions. To keep this simple, we will first define theology in monotheistic terms. Theology is made of two Greek words: "theos," which means God, and "logos," which means "word." Literally, theology is "words about God," or the study of God. Notice that "logos" gives the suffix "ology," which means "the study of." Therefore, "biology" is the study of "life," which is "bio."

To say, however, that theology is the study of God may not clarify things. There seems to be no way to study God directly. God cannot be seen. Most believers do not believe that God speaks to them directly. There is no way to interview or email God.

So, what can we do? One answer is to say that although one cannot study God directly, one can study what humans experience in their religious faith. Therefore, theology can be defined as "the critical reflection on the human experience of God." "Critical" means to take a serious and honest look at something.

No definition is perfect. The difficulty with this definition is how does one know what is an authentic experience of God and what is not authentic? People have done a lot of crazy things in the name of religion. Thus, an alternative definition of theology could be "the critical reflection on what humans claim to be their experience of God."

Another possible definition is that theology is a "reflection on the divine." Yet another is to say that "theology is the thinking part of a religion." There are many parts to religions: ceremonies, organizations, and moral beliefs. Theology is the thinking out and explaining of the beliefs of a religion. Notice that these definitions of theology describe it as a process.

FIGURE 2.1 Saint John the theologian

A final definition is that "theology" is the inner logic within a religion. Religions start with certain beliefs that form the basis of the religion. Theology is the inner logic that comes with these beliefs.

For example, in Islam, one starting belief is that Muhammad is the final revelation of God. Muslim theology looks at the Qur'an, which was revealed to Muhammad, and at traditions about Muhammad called Hadiths. From these sources Muslim theology works out how Muslims are to live out their faith.

Two other words come from theology. It can be an adjective: "theological." Also, a person who does theology in a serious way is called a "theologian."

The word "theology" can also be used for non-monotheistic religions in which it refers to the beliefs, concepts, and inner logic of a religion such as in Hindu and Buddhist theologies.

Some tribal religions and folk traditions reject the concept of theology. For some, the spirit world is to be lived and experienced. Since the spirit world is beyond explanation, any attempt to analyze it and create a theology of it goes against the very nature of the spirit world.

B. DOCTRINE, DOGMA, APOLOGETICS, CATECHESIS

Other terms are also helpful since they describe efforts to list or explain the theological beliefs of religions. "Doctrine" and "dogma" are words used for the teachings of some religious groups. For some people dogma carries a negative feel; to others it implies a rigidity of thought. But the word also has a neutral meaning.

For most people doctrine and dogma mean the same thing: the teaching and beliefs of a religion or a church. Some groups have spelled out their doctrine in great detail, such as the *Catechism of the Catholic Church*. If you are interested, it can be viewed online.

"Apologetics" is a helpful word. It resembles the word "apologize" but has a different meaning. The word comes from early Christianity when writers defended their faith in works called "apologies." For example, Justin the Martyr, who lived in the second century, wrote his *First Apology* and *Second Apology* to defend Christianity.[1] Apologetics is speaking or writing to defend one's religious beliefs or to explain it to people who disagree with it or who do not understand it. In this sense, apologetics is not about saying "I'm sorry."

Here are additional words used in some Christian traditions. "Catechesis" is the basic teaching of a religion given to people joining a religion. A person in such a program is called a "Catechumen." A book of the basic teachings is called a "catechism." A most famous example was the *Baltimore Catechism* used by millions of American Roman Catholics up to the 1960s. Martin Luther wrote both a *Large Catechism* and a *Small Catechism* in the 1500s.

C. HERESY AND ORTHODOXY

Since in most traditions there are disagreements over what is the correct belief or theology, two important words need to be defined: "heresy" and "orthodoxy." Heresy means wrong belief and orthodoxy means right belief. Since heresy is wrong belief, one who holds the wrong belief is a "heretic," and views that are wrong are called "heretical."

Orthodoxy means right belief, which is also called "orthodox" belief. People who hold the right belief are called orthodox.

Note that the word is used in the title of certain groups. For example, among Christians there are denominations such as the Greek Orthodox and the Russian Orthodox. Among Jews, one branch is called Orthodox Judaism, and its followers are called Orthodox Jews.

One last and very important thing must be noted about the words heresy and orthodox. These are not terms of fact but of judgment. Therefore, the terms depend on who is using them. One person's orthodoxy is another person's heresy. (Note that whether a place is east or west depends on where you are standing.) Judgments of heresy and orthodoxy depend on whom you are asking.

D. DENOMINATIONS, SECTS, AND CULTS

The following words are important for trying to organize all the religious groups that exist. Within each major religion there are various groups and divisions. What do we call the different pieces?

---

1   There are also non-Christian examples such as Plato's *Apology* in which Socrates defended himself.

1. Denomination

This word is helpful in Christianity where different kinds of Christians have created separate organizations or share a common history. There are Methodist, Lutheran, and Baptist denominations. And many more exist. Just take note of all the church buildings as you drive around and look at the signs out front.

The word "denominate" means to give a name to something. *Nomen* is the Latin word for name. So "denominations" are names given to different groups within a religion.

In American Christianity, however, there is a reaction against this term by some churches. Some groups see themselves as "true Christians" and not just one group among many, so they reject the term "denomination" and call themselves "nondenominational." This means that they are not part of a traditional denomination such as Lutheran, Methodist, or Baptist. Also, many nondenominational churches are independent congregations.

There was a similar movement in the 1800s to just be "Christians," and so the Disciples of Christ was created. Today this group is seen as one more Christian denomination.

For this book the word denomination is used simply to mean an organized group within a major religion or a group within a major religion that has a common history.

2. Sect

Another term for a religious unit is "sect," which is harder to pin down than "denomination." It is useful when the religion itself lacks many organized groups. Christianity is filled with many organized groups that we can separate as denominations. Most Buddhists do not belong to organized groups with membership lists. Yet in Buddhism there are groups that have different beliefs or follow a specific teacher. The word sect could be used to describe these various groups. In Mormonism there are various splinter groups that can be called sects.

Sometimes the word sect seems to have a negative feel. Some people use it to refer to those who have the wrong beliefs, while others might be offended if someone called their religious group a sect.

Words such as denomination and sect are attempts to organize the study of all the varieties within religion. Try sometime to divide all the things we call sports into categories. You may find it difficult.

3. Cult

The word "cult" has a long history in English and it refers to a group of people devoted to a particular religious place or person or cause. This use of the word is simply a description with no negative judgment. For example, in Italy one could speak of those Catholics who were devoted to Saint Francis of Assisi as the cult of Saint Francis. Ancient Romans who prayed to the Egyptian goddess Isis belonged to the cult of Isis. However, the use of the word has taken on a negative meaning.

The word has been used for several groups such as the People's Temple, the Branch Davidians, and Heaven's Gate. These religious communities came to disastrous ends.

Today the word is used for groups in which a leader has a very strong, unhealthy, emotional control over members of the group. Most people use the word to describe a religious group that controls the entire life of members and controls their thinking. Typically, members of a cult are not allowed to question the leader or to leave the group. Often the members live together in a place isolated from the rest of society. Often the leader's influence on members includes inappropriate sexual relations with many of the members.

Keep in mind that cult is a loaded word with many associations. Since there is no precise definition, cult is more of a word of negative judgment and should be used very carefully. Often the community space where such a group lives is called a "compound," which is another loaded word.

One goal of the study of religion is to get people to think and speak in a more precise way. Notice in life that some words help us clarify and make sense of things; other words add to the confusion. Being careful with words such as sect and cult can improve the discussion.

E. CHURCH

"Church" is an ordinary word, mostly used by Christians, with several meanings. Often these meanings reflect different theological views, and often Christian denominations have different understandings of the word.

For a Christian the word church can mean a building, a local church community, or the entire denomination. Thus, for example, a person could say, "My church meets in an old church built in 1890 and we are members of the Lutheran Church." Notice the three meanings of the word. The first meaning of church is the local community of believers, the second meaning is the building, and the third meaning is the denomination.

Christians have argued over the meanings of the term. For Catholics the term often means the institution of the Catholic Church. When a Cath-olic says church, often the pope comes to mind.

FIGURE 2.2 A Christian Church

When a Protestant says church it often means the people coming together to pray and worship.

F. DIVINITY, DIVINE, DEITY, AND DEMIGOD

"Divinity," "divine," "deity," and "demigod" are four words often used in discussing various religions. For polytheists, a divinity is a god. Since they believe in many gods, there are many divinities. Monotheists believe in only one divinity: God. The adjective "divine," has several meanings. It can mean "very good." Sometimes we say, "You look divine!" or "This tastes divine." There is even a candy called Divinity Fudge.

"Divine" can also mean to be "like" God or to be godlike. But you have to be careful about the meaning of "like." To be like something is not to be it. In other words, if someone is "godlike" it means he or she is not God, but in some aspect similar to God. The final meaning is that to be "divine" means to be God. God is divine.

The word "deity" is pronounced with a long "e" sound: "dee-it-tee," or with a long "a" sound: "day-it-tee." It is based on the Latin word for God, *Deus*. So deity is another word for God. For monotheists, God is the only deity. In polytheism, a deity is any god or goddess. The plural is "deities."

In mythology there are beings called demigods. Demigods appear in many Greek myths. A demigod is usually half divine and half human. In many Greek myths the god Zeus is the father, and a human woman such as Danae is the mother. The child is a demigod such as Perseus, the son of Danae. A demigod often has special abilities or powers.

Usually in Greek mythology a demigod is mortal and will eventually die. But there are exceptions in Greek mythology.

But do not get demigod confused with the word "demagogue." A demagogue is a leader or speaker who gets people all fired up, often for the wrong reasons.

FIGURE 2.3 Perseus On Pegasus Hastening to the Rescue of Andromeda, by Frederic Leighton (1895-96)

G. MORTALITY AND IMMORTALITY

Two words need to be clarified: "mortal" and "immortal." To be mortal is to have to die. Humans and animals are mortal; they all die. "Im" means "not," so immortal means "not die." In most religions, God or the gods cannot die.[2] Monotheists believe that God is immortal; God lives forever and cannot die.

Polytheists believe their gods cannot die. In fact, a big difference between gods and every other living thing is that gods cannot die, but everything else can.

Regarding humans, it can get complicated. In most religions it is thought that the human body is mortal and it will die. Some people, however, believe humans have souls that will not die. Thus, humans have immortal souls. Many people believe that after a person's mortal body dies the immortal soul leaves the body and lives in heaven with God (or hell if they were bad).

Mortal refers to death. Look at the French word for death, *mort*. The Spanish word is *muerte*. The English words morgue, mortician, and mortuary have the same root. Morticia was the wife of Gomez Addams in the movie and old TV show *The Addams Family.*

And there is the word "mortgage." In a mortgage you "kill the loan off" over time. It does not mean, "Getting this mortgage paid off will be the death of me!"

In religious traditions there are a few people who did not die. Utnapishtim, in the ancient Mesopotamian story the *Epic of Gilgamesh*, was immortal. Elijah, in the Hebrew Scriptures/Old Testament, was taken into heaven in a fiery chariot and did not die. Some Christians believe in the Assumption of Mary, the mother of Jesus, that she was taken bodily into heaven without dying.

H. SPIRITUAL, SPIRITUALITY, SPIRITUALISM

1. Spiritual

"Spiritual" is a difficult word to define since people use it in many ways and often to describe things that are very hard to describe. The first question about a "spiritual experience" is whether it is something that is just an emotional experience within a person, or an experience within a person of something that is greater. In other words, is the spiritual experience just the emotions and thoughts within a person or is it an experience of something beyond such as God, an angel, or a higher power? Some people talk about spiritual experiences that are powerful emotional experiences but without reference to any beings such as God, an angel, or a higher power.

---

2   In the *Star Trek* series, the Klingons actually killed their gods.

Sometimes people use spiritual as an alternative to "religious." Some might say, "I am spiritual, not religious." What this typically means is that a person has a belief and perhaps an experience of God or some higher power but not as part of a religious group. In fact, some people do not find God in organized religion and regular religious services. They find God on their own.

2. Spirituality

"Spirituality" is a label for one's own personal religious experience or religious devotion. What a person experiences in going to a synagogue, church, mosque, or temple could also be part of his or her spirituality.

A person could, however, regularly go a synagogue, church, mosque, or temple and not get anything out of it. If that person also lacked a private prayer life, he or she would not have a spirituality. Another person with a private prayer life would have a spirituality.

Use of the term spirituality is somewhat recent. It became more commonly used around the mid-twentieth century. Older words were used to describe a person's religious faith, such as "devotion" or "piety." If you had piety you were a "pious" person. The reason spirituality was not used in the past was that it sounded much like the word "spiritualism." Most religious people rejected spiritualism.

Keeping the Words Straight in Your Mind

If you find all these words confusing just remember that in life we often separate similar-sounding terms. An eight-year-old child who likes baseball can easily explain the difference between a double, a double play, and a doubleheader.

3. Spiritualism

Spiritualism is the tradition of trying to contact the spirits of dead people. Sometimes the goal is to get guidance for the living from the dead spirits. Sometimes the goal is to communicate with loved ones who have died. (The popular 1990 movie *Ghost* is a story about contact with the dead. But keep in mind it is a movie with a made-up story.) Spiritualism is described in more detail in Chapter 16.

I. SOULS AND SPIRITS

The words "soul" and "spirit" are often used in religion. They are not easy words to define nor explain. For many people these are two words for the same thing. Your spirit is the same thing as your soul.

But there are some Christians, who after reading the Epistles in the New Testament, say that humans have both a soul and spirit. (An epistle is a letter. There are twenty-one of these letters in the Christian Bible.) A number of websites explain the different views.

In this book, soul and spirit will be used interchangeably. This means they are being used as two words for the same thing and that a person only has one.

Usually the concept of a soul is understood as something within you that is different from your body. Many in different religions believe you have a soul and that when your body dies your soul leaves your body. For example, many monotheists believe the soul of a good person goes to heaven when that person dies and continues to exist forever. When a person dies the body clearly does not go to heaven. A body is either buried where it rots away or cremated (burned) and turned to ashes. So, what goes to heaven? For many religious people the answer is clear: "The soul goes to heaven."

1. Animal Souls?

Do only humans have souls? Most monotheists such as Christians, Muslims, and Jews think of the soul as something that only humans have. But other views exist.

Animists such as Native Americans believe both humans and animals have souls. Animists often typically use the word spirit instead of soul. For animists who lived by hunting it was important to treat killed animals such as bison, elk, caribou, seals, and walruses with respect so as to welcome the spirit of the animal into the human world, or to thank the spirit of the animal for giving its life so that humans can eat.

Animists also have a less defined notion of what is a spirit. Thus, natural places such as streams and mountains can also have spirits.

2. Reincarnation

Hindus—followers of Hinduism—believe humans have souls. When a human dies the soul leaves the body and goes into another human body. This is the Hindu belief in reincarnation. But animals also have souls and these are the same souls that can be in human bodies. If a person lives a bad life that person's soul can go into an animal. Animal souls will eventually be reborn as human souls. We will discuss reincarnation more in Chapter 8.

J. IMMANENCE AND TRANSCENDENCE

Two important words in religion are "immanence" and "transcendence." Immanence is the idea that the divine reality is present in the physical world. Transcendence is the idea that the divine presence is beyond the physical world. Although these words can be used in most religions, here are two monotheist examples of the words.

A monotheist who speaks of finding God in nature or finding God in one's heart is speaking of immanence. A monotheist who speaks of God as creator of the universe and the final judge of everyone is speaking of transcendence. These two words are nouns. The adjective forms of these words are "immanent" and "transcendent." To put this simply, an immanent God is close, accessible, loving, and welcoming. A transcendent God is distant, far away, and to be feared.

Having learned these key vocabulary terms, you are now ready to learn a few more basic tools to study religion.

DISCUSSION QUESTIONS

1. What new vocabulary terms did you learn?

2. Can you name some of the churches or other religious buildings near where you live? Are there some buildings near you that you are unclear what religion or denomination meets there? Can you find out what they are?

3. Have you ever met people of different religious backgrounds than your own?

4. What do you think about the existence of souls? Do humans have them? Do animals have them?

5. Have you seen any movies about people with religious beliefs other than your own?

Credits

- Fig. 2.1: Source: https://commons.wikimedia.org/wiki/File:Ritzos_ Andreas_-_St_John_the_Theologian_writing_his_Revelations_on_an_ open_scroll_-_Google_Art_Project.jpg.
- Fig. 2.2: Source: https://commons.wikimedia.org/wiki/File:Second_Free_ Baptist_Church.jpg.
- Fig. 2.3: Source: https://commons.wikimedia.org/wiki/File:Leighton,_ Frederic_-_Perseus_On_Pegasus_Hastening_To_the_Rescue_of_Androm- eda_-_1895-96.jpg.

CHAPTER 3

BASIC TOOLS FOR STUDYING RELIGION

A. ELEMENTS OF RELIGION

Sometimes people describe four basic elements of each religion. These are called the Four C's: *creed*, *code*, *ceremonies*, and *community*. Each religion has these elements if you look for them.

1. Creed

"Creed" refers to the beliefs of a religion. Every religion has a set of beliefs. For some religions their creed is not written down. Baptist Christians, for example, reject written creeds although they have a set of religious beliefs. Other religions actually have a written statement called a "Creed." The most famous is the Christian statement the *Nicene Creed*.

2. Code

"Code" refers to the moral rules of each religion. All religions have beliefs on what is right and wrong. Several religions base their moral code on the Ten Commandments. But each religion has rules on how to live one's life and for how to follow its religion. This means there are two types: 1) moral rules on how to live, such as "Do not kill" or "Do not steal"; and 2) rules on how the religion works, such as "Be quiet when in church" or "In this church the local minister is appointed by the bishop."

3. Ceremony

"Ceremony" refers to the rituals of religion. Some examples of common religious rituals include baptism, weekly visits to a mosque, a Jewish bar mitzvah, or visiting a Hindu temple to pray. A ceremony can also be a simple prayer service.

Even groups that say, "We don't do rituals," usually have some type of service that follows a set pattern. This is a ritual even if it is simple. Rituals can be simple or they can be very elaborate.

A ritual is a repeated way of doing something that gives meaning. Rituals are important for people and are not limited to religion. Singing the national anthem before a baseball game, for instance, is a ritual. Many people find it meaningful although it has no effect on the actual game. Many people have rituals around holidays such as Thanksgiving. Often family members resist changing the rituals since they have so much meaning.

Here are the various categories of religious ceremonies with some examples:

Daily rituals

Daily prayer

Weekly rituals

Going to church on Sunday, or a synagogue on the Sabbath, or a mosque on Friday

Seasonal rituals

Rosh Hashanah (Jewish New Year) in the fall
Passover in spring
Christmas
Easter
Holi (a Hindu festival in spring)

Rituals to mark life stages

Birth
Adulthood
Marriage
Death

Special Events

When a new bishop is installed,
Memorials to mark tragedies, such as those after 9/11

4. Community

A "community" is the group that comes together for the rituals of a religion. Many communities ask their members to register at the local church or synagogue. For many religious people their local church, mosque, synagogue, temple, or meeting place is their primary religious community.

Many religious communities are more structured, while some communities are informal. For example, some small churches are made up of people who live near a church that has no connection to other churches.

For Roman Catholics it is very different. A Catholic is a member of a local parish that is then part of a bigger area called a "diocese" or "archdiocese." But every diocese

FIGURE 3.1   Saint Peter's Basilica in Rome.

and archdiocese is part of the greater Catholic Church headed by the pope in Rome. Many Catholics feel part of a greater community.

A Catholic on vacation may go to church in a different city but find the service almost exactly like the service in his or her home parish. Many Catholics who visit Vatican City, the headquarters of the Catholic Church in Rome, feel this is the headquarters and symbol of the church to which they belong.

FIGURE 3.2   The Ka'ba in Mecca.

The Muslim sense of community varies from place to place but the basic element of community is the local mosque. However, once in a lifetime a good Muslim is expected to make a pilgrimage, called the "Hajj," to the city of Mecca in Saudi Arabia. Here a pilgrim often has a powerful experience of being part of the world-wide community of Islam called the Ummah.

Most religion is practiced within communities of people. But there are some exceptions. Sometimes religious monks live complete solitary lives, but such people are rare. More commonly, monks who spend a lot of time by themselves in prayer are still connected to other monks doing the same thing.

B. COUNTING MEMBERS

No one has figured out a perfect way to count how many people belong to specific religions. There are, for instance, many kinds of Christians. One Christian group is called "Methodist." So, if you wanted to count how many Methodists there are, who would you count? Would you only count those who are registered as members of the church? But what about registered members who do not go to church very often? Would you count inactive members or not? Would you count those people who are not registered members but still go to church, or non-registered members who still believe in the teachings of Methodism? And to further complicate it, there are people who claim to be Methodist but have not set foot in a church for many years.

The problem is even more complicated for Buddhism. Typically, in Buddhist countries there are few religious organizations with membership lists. Attendance at ceremonies and shrines is left up to the individual, and many religious practices are private or done within the family. How do you count the number of Buddhists in the world?

Judaism also shows how difficult the question can be. Among Jews there is great disagreement over who is a Jew. It can be defined as an ethnic heritage or a religious heritage. One definition is that a Jew is someone with a Jewish mother. But this says nothing about religious beliefs.

Jews can be defined as a people but that does not give much information. Many Jews are not religious, and some Jews do not believe in God. And to further complicate the problem, some Jews are uncomfortable trying to count who is Jewish because of the Holocaust in Europe under Nazi Germany in the 1930s and 1940s when the Nazis used census records to create lists of Jewish people to be eliminated.[1] (The question of "Who is a Jew?" will be covered in Chapter 5.)

---

1   The Nazis tried to eliminate other groups as well, including Jehovah's Witnesses, Roma (also known as Gypsies), homosexuals, and political opponents.

Therefore, any reference to how many people belong to a religion is a ballpark estimate, unless the number is stated as something that is countable, such as registered members.

Here are some current numbers (as of 2012) of people in the various religious groups that have more than ten million followers.[2] But these numbers are how many people are identified as being part of each religion. These numbers do not try to sort out people who are active in their religion from those who are not.

TABLE 3.1   Number of People in Various Religions

WORLD POPULATION	7.2 BILLION
Christianity	2.4 billion
Islam	1.8 billion
Nonreligious	1.2 billion
Hinduism	1.15 billion
Buddhism	521 million
Chinese traditional religion	394 million
Ethnic religions	300 million
African traditional religions	100 million
Sikhism	30 million
Spiritism	15 million
Judaism	14 million

The "Nonreligious" category includes atheists, agnostics, and nonbelievers. This group is hard to measure since these people typically do not belong to any organization and they use different ways to label their views. This group, however, is a growing percentage of the population in America. Sometimes, nonreligious people are called "nones" because they are not affiliated with any organized religious group. If they had to take a survey about belonging to a religion, they would answer "none of the above."

---

2   These numbers are based on *"The Global Religious Landscape." The Pew Forum on Religion & Public Life, Pew Research Center.* December 18, 2012. The Wikipedia article "List of religious populations" is based on the Pew Study.

Some Big Numbers

When talking about numbers, the size of the Roman Catholic Church should be noted. In the religion called Christianity there are many denominations. The biggest Christian denomination is the Roman Catholic Church, which has about 1.228 billion members. That makes it the largest Christian denomination. It is also the largest organized religious group in the world; no other group comes anywhere close.

The number of Muslims is larger than the Catholic Church, but Muslims typically are not part of any organization. Most mosques are independent of one another.

Also note that the number of Roman Catholics is slightly more than the population of India, the second-largest country, which in 2011 numbered 1.210 billion. In all of human history, the only thing larger than the Roman Catholic Church, in terms of people, is the nation of China, at 1,375 billion. (Granted, this is comparing apples to oranges, it is still interesting to consider the scales involved.)

Also notable is that the Jewish faith is small compared with other religions, although the Jewish religion and the Jewish people have had much influence despite the small numbers.

Finally, an interesting trivia question: What country has the largest Muslim population? The answer is surprising: Indonesia in the South Pacific. (Go online and find a map if you do not know where and how big it is.)

Muslims are found throughout the world. For some people the stereotype of a Muslim is someone from the Middle East. Islam both began and grew in the Middle East but today it can be found everywhere across the globe. Thus, the following point must be emphasized: *Although the majority of people in the Middle East are Muslim, by far more Muslims live outside the Middle East than in the Middle East.* There are huge Muslim populations in Africa and Asia, and large and growing populations in Europe and North America.[3]

C. ATTITUDE

It is helpful to have an open attitude when studying other religions. The fact that you are reading this book indicates you probably already have this attitude. The goal is to try to understand each religion on its own terms and to see why people in that religion believe the way they do. The beliefs of other religions make sense to the people in those religions. A student of religion needs to understand why people in other religions think the way they do.

---

3   Another common stereotype is that all Arabs are Muslims. In fact, "Arab" is an ethnic group and although most Arabs are Muslims, there are also many Arabs who are Christian. Also, Arab Christians can trace their faith back to the earliest periods of Christianity.

It must be said, however, that trying to understand another religion does not mean you have to join that religion or give up your own beliefs. A few people are afraid of studying other religions out of fear they will abandon their own faith and join another religion. That does not occur often.

The goal is to learn how others think. But you can still disagree! To understand someone else's view does not mean you have to embrace those views. The goal is to understand a different set of ideas. There is a desperate need in our time and culture for people to understand the other side. The intense political and cultural struggles of our time could be diminished if this were occurring. However, understanding others views, and why people think the way they do, does not mean you cannot still hold on to your views.

For instance, a devout Christian can learn in detail the beliefs of Islam—and develop an understanding and respect for Islam and Muslims—and still not accept the fundamental Muslim belief that Muhammad received the final revelation from God. On the other hand, a Muslim can understand the basics of Christian belief yet not decide to become a Christian.

The necessary attitudes are an openness to other religious traditions and curiosity about them. Studying religion also requires imagination. We need to imagine how other people see the world. This is a valuable skill in today's world.

One last point is that when devout believers study other religions they often come to better understand their own beliefs.

1. Tolerance

One goal of studying religions is to help people become more tolerant of the differences of others. In many places in both America and Europe, the culture surrounding people has become more diverse. For much of American history many Christians lived amid other Christians. Now many Christians find Muslims and Hindus in the world around them: as neighbors, at work, etc. Many Muslims and Hindus who now live among people of many faiths have parents or grandparents who emigrated from places where everyone had the same culture and religion.

2. The Limits of Tolerance

Understanding, tolerance, and respect for other people—despite our differences—are important and necessary values for our future. But it has to be conceded there are limits to tolerance. Some people have practices that seem to be wrong even if they do not seem wrong to those doing them. Female circumcision is such a practice.

Many people have never heard of this practice and do not know about it, but it exists in some African tribal cultures. A female circumcision, or clitorectomy, removes the clitoris of a young female. It is often done as part of an initiation ritual when a girl becomes a woman. The clitoris is removed with a knife without any anesthetics. (The clitoris is a pea-sized bundle of nerves above the urethral opening, which is above the vagina.)

Male circumcision has a long history and is part of several religious traditions. (A circumcision removes the foreskin from a male penis.) For Jews, circumcision is the bris ceremony, performed when a boy is eight days old. Male circumcision, if done properly, can be painful, but since it is simply removing excess skin and muscle, there are typically no long-term problems.[4] Most people do not have moral objections against male circumcision, but removing the clitoris of a woman removes her later ability to have pleasure during sex. As seen by many people, a clitorectomy is a mutilation of a woman's body that has no justification. It is also seen as a violation of women's rights and women's bodies. Lastly, the experience of a young woman having this done can be quite traumatic.

If the reader is unclear what the words "clitoris," "circumcision," or "foreskin" mean, the articles in Wikipedia with drawings and photos can be helpful.

Another example of a practice seen as wrong by many people is the mistreatment of women by groups such as the Taliban, in Afghanistan. They forbid women to get education and in some cases have thrown acid in the faces of women trying to get an education.

Developing a general attitude of tolerance toward other religions does not require one to accept everything done in the name of religion. Practices that violate human rights can be opposed. Concerned people around the globe are raising awareness about issues such as female circumcision and the treatment of women by the Taliban. The hope is that global awareness will force a change in attitudes by those doing these practices.

A final word of caution must be given. History has many examples of outsiders seeing local religious cultures as wrong and using that judgment as an excuse for invasion, conquest, and domination. Sadly many examples can be given: the Spanish conquest of Central and South America, British conquests around the globe, other European conquests in Africa and the Mideast, and the American conquest of the Native Americans. Often cultural conquest was used to justify political and economic conquest.

The lesson is that raising awareness of unjust practices done in the name of religion is a good thing; however, conquering or dominating other cultures to stop such practices can be a violation of the rights of those practicing their religion. Conquests often create greater injustices than the local practices that were used to justify conquest.

---

4   There are some people who question the morality of male circumcision.

3. Extremists Are Extremists!

Extremists by definition are at the extreme. They are not in the middle. They are not typical. They are not normal. When we hear about religious extremists we have to keep in mind they are not typical representatives of a religion.

The vast majority of Muslims in America saw the September 11, 2001, attackers as extremists who did not represent true Islam. Most American Muslims saw the 9/11 attacks as an attack on themselves and their country.

During the US occupation of Iraq, extremists conducted many suicide bomb attacks. Most of the victims were Iraqi Muslims.

The extremist group ISIS, which has conquered parts of Syria and Iraq with great brutality, does not represent typical Muslims by any means. The vast majority of Muslims do not agree with the group's methods. Also, most of the victims of ISIS are, in fact, Muslims.

Most Christians see the members of the Westboro Baptist church as extremists. The Westboro Baptists are the group that shows up at funerals for American soldiers with protest signs such as "YOU ARE GOING TO HELL" and "AMERICA IS DO OMED." Most Christians understand these are not typical Christians.

Also, most Christians hope that non-Christians will see that the Westboro Baptists do not represent typical Christian values. In the same way, most American Muslims hope that non-Muslims will see that Muslim extremists are not typical Muslims.

In many ways the typical Muslim is a lot like the typical Christian, Jew, Hindu, Sikh, etc. Most religious people want to live in safe, secure, and peaceful places where they can raise their families, be prosperous, and live out their religious faith.

D. WHICH RELIGION IS THE RIGHT ONE?

"What if we pick the wrong religion? Each Sunday we're just making God madder and madder."
—Homer Simpson

In human history there has been much arguing, fighting, injustice, and even killing over the issue of which religion is the right one. Most people believe their religion is the right one. Why belong to a religion if you do not believe it is the right religion? But many people also assume their religion is the right one in God's eyes (this is a monotheist example). Throughout history some have gone further and used this belief to force their religion on others.

Much injustice has been done forcing religion on other people. To many people, it is wrong to do it. The principle of religious freedom rejects forcing religious beliefs on people. Most people around the world accept this principle. Fortunately, many people do not feel the need to force their religion on other people even if they believe other people are wrong.

But even if you reject forcing your religion on someone else, how do you prove that your faith is the right one in God's eyes? If you cannot convince someone that your religion is the right one, how do you prove to him or her that you have the right religion? The answer is that you cannot. God does not send signs to show which religion is the right religion—at least not signs that would convince members of the "wrong" religions that they are wrong.

If you cannot convince someone that your religion is the right one and you accept the moral principle that it is wrong to force religion on another, then you have to accept that others hold different religious beliefs. So how should a religious person think when faced with people with different religious views? Here are some options. (Some of these are based on monotheist views but are easily adapted to other views.)

1. Intolerance
2. Religious Relativism
3. Religious Belief with Tolerance
4. All Religions Are One
5. Accept the Mystery of It

1. Intolerance

The first option is to be intolerant of other religions. A religiously intolerant person might think, "My religion is right and other religions are wrong. If they are close to my religion they are less wrong. But the more different they are from my religion, the more wrong they are." Religious intolerance is often linked to the view that there is only one true religion that can get people into heaven.

Intolerant people often show their intolerance in subtle or not-so-subtle ways. Religious intolerance runs the gamut from unfriendliness to discrimination to violence, ethnic cleansing, and war.

The whole point of studying religions and reading a book such as this, however, is to reject religious intolerance.

2. Religious Relativism

A second option is "religious relativism," which is to say that religion is up to each individual: "My religion is fine with me; your religion is fine with you. That is OK." Religious relativism holds that all religions are equal and no religion is better than another. This attitude is common among many people.

But many people find this an unsatisfactory answer: "My religious beliefs are so important to me that it is hard to believe they are just as good as everyone else's." For example, a Christian who believes Jesus is the Son of God, sent by a loving Father to come to earth to save humans from their sin, might find it hard to accept other religious views as "just as good."

3. Religious Belief with Tolerance

The third option is to believe your religion is the right one and to hold to that. You respect other people's faith and show tolerance and understanding, but you still hold to your beliefs as the right ones. People of strong religious faith can follow this option and need not feel guilty for being true to their beliefs: "My religion is right. You can hold to your beliefs, but I still believe my beliefs are the best." But along with a commitment to one's religion there is a tolerance and acceptance of other religions. There is also a willingness to study and understand other religions and look for areas of common ground with people of other religions to solve some of the problems in our world.

4. All Religions Are One

A fourth option is to believe that "all religions are one." There are several versions of this view. One is the idea that all religious faiths are praying to the same divine reality. Therefore, Muslims, Christians, Jews, Hindus, Sikh, most Buddhists, and followers of native traditions are all worshiping the same divine spirit.[5]

The other version is to hold that all religions are pursuing the same ultimate truth. There is a group that promotes this view: the Vedanta Society. This group, which is an offshoot of Hinduism, believes in the saying, "Truth is one, sages call it by various names."[6] A sage is a teacher. Although religions have different names, they honor the same truth.

5. Accept the Mystery of It

A fifth option is to accept the mystery of the problem and not worry about it. For example, one could believe in God and be aware of all the various religions that have members—most of whom seem to be faithful people trying to live moral lives—and not need an explanation on how it makes sense. It is a mystery. In this view one might believe we cannot know how God looks at all the different people in all their religions. One might even think, "I will leave it to God to sort this out." Along with this view would go attitudes of tolerance, understanding, and respect.

---

5   There are various Buddhist groups. Some Buddhist groups believe in a divine presence in the universe, some do not.

6   This saying is from the *Rig-Veda*, an ancient Hindu writing.

E. ANALYZING AND CATEGORIZING RELIGION

This book is designed to help people study religion. It tries to explain things in a simple and straightforward way. Part of the strategy involves defining terms and sorting things into categories. Most students should find this helpful.

This way of thinking, however, is alien to some religious people. For people who practice tribal religions, such as some Native Americans and thinkers in some Asian religions, this way of thinking is wrong. Trying to explain, make sense, and put into categories a spiritual reality violates the spiritual reality. It would be like trying to love someone by staring at his or her X-rays and CAT scans. A person is not what is seen in his or her X-rays. Similarly, religious faith or a spiritual experience cannot be explained and analyzed. To analyze it is to miss what it really is.

This book and its analysis of religion are not for everyone, but many will find the book helpful. Many people will find the words they have heard over the years clarified and explained. Readers will now be able to ask better questions and sort out and compare different religious ideas and practices. Such comparison helps us see what is different about various religions and, of more importance, to see what religions have in common.

DISCUSSION QUESTIONS

1. Can you give some examples of nonreligious rituals?

2. Can you offer some examples of the Four C's in religions with which you are familiar?

3. What did you find interesting about the size of various religions around the world?

4. What are you views on religious tolerance?

5. Can you provide some examples in which people failed to show religious tolerance?

Credits

CHAPTER 4

QUESTIONS ABOUT GOD FOR MONOTHEISTS

A. DO YOU CAPITALIZE GOD?

Many of us were trained using the common grammatical method for English that when you speak of the one God, the word "God" should be capitalized. When you speak of other gods, such as those in Greek mythology, the word "god" is not capitalized. Some religious writings even go so far as to capitalize pronouns for God such as "He" or "His."

These rules were possibly decided by Christians to emphasize their belief that there was only one god and that figures such as Zeus and Apollo were false gods, and therefore "god" should not be capitalized. Another reason could be that "God" is a name or proper noun, and a "god" is a common noun.

This book will follow the standard grammatical use of capitalizing "God" as a proper noun in describing monotheism, and not capitalizing "god" or "gods" as common nouns when describing polytheism.[1]

B. WHAT IS THE GENDER OF GOD?

Traditionally, God has been described as male, especially when the term "Father" is used for God. Male pronouns were often used for God such as in the King James version of Psalm 23: "The Lord is my shepherd; I shall not want. He maketh me to lie down in green pastures: he leadeth me beside the still waters." In recent decades inclusive language has become standard when speaking about men and women. Some people have stopped using male pronouns for God by simply avoiding pronouns for God. That is what this book has done. A number of religious songs have been changed to take out the male pronouns.

Some people want to go further and speak of God as "Mother" or as "Mother/Father" and use the pronouns "she" and "her." For some this is not just a change in labels but a change in the way they think about God.

---

1   I am also using these rules for fear that my third-grade teacher will come back from her grave and haunt me if I do not follow them.

Others object to such changes, thinking it is too close to pagan beliefs about a "Mother Goddess" or "Mother Earth." Very likely the writers of the Hebrew Scriptures/Old Testament would have objected to any Mother/Father imagery for God because the ancient faith of the Israelites defined itself as very different from the religion of Baal, which believed in a male god Baal and a female goddess Asherah.

Another way to look at the gender issue is to say that God is beyond gender and any labels put on God are inadequate human attempts to describe God, who is beyond exact description.

Give these questions some thought. What is the gender of God? Does God even have a gender? This issue will not be settled soon; discussions on it will continue.

C. IS GOD A HIGHER POWER?

Some people use the term "Higher Power" instead of the word "God." People using the term can have a wide range of different ideas about what is the Higher Power. And people using the term can be monotheists or pantheists, or people who have not thought out their own religious ideas.

There are practical reasons for using the term Higher Power. For example, the term is often used in Alcoholics Anonymous. The second of the *Twelve Steps* states, "Came to believe that a Power greater than ourselves could restore us to sanity." In a diverse group such as AA, referring to a Higher Power is broad enough and vague enough to apply to all kinds of religious beliefs. What AA wants to avoid are discussions on the details of religion that could lead to disagreements and divisions and would distract people from dealing with their addictions. The goal in AA is to support a spiritual view of life but not any one specific religion.

Another reason for using the term Higher Power is theological. The term speaks of a divine being in very broad terms because such a divine being is beyond any neat categories. According to this view, putting labels such as "God," "Father," or "Creator" should be avoided since they put limits on what is limitless.

Also, many people use the term Higher Power because they want to get away from traditional ways of thinking about and labeling God. Such people may have grown up in a religious environment that they later rejected; however, they want to hold on to religious belief on their own terms. For example, for those who grew up in a religion where God was presented as judgmental and punishing, a Higher Power can be seen as an accepting and forgiving presence.

But keep in mind that the term Higher Power is vague and nonspecific. When several people refer to a Higher Power they may have very different ideas on what it means. People can work out in their own minds what this Higher Power is like and what the Higher Power requires of them. Perhaps that is the beauty and use-fulness of the term.

D. WHERE IS GOD?

Among polytheists, many of the gods were local gods. In ancient Mesopotamia, for example, each city had its own god and a temple for that god. Anu the sky god was the god of the city of Uruk. Ellil, the god of wind and storm, was the god of the city of Nippur.

One strategy of the Romans when building their empire by conquering peoples was to incorporate the conquered local gods into the Roman pantheon. This had a religious strategy. The idea was to encourage the people to keep worshipping the local gods so they would be happy and side with the Romans. It also was part of a political strategy to reduce the resentment of conquered peoples.

Monotheists typically say that God is everywhere. Yet, often they have special places where God is believed to be present in special ways.

In ancient Israel it was believed that God was especially present inside the ancient Temple in Jerusalem, in the central room called the Holy of Holies. It was so filled with God that no one could go there except the high priest, and only once a year. When he entered, a rope was tied to him so that if he was struck dead by being in the presence of God his assistants could drag out his body without them having to enter the Holy of Holies.

In Islam, the sacred place to visit is Mecca during the Hajj pilgrimage. The center focus is the Ka'ba, a cube-shaped building about 40 feet in each dimension. When Muslims pray around the world they always face Mecca.

Roman Catholics often view Jesus as especially present in the church when consecrated hosts

FIGURE 4.1 The Temple of Solomon in ancient Jerusalem.

are in the tabernacle in the front of the church. A red candle in the church front indicates the presence of such consecrated hosts. Many Catholics genuflect when entering a church as a sign of recognizing the presence of Jesus.

For monotheists, the belief that God is everywhere—yet there are special places to encounter God's presence—is not exactly a contradiction; rather, it is thinking in two overlapping ways.

There is a legend about Guru Nanak, the founder of the Sikh religion. It was said that he made the pilgrimage to Mecca, and that during his sleep he was awakened by an angry guard for sleeping with his feet toward the Ka'ba. This was disrespectful to Allah. (In many parts of the world showing the bottoms of one's feet to someone is considered a great insult.) Guru Nanak responded, "Then point my feet in a direction where God is not."

E. HOW BIG IS GOD? (AND RELATED QUESTIONS)

How big is God? This seems a strange question. Many people might say, "God is infinite, beyond any measure," or "God is bigger than the universe," or "God is so big we cannot even imagine it." So why even bother with the question?

Many people believe God created the universe. This would mean that somehow God is bigger than the universe. So, how big is the universe and how much do we know about it?

The universe is a big place that is getting bigger. Science measures the universe as 92 billion light years across. A light year is six trillion miles. The universe is 92 billion x six trillion miles across! Imagining a God who created such a universe requires a big image of God. Also, science puts the age of the universe at 14 billion years. This also requires us to stretch our images of God. Biblical fundamentalists who believe the earth is only 6,000 years old have a smaller image of God.

How much do we know about God? First, we have to ask how much we know about the universe. It turns out we only know a tiny fraction of the universe. There is so much we do not know about our own planet. Tens of thousands of species of plant and animal life have never been cataloged. For example, there are tens of thousands of different kinds of wasps, most of which have not been catalogued. And this is just one insect!

We only know a tiny bit about our universe. Our solar system is in the Milky Way galaxy, which has somewhere between 200 billion and 400 billion stars. Yet the Milky Way is just one galaxy. There are anywhere from 100 billion to 200 billion galaxies in the universe. The earth is a tiny, tiny part of the universe and we do not even know the earth very well!

Yet, when some people talk about God they seem to speak as if they know everything about God. Some people make all kinds of judgments in God's name about the world around them. But if we only know a little bit about the universe then maybe we only know a little about the God of the universe.

One last question: Is the earth the center of the universe? For most of human existence, people believed the earth was the center of the universe. They also had a very small idea about the size of the universe. Many humans thought the earth was the physical center of the universe and the theological center. It was easy to believe the whole point of creation was to ensure that humans could exist on earth. But if the universe is so vast, and has existed for so long, then it becomes hard to imagine that the whole purpose of the universe revolves around human beings who have existed for the tiniest speck of time in the tiniest speck of space.

F. DOES GOD LIKE BLACK CLOTHES?

An interesting question is why some religions see the color black as an important religious sign. Catholic priests when not in church wear black shirts, pants, and jackets. In the past many Catholic priests wore a black tunic called a cassock, and some more traditional priests wear them today; however, the outfits Catholic priests wear at Mass—the most important Catholic service—are often very colorful. (These clothes are called "vestments.") Some Catholic nuns wear

FIGURE 4.2 Lancaster County Amish

traditional outfits called habits that are black. (Habits can also be brown, blue, or white.)

Often black is used as a symbol of being separate from the ordinary world and of being dedicated to God. Among Hasidic Jews, black clothes are the norm. Amish men typically wear black pants, jackets, and hats. The Amish want to get away from anything that is decorative. Even the Amish horse-drawn buggies are black.

The interesting question is "Does God like black clothes?" or "Does God see it as more holy to not be colorful." If nature is a fundamental revelation of God, then what does one see in terms of color in nature? One finds abundant color in nature: sunsets, wildflowers, all the various birds, the various colorations of animals, and the colors of stones and gems. Nature is filled with color. In fact, true black is hard to find in nature.

There are black birds such as the grackle. But grackles have an iridescent purple around their necks and when the light hits their black feathers they glisten with the rainbow effect. (Do an online search for "grackle" to see for yourself.)

The same can be said for a lump of coal, which is very black, but when light hits black coal it often makes a rainbow on the surface of the coal. And nature is filled with totally ostentatious animals such as the peacock. Someone might ask, "What was God thinking when God created the peacock?" So why then do some religions insist on black clothes?

G. IS GOD A GOD OF LAW OR LOVE?

For some religious people, God is a god of rules and laws. God helps people by giving them laws and holding people accountable for not following them. In some religious traditions much time and energy is spent trying to figure out the rules and how to obey them.

Often religious traditions that emphasize the laws of God also include an emphasis on the human failure to follow the laws. And often such an emphasis brings a sense of guilt, shame, or inadequacy to people. God is seen as harsh and judgmental. God is to be feared. Many people have left various religions because of this emphasis on rules and punishments.

The opposite view is that the whole point of religion is to believe in a God of love, acceptance, and forgiveness. One theme in the Hebrew Scriptures/Old Testament is that although the people continually broke God's laws, they were continually forgiven by God. Some people note how frequently Jesus talked about forgiveness.

So, which is the right emphasis for understanding God? What do you think?

H. DOES GOD WANT UNIFORMITY OR DIVERSITY?

1. Uniformity

In many religions there is a great emphasis on uniformity. Things have to be just one way and if things are done differently it is considered wrong. Sometimes there is animosity toward religious groups that are very similar yet disagree on secondary issues. For example, in Islam there is a growing divide between Sunni and Shia Muslims, even though they agree on the importance of the Qur'an, the Five Pillars, and all the essentials of Islam. In Christianity, many denominations have split, sometimes repeatedly, over disagreements on issues of doctrine. Among some Christians the attitude is not uncommon that "our denomination is the true version of Christianity and other denominations are wrong."

Traditions with rituals often have detailed rules about the rituals. Christians such as Roman Catholic, Orthodox, Anglican, and Episcopalian have extensive rules regarding Eucharistic services on such things as the exact sequence of the service, the exact words to be said in many parts of the service, the color of vestments a priest should wear on specific days, hand positions of the priest, where items should be placed on the altar, and the kind of music that can be used. In some prayer books used for services the prayers to be said are printed in black while the instructions on what to do, such as hand positions, are printed in red. They are called "rubrics." The word means "red" as in "ruby."

A number of religions identify themselves with the word "Orthodox." This reflects their view that their approach is the right one and can imply that other approaches are not the correct ones. Lastly, in those traditions that insist on uniformity, a common attitude is the assumption, "This is the way God wants it to be."

2. The Diversity of Nature

Does nature tell us anything about God? Does nature reveal anything about God? Or is God beyond the natural world? This is an important question because one of the elements of nature is its great diversity. Nature is incredibly diverse. There are countless species of insects. So many kinds of insects exist that we have not even been able to classify and catalog them all. There are so many different kinds of beautiful birds that are so varied across the world.

Yet in so many religions there are people who think everything has to be a certain way. With certain rituals some people insist that things be done in an exact certain way and think that God would be offended if things are not done in that precise way. If God created a universe filled with great unimaginable diversity, why would not the religious experience of people also be very diverse?

Some people even wonder whether the insistence on uniformity in some religions is a kind of idolatry. Is it a kind of false god to insist that everything has to be one certain way? It is also interesting to note that people who insist on things being a certain way seem to like that certain way. Looking at some people it is hard to tell the difference between their way and what they say is God's way.

I. WHY DOESN'T GOD CLARIFY THINGS?

For millennia religious people have argued over many, many, things. Religious groups with very similar views often have very hostile arguments and divisions over very small points. For example, Christian churches have sometimes split over small points of doctrine and practice. An outsider might think "You are so similar on so many points. Why can't you get along and work together?"

So why does God not clarify things? For Christians, why does Jesus not send a clear message to arguing groups about who is right and who is wrong? There is no answer to this question. It is just something interesting to think about

---

DISCUSSION QUESTIONS

1. What do you think about the gender of God?
2. What does the term "Higher Power" mean to you?
3. What do you think about God and the universe?
4. What is your definition of God?
5. Do you think of God as a God of love or a God of law?

Credits

- Fig. 4.1: Source: https://commons.wikimedia.org/wiki/File:Jerusalem_Modell_BW_3.JPG.
- Fig. 4.2: Copyright © it:Utente:TheCadExpert (CC BY-SA 3.0) at https://commons.wikimedia.org/wiki/File:Lancaster_County_Amish_03.jpg.

CHAPTER 5

JUDAISM

THE NEXT STEP in exploring religion is to learn about the major religions and traditions. The next three chapters will cover the Western religions in the order they developed historically: Judaism, Christianity, and Islam. Chapter 8 will cover the Eastern religions of Hinduism, Buddhism, and religion in China. Chapter 9 will briefly cover other important religions including Sikhism. This chapter is about Judaism.[1]

A. OVERVIEW

Although small in numbers, the religion of Judaism has had a great influence on the world. There are about 14 million Jews. Someone who follows Judaism is called a Jew.

Judaism, as are all religions, is very diverse. In fact, there is an old Jewish joke that if there are two Jews in a room there will be three opinions. Yet the general outlines of what most religious Jews believe and practice can be described.

Judaism as a religion is based on belief in one god. The name of God in English is rendered as "Yahweh." The word is based on four Hebrew consonants יהוה. Strict Jews will not speak the word out of respect for God and to follow the commandment: "You shall not take the name of the Lord in vain." Strict Jews will also not write the word and would even object to printing the English word, such as in this paragraph. Some strict Jews even write the word "God" as "G-d."

Central to Judaism is the belief that God chose as his people the ancient people of Israel. They were not chosen for their greatness, rather they were chosen because for their very insignificance and weakness.

---

1   For a more thorough exploration of Judaism see Stephen M. Wylen, *Settings of Silver: An Introduction to Judaism* (Mahwah, NJ: Paulist Press, 2014).

B. WHO IS A JEW?

As previously stated, in Judaism there is a great diversity of opinion on many things including the important question, Who is a Jew? The definition of a religious Jew is someone who holds the beliefs of Judaism. This would include someone who did not grow up Jewish but converted to Judaism.

Most Jews were born Jewish. A child born of Jewish parents is a Jew. If only the mother is Jewish the child is considered a Jew. For many Jews if only the father is Jewish then the child is not a Jew until he or she makes a religious conversion.

To further complicate the issue, many people who were born Jewish do not hold religious views. Some are agnostics or atheists yet they are still considered Jews. Often the term "ethnic Jew" is used for someone who was born Jewish but does not hold Jewish religious beliefs or follow Jewish practices. Ethnic Jews are also called "nonreligious Jews," "non-observant Jews," "nonpracticing Jews," and "secular Jews."

C. THE JEWISH BIBLE

Jewish faith is based on the Jewish Bible which is called the Bible or the Tanakh. (Non-Jews sometimes refer to the Jewish Bible as the Jewish Scriptures or the Hebrew Scriptures). The writings in the Jewish Bible are the same writings as the Christian Old Testament.[2] Jews, however, typically do not like the term "Old Testament" for their bible since it is a Christian term.[3]

The Jewish Bible describes several key events starting with the call of Abraham and the promises made to him. The story of Abraham is set about 1800 BCE.[4] He was called to leave his home in Mesopotamia (modern Iraq) and go to the land of Canaan (roughly the area of modern Israel and the Palestinian territories). God made two promises to Abraham: 1) he would have numerous descendants, and 2) his descendants would own the land of Canaan. At the time Abraham did not have descendants and he was a visitor in the land.

The next important events have to do with the story of Moses, set about 1300 BCE, and several hundred years after the time of Abraham. Abraham did have

---

2   The Protestant Old Testament.

3   For a Christian overview of the Old Testament, see Bernard A. Asen, "The Old Testament," in J. J. Mueller, ed., *Theological Foundation: Concepts and Methods for Understanding Christian Faith* (Anselm Academic, 2011).

4   The dates listed for these biblical stories are based on scholar's attempts to establish the historical settings for the stories. However, there is much uncertainty about the earliest stories as to what actually happened and when it happened.

FIGURE 5.1 A Torah scroll

descendants, and they became the 12 tribes of Israel. During a famine in Canaan they went to Egypt and stayed. By the time of Moses, the descendants had been enslaved by the Egyptians.

Moses was called by God to lead the people out of Egypt. This event is called the Exodus. After Moses led the people out of Egypt, the story is told that he went up Mount Sinai and encountered God. God gave Moses the law, starting with what are known as the Ten Commandments.[5]

But other laws were also given. According to Jewish tradition, God gave 613 laws. The laws are found in the first five books of the Bible: Genesis, Exodus, Leviticus, Numbers, and Deuteronomy. These books are called the "Torah." The word Torah means "instruction" but it is commonly translated as "law."

The word Torah, however, is used in several ways. Torah can mean the first five books. It can also mean the law in the books. It can mean the laws in the Bible and the centuries of interpretation and commentary on the law. The Torah is also called the "Law of Moses," though many historians and bible scholars believe the laws were compiled over many generations after the time of Moses. Because of the link to Moses, the law is often called the "Mosaic Law."

The rest of the Jewish Bible relates the story of the creation of the Kingdom of Israel with the first kings Saul, David, and Solomon (c 1040 BCE to c 922 BCE). Then the kingdom split into two parts: a northern kingdom called Israel and a

---

5   In the Mel Brooks comedy movie *History of the World, Part 1,* God originally gave 15 Commandments. Check it out on YouTube.

southern kingdom called Judah (922 BCE). The northern kingdom was conquered in 721 BCE by the Assyrians and only Judah survived. From that moment on the people of Israel were called "Jews." (The word "Jew" comes from the word "Judah.") Then the Jews were conquered by the Babylonians (587 BCE), Greeks (332 BCE), and Romans (63 BCE).

The Jewish Bible contains a book of prayers called Psalms, a book of guidance called Proverbs, and books of the messages of prophets warning the people of their failure to follow God's laws.

The Jewish Bible is divided into three sections: the books of law called the Torah, a section of books on the prophets called the Neviim, and a section of other writings called the Kethuvim. "Torah" means "law, "Neviim" means "prophets," and "Kethuvim" means "writings." A prophet is one called by God to speak for God. The first letter of the name of each section—T, N, and K—have been turned into the word "Tanakh," which is another name for the Jewish Bible.

The religion of Judaism is monotheism. It is based on belief in the God of Israel and following the law of God. Many Jews believe faithful Jews will go to heaven to be with God when they die; however, the Hebrew Scriptures do not say much about the afterlife so Jews have different ideas about what happens after one dies. Most Jews do not believe in a hell where souls stay for eternity to be punished.

D. JEWISH LAW AND THE MAJOR DIVISIONS OF JUDAISM

The Jewish faith tradition is based on the Jewish Bible and also on a collection of writings known as the Talmud. A standard Talmud is more than 6,000 pages long and is published in several volumes. The Talmud is commentary on the law.

If you make a rule, it may sound simple, but interpretation can get complicated. A parent may tell a child, "Don't talk to strangers." But if the child gets lost should not the child talk to someone? Laws need interpretation.

The Talmud is centuries of trying to figure out how to interpret the commandments such as "Keep the Sabbath holy." The Sabbath is the day of rest. No work is to be done. Many Jews follow extensive rules so as to not work on the Sabbath, and many Jews will not drive cars or use electricity on the Sabbath.

In Judaism today, there are three major groups: Reform, Conservative, and Orthodox. (There are also other smaller groups.) These groups differ on how strictly they follow the Law of Moses.

Orthodox Judaism is the strictest group in following the Law. Orthodox Jews are bound by all 613 laws in the Torah and do not believe that God's requirements have changed since ancient times. To outsiders, following these ancient laws seems a burden. To Orthodox Jews the laws are seen as a gift from God.

The laws have a huge influence on one's life, such as food laws. For example, in the Bible it states, "You shall not boil a kid goat in its mother's milk" (Exodus 23:19). Apparently, there was an ancient delicacy of taking a baby goat and cooking it in its mother's milk. It was forbidden in the Bible. But who serves this today? No one is planning to open franchised restaurants serving it. Thus, the interpretation is that meat and dairy products should not be eaten together. This is one of the food laws called "kosher laws."

Eating kosher is following Jewish food laws. In a kosher kitchen in a home or restaurant there will be two refrigerators, two sinks, two dishwashers, and two sets of dishes. One of each of these is for meat products and the other one of each is for dairy products to ensure they never mix.

Other kosher food laws ban the eating of pork or any kind of seafood that does not have fins and scales. Regular fish are fine, but lobster, shrimp, clams, catfish, squid, and the like are forbidden.

Reform Jews insist the moral laws of God, such as "Do not kill," should be followed, but that other rules, such as food rules, applied to ancient times and are not relevant today.

Conservative Jews are in between. They are stricter than the Reform Jews in following the rules but less strict than Orthodox Jews. Many conservative Jews follow the kosher rules and many do not.

E. HASIDISM (HASIDIC JUDAISM)

Another important Jewish group are the Hasidic Jews. Hasidism is a movement within Orthodox Judaism that began with the teaching of Israel Baal Shem Tov in Eastern Europe in the 1700s. Hasidic Jews take the laws of the Torah very seriously yet they emphasize a loving and joyful following of the laws in the Torah. Hasidic Judaism includes an emphasis on mystical prayer, which is praying in such a way as to directly experience God.

Hasidic Jews, similar to many Orthodox Jews, often wear distinctive outfits, mostly in black with long coats and black hats for males. Hasidic males also have traditional hair curls on each side of their head.

F. JEWISH RITUALS

The Jewish religion has many rituals and celebrations. These rituals can be divided into three groups: the Sabbath service, seasonal rituals, and rituals to mark important points in life.

1. Sabbath Service

Perhaps the most important Jewish ritual is the Sabbath, the day of rest. It starts on Friday at sundown and ends on Saturday at sundown. (Modern people with clocks start the day at midnight. Jewish customs follow ancient customs when no one had clocks.)

The key to the Sabbath is a family meal at home, which begins with the lighting of a candle and a blessing. Many Jews then go to synagogue services on Friday evening or Saturday morning.

2. Seasonal Rituals

Here is a list of the major Jewish seasonal ceremonies with brief descriptions. The dates to celebrate these holidays are based on the Jewish calendar so they are not on the same day each year on the regular calendar.

Rosh Hashanah is the New Year's celebration held in fall. During the synagogue celebration a ram's horn, called a "shofar," is blown to announce the New Year.

Rosh Hashanah begins a ten-day period called the High Holy Days ending with Yom Kippur, the Day of Atonement. "To atone" means to make up for doing something wrong. Yom Kippur is remembered with a 24-hour fast. It is a day to reflect on one's failure to live up to God's law during the past year.

Passover is a meal that remembers the Exodus from Egypt. Passover is usually celebrated on the first full moon after the spring equinox. The meal is called a "seder" and includes lamb or fish, unleavened bread called "matzah," bitter herbs, and a paste of apples and nuts called "haroset." In the Exodus story the Hebrews ate a meal before leaving Egypt. They did not have time to let the bread rise so they ate unleavened bread (bread without yeast). The bitter herbs symbolize the bitterness of slavery in Egypt. Haroset symbolizes either the food the slaves ate or the mortar between the bricks that the Hebrews made while slaves. The seder meal includes blessings and readings of the Exodus story of Moses leading the Israelite slaves out of Egypt.

Shavuot remembers the giving of the Law of Moses. This celebration is also called Pentecost. "Pent" means five, as in the word "pentagon" for a five-sided figure. Here it means 50 days after Passover. But 50 is not a biblical number. The numbers 7, 12, and 40 are important symbolic numbers in the Hebrew Scriptures, so why 50 days? The key to understanding this is to know that another name for Shavuot is the Festival of Weeks. Using the importance of the number seven, Shavuot is seven weeks after Passover. After completing seven weeks ($7 \times 7 = 49$), the next day would be the 50th day.

Sukkot remembers the wandering of the Israelites for 40 years after they left Egypt. During this time they lived in tents. Sukkot is celebrated in the fall by building a shelter in one's home or at the synagogue. Jews then eat meals or even sleep in the Sukkot booth.

FIGURE 5.2 A sukkah for Sukkot

Hanukkah (also spelled Chanukah and Hanukah) is an eight-day celebration that takes place between late November and late December. Hanukkah remembers the story of the Maccabean revolt. In 332 BC the Greeks conquered the Kingdom of Israel and it came under Greek control. Later, Greek kings tried to crush and remove the Jewish religion including taking the Temple in Jerusalem and converting it into a Temple of Zeus.

The Jews revolted and in 165 BC they retook the Temple and rededicated it to their God. There is a legend about the lamp stand in the Temple called the menorah. The Jews relit the seven lamps on the menorah and although they only had enough oil for one day, by a miracle the lamps stayed lit for eight days.

FIGURE 5.3 The menorah depicted in a stain glass window.

FIGURE 5.4 The Eighth Night

Jews remember Hanukkah with a candelabrum of eight candles for the eight days of Hanukkah and a ninth candle to light the others. Each day's celebration includes blessings, prayers, songs, gifts, and games.

Purim is a joyful and festive celebration in March that remembers the story of Esther in the Hebrew Scriptures. Esther was the Jewish queen of Persian King Ahasuerus. An evil adviser to the king, Haman, got Ahasuerus to pass a law that all Jews should be executed. Mordecai, the uncle of Esther, told her to intervene with the king, which she did. The king changed the policy and saved the Jews. In the end, Haman was executed on the scaffold he had built for the Jews.

3. Life Stages

Jews have rituals to mark important stages in life: birth, becoming an adult, marriage, and death. For infant males, a ceremony called a brit milah takes place on

FIGURE 5.5 A bar mitzvah

the eighth day of life. The ceremony is a circumcision performed by a trained person called a mohel.[6] For girls, there is a naming ceremony called a simchat bat.

The ceremony for becoming an adult is called a bar mitzvah and takes place when a boy is 13 years old. Bar mitzvah means "son of the covenant," which means that a boy is now bound by all the Laws of Moses. The ceremony involves reading aloud

---

6 A circumcision removes the foreskin of the male penis. See the Wikipedia article "Circumcision" for more information.

from the Torah in Hebrew in a synagogue. Reform Jews and some Conservative Jews also have a similar ceremony for girls called a bat mitzvah.

Marriage involves several details. Before the wedding ceremony the groom signs a contract, called a ketubah, that outlines his duties as a husband. The wedding takes place before a rabbi and under a canopy called a chuppah, which represents heaven or the home that the couple will create. As the bride enters she walks three or seven times around the groom. The ketubah is then read and the groom gives the bride a ring. Sometimes the wife also presents a ring to the groom. Seven blessings are given. Then the couple drink from a class of wine and the glass is broken to remind them that the joy of life must be tempered.

Among Jews there are a number of practices regarding death. Many Jews do not believe in embalming bodies, seeing it as a desecration of the body. Many Jews do not conduct a wake with the viewing of the body (cremation is forbidden). Instead, bodies are washed and then buried fairly quickly with a private service for just the immediate family. Then for the next week the family "sits shiva." They stay at home in mourning while extended family and friends visit and share their grief. The kaddish is a special prayer said for the dead.

G. IMPORTANT MORAL TEXTS IN THE HEBREW SCRIPTURES

Two passages from the Hebrew Scriptures/Old Testament are particularly important for addressing moral issues for both Jews and Christians: the Ten Commandments and the rule of "an eye for an eye." Although this chapter is on Judaism, both Jewish and Christian views on these important texts will be examined. Both Jews and Christians consider these texts important but there are often different answers on how to interpret them between Jews and Christians. Also, among Jews and among Christians different ideas exist on how to apply these texts to current moral issues.

1. The Ten Commandments

The Ten Commandments are the most famous moral code, and are found in the Hebrew Scriptures/Old Testament. The commandments are found in two places: Exodus Chapter 20:1-17 and Deuteronomy 5:6-21. In two stories, Moses goes up a mountain and receives the commandments. There are slight differences between the two versions. (If you have never read these important passages you can look them up in a Bible or go online and read them.)

The Ten Commandments are the foundation of morality for both Jews and Christians. In the actual texts the rules are not called the Ten Commandments, nor are they numbered as ten in the biblical text. In some cases it is even difficult to figure out where one commandment stops and the next commandment begins. As a result, there are different lists of the commandments. The Wikipedia article on the Ten Commandments has a chart showing various versions.

Here is a typical Jewish version:

1. I am the Lord your God, who brought you out of Egypt.
2. You shall have no other gods. You shall have no graven images or likenesses.
3. You shall not take the Lord's name in vain.
4. Keep the Sabbath holy.
5. Honor your father and mother.
6. You shall not kill.
7. You shall not commit adultery.
8. You shall not steal.
9. You shall not bear false witness.
10. You shall not covet your neighbor's wife or possession.

Here is a typical Protestant Christian version:

1. I am the Lord your God, you shall have no other gods.
2. You shall have no graven images or likenesses.
3. You shall not take the Lord's name in vain.
4. Keep the Sabbath holy.
5. Honor your father and mother.
6. You shall not kill.
7. You shall not commit adultery.
8. You shall not steal.
9. You shall not bear false witness.
10. You shall not covet your neighbor's wife or possessions.

Although many people follow the Ten Commandments there is disagreement on a number of key issues. As will be discussed in Chapter 15, people disagree on the use of images and statues in religion.

The commandment on the Sabbath is understood in different ways. The word "Sabbath" refers to Saturday. For Jews the Sabbath is the holy day starting at Friday sundown and going to Saturday sundown. Christians moved the holy day to Sunday because of the belief that Jesus rose from the dead on a Sunday, and perhaps to be different than Jews. Christians changed the meaning of the word Sabbath, and some Christians have even reworked the commandment to state, "Keep the Lord's day holy." But one group of Christians, the Seventh-day Adventist Church, follows the Jewish definition of the Sabbath as Saturday. Seventh-day Adventists go to church on Saturday.

Perhaps the greatest controversy is over the commandment "You shall not kill." It is not simple to interpret this commandment. Some people such as the Amish and the Quakers understand it to ban all types of killing of humans. They would point out that although the Old Testament read "an eye for an eye," Jesus rejected "an eye for eye."

Other people interpret the commandment to prohibit murder. Some even write the commandment as "You shall not murder." But what is murder?

"Murder" is a common word yet most people have not thought about what is meant by the word. It turns out the word is not just a label for killing a human being, but it also includes the judgment that a particular act of killing a human being is wrong. The meaning of the word "murder" is that a murder is an "unjustified intentional killing" of a human by another human.

Suicide does not fit the definition. The word "intentional" is in the definition. Accidentally killing a person is not committing murder. But the word "unjustified" is also part of the definition. Some people believe that some intentional killing is justified, such as in capital punishment and in warfare.

But people disagree on when killing is unjustified. Most people want to justify some kind of killing of humans. Here are some examples in which some people justify the intentional killing of humans: war, capital punishment, police officers acting properly in the line of duty, self-defense, and mercy killing.[7] (This is just a list of examples some people cite as justification for taking human lives. People will disagree on what should and should not be on the list.)

---

7 To keep this simple I have left out the examples of abortion and euthanasia. For abortion there are several moral issues involved. Is abortion justified? If abortion can be justified then when is it justified? Is it a human being that is killed when an abortion takes place? When does the fetus become a human being? The term "euthanasia" is often used for a range of actions including such things as turning off life support on a brain-dead person, refusing further chemotherapy for a terminal patient, and physician-assisted suicide. Each of these examples provides a different set of moral questions. To further complicate the discussion, the word euthanasia is used differently by different people. It is beyond the scope of this book to sort out all of these various issues.

Unfortunately, the Bible does not give detailed answers on many of these moral questions. Religious people down through the centuries have given different answers. The Hebrew Scriptures/Old Testament offer stories that justified warfare and capital punishment. In the New Testament, Jesus rejected violence. Chapter 6 includes more on his views.

As cited before, groups such as the Amish and the Quakers, and religious pacifists, see all intentional killings of human beings as wrong. Many point to the teachings of Jesus. Also, people who oppose all killings would point out that killing people often does not really solve problems. Capital punishment does not make us safer. It does not lower murder rates. Wars often lead to more wars.

A final question comes up regarding the Tenth Commandment: What does the word "covet" mean? One definition is "to desire wrongfully." But this definition begs the question of what is the difference between wrongful desire and desire that is not wrongful. The problem is agreeing on what is the boundary. Seeing a married woman as attractive is one thing but at what point does that turn into wrongful desire? You may appreciate your neighbor's new car and wish you had one, but at what point do you start coveting the car?

The point of the command (or commands), which is an important point, is that it is not just one's actions in wrongfully taking someone's property that are bad. If we have the intentions, even if they do not result in actions, the intentions can be morally wrong.

2. An Eye for an Eye

> But if injury ensues, you shall give life for life, eye for eye,
> tooth for tooth, hand for hand, foot for foot, burn for
> burn, wound for wound, stripe for stripe.
>
> Exodus 21:23-25

"An eye for an eye" is known as the *lex talionis*, the law of retaliation. It is found in the Hebrew Scriptures/Old Testament in Exodus and in Deuteronomy. It showed up earlier in the ancient Babylonian law code of Hammurabi. This ancient moral principle has had great influence down through the centuries. Even today people sometimes cite it as a moral principle. But the concept is often understood.

First, in the history of human development "an eye for an eye" was a step forward. It limited retribution to an equal amount. So, if you broke my arm, I could break your arm but I could not kill you. If you poked my eye out I could then poke out your eye, but again I could not kill you. If you killed my brother, my family could kill you, but we could not wipe out your entire family or village. This was progress.

Second, in the ancient world "an eye for eye" typically meant a money settlement proportionate to the injury. A small injury required a small money settlement; a big injury required a bigger money settlement. Today the same principle is followed in lawsuits over injuries and workers' compensation settlements.

Ancient people were smart enough to understand that if you break my arm and I break your arm, then there are two people who cannot do any work. Even in the case of killings, there would often be a cash settlement rather than killing someone in return. This became known as blood money.

This custom still exists. During the American military action in Afghanistan there were several instances when people were killed and the United States government made a money settlement to the family.

"An eye for an eye" is used by some people today as a justification for capital punishment although when originally used there were no prisons. Today the option exists of putting convicted murderers in prison for life.[8]

The problem with retaliation and revenge is that we tend overvalue injuries to ourselves and undervalue injuries to others. On a simple level, for many people it is significant when their feelings are hurt; when other people's feelings are hurt it is insignificant. So, we tend to measure injuries differently. In revenge, one is trying to "even the score." But how can you do that if there is no agreed-upon measurement?

There have been a number of retaliation feuds such as the famous Hatfield/McCoy feud during the 1800s in Kentucky and Virginia. If a Hatfield killed a McCoy then the McCoy would kill a Hatfield to even the score. However, the Hatfields would not see the score as even and settled. Instead, they would have a need for revenge over the latest killing of a Hatfield and so they would kill another McCoy, which would set up another killing of a Hatfield ... and on and on.[9]

The Jewish Talmud contains a discussion of *Lex talionis*. The Torah text is understood to require a money settlement and not physical injury as retaliation. The law of *Lex talionis* has also been discussed in Islam and Christianity.

The Qur'an, the holy book of Islam, also addresses "an eye for an eye" and refers to its place in the Hebrew Scriptures.

> *In the Torah We prescribed for them a life for a life, an eye for an eye, a nose for a nose, an ear for an ear, a tooth for a tooth, an equal wound for a wound: if anyone forgoes this out of charity, it will serve as atonement for his bad*

---

8   Life imprisonment is also cheaper than capital punishment.

9   I am using the Hatfield/McCoy example in a theoretical way and not getting into the nitty-gritty details of the actual history.

*deeds. Those who do not judge according to what God
has revealed are doing grave wrong. (Qur'an, 5:45)*

Jesus totally rejected the concept of "an eye for an eye."

*You have heard that it was said, "An eye for an eye and a
tooth for a tooth. But I say to you, offer no resistance to one
who is evil. When someone strikes you on the right cheek,
turn the other one to him as well." (Matthew 5:38-39)*

This is one of several of the Mosaic laws that Jesus reworked and reinterpreted; however, when Jesus said "turn the other cheek" he seemed to be describing some sort of insult situation, especially with the detail of being slapped on the right cheek. This seems to imply a backhand blow. What Jesus does not do is explain how this principle would apply to such moral issues as killing in war, capital punishment, and self-defense. For nearly 2000 years Christians have argued over how to apply "turn the other cheek" to such moral issues. The central point, however, is that Jesus rejected "an eye for an eye" and retaliation as a moral principle.

Lastly, Mahatma Gandhi, the Indian leader, noted "an eye for an eye will only make the whole world blind." Martin Luther King Jr. repeated this idea, saying, "The old law of an eye for an eye leaves everyone blind." In the musical *Fiddler on the Roof*, Tevye comments, "Very good. That way the whole world will be blind and toothless."

DISCUSSION QUESTIONS

1. What did you learn about Judaism?

2. If you are not Jewish, where have you encountered Jewish people? Where is the closest Jewish synagogue? (You could do an online search to find one.)

3. Which Jewish rituals are the most interesting? How do the Jewish rituals compare to the rituals of other religions?

4. What are your thoughts on the Ten Commandments? Are there other moral rules that you think should be added?

5. How do you understand the commandment "You shall not kill"?

Credits

- Fig. 5.1: Copyright © Lawrie Cate (CC by 2.0) at https://commons.wikimedia.org/wiki/File:Torah,_the_Jewish_Holy_Book.jpg.

CHAPTER 6

CHRISTIANITY

THIS CHAPTER EXPLORES Christianity, which is the religion based on faith in Jesus. The first section explores details about Jesus. Both believers and nonbelievers could agree on this information. The next two sections describe the Christian beliefs about Jesus, which Christians hold but non-Christians do not hold. Later sections discuss the Christian Bible, Christian rituals, and the major divisions of Christianity.[1]

A. JESUS

1. Background

His name was Jesus. In his time people would have called him "Jesus of Nazareth" or "Jesus, son of Joseph." During his public career Jesus avoided giving himself titles other than "son of man." This title seems to be a humble one but no one is quite sure what Jesus meant by it.

We have a limited amount of information about Jesus. Our main source would be the four Gospels: Matthew, Mark, Luke, and John. Matthew, Mark, and Luke—the Synoptic Gospels—provide the most detail about Jesus.[2] Other writings in the New Testament, such as the letters of Paul, offer very little information on the life of Jesus.

Jesus is mentioned very briefly in the writings of Josephus, a Jewish historian, and in the Jewish Talmud, but it is debated how much these references tell us about Jesus and they do not add much our knowledge. Also, there are about two dozen early writings that did not make it into the Bible. Such writings include the Gospel

---

1   For a more thorough exploration of Christianity, see "Chapter 9, Christianity," in Mary Pat Fisher, *Living Religions.* 6th ed. (Upper Saddle River, NJ: Prentice-Hall, 2005). Also see John Renard, *The Handy Religion Answer Book* (Canton, MI: Visible Ink Press, 2015), 59–119.

2   It is beyond the scope of this book to go into the complicated question of why the Gospel of John is so different and the question of the accuracy of the details in the Synoptic Gospels.

of Thomas, the Infancy Gospel of Thomas, and the Gospel of Peter. Christians have differing views on whether these writings add details to our knowledge of Jesus or distort the message of the four gospels in the New Testament.

Our best guess for the years of the life of Jesus would be from 6–4 BC (BCE) to 27–33 AD (CE). Jesus lived in the region called Palestine in what at the time was the Roman province of Judaea. Today this is modern Israel and the Palestinian territories. Jesus was a Jew. But what language did Jesus speak? He probably spoke Aramaic, the language of the common people.

Although the Romans spoke Latin, Greek was an important language in the Roman Empire for business and literature. Did Jesus know any Greek or Latin? We do not know. The best guess is that he did not since he was probably uneducated. Very likely, he did not know much Hebrew; however, there is no way to know with certainty. After his death the Christian New Testament was written in Greek.

Jesus lived in an area under Roman control, though the Romans kept Jewish kings in power (e.g., Herod the Great, Herod Antipas). The Roman governor, Pontius Pilate, would decide to execute Jesus.

Almost nothing is known of the early life of Jesus. The Gospels of Matthew and Luke have infancy stories about Jesus. It is impossible, however, to know how accurate the stories are since the gospel writers were trying to make theological points about Jesus. For example, did the Magi—the Wise Men—actually visit Jesus, or was this detail made up by the writer of Matthew's Gospel to make the point that Jesus came for the whole world? Also, the gospels were written about 70 years after the birth of Jesus. There would have been no written records of the early life of Jesus.

2. Public Ministry of Jesus

We know about Jesus when he went public and began his ministry, about the age of 30, according to the Gospel of Luke. His public ministry began with his baptism. The three Synoptic Gospels describe the baptism of Jesus.

There are three main elements concerning what Jesus did. He gathered followers, he taught people, and he healed the sick. Jesus gathered an inner circle of twelve men called the Apostles. The choice of twelve was symbolic of the twelve tribes of ancient Israel. But there were other followers, including women.

Jesus's style of teaching was to tell stories or give short sayings. Three gospels offer us a picture of how Jesus taught: Matthew, Mark, and Luke. One of the themes of the preaching of Jesus was seeing God as Father. Jesus used the word "abba" for God. "Abba" means "father."

Jesus also taught about the "Kingdom of God." It is not totally clear what Jesus meant by the Kingdom of God and readers of the gospels have argued extensively over the meaning of the term. What Jesus was not talking about was a heaven after death. Nor was he talking about some interior religious experience. What Jesus seemed to be talking about was a changed set of relationships between people and a changed relationship with God the Father in the present time.

Part of his Kingdom of God was a rejection of the values of the world. Jesus rejected wealth and power. Jesus spoke about loving enemies. He taught "Blessed are the poor" and "Blessed are the meek." He also gave his own interpretation on how to live the Laws of Moses.

The core teachings of Jesus can be found in the Gospel of Matthew, chapters 5–7, and the Gospel of Luke, Chapter 6, verses 20–42. Get a Bible or find a Bible online to read these important passages (it will only take about ten minutes).

Also, Jesus healed people. All the gospels speak of this. People have different views on how Jesus healed and what to call his healings. Some call them "miracles" or "signs." In some cases the healings are described as driving out demons. In the ancient world, without medical science, demons were given as an explanation of medical illnesses.

3. Crucifixion

Jesus eventually got into trouble with the religious authorities, who turned him over to the Romans to be crucified. The Romans probably saw Jesus as a potential leader of an uprising against Roman authority. At the time there were a number of Jewish figures called "messiahs" who wanted to free Israel from Roman rule and establish a Jewish kingdom. The word messiah was also used for a Jewish king.

The Romans, however, misunderstood the message of Jesus. Jesus preached a Kingdom of God with the values of "Blessed are the meek" and "Turn the other cheek." In the Gospels of Matthew and Luke political power is a temptation from the devil that Jesus rejects (Matthew 4:1-11, Luke 4:1-13). The devil offered Jesus the kingdoms of the world if Jesus would bow down and worship the devil. Jesus rejected the devil and his offer of political power.

When crucifying someone the Romans would put a sign on the cross stating the charges against the person. For Jesus, the sign read "Jesus of Nazareth King of the Jews." This sign charged Jesus with the political crime of being a messiah. The sign in Latin would be *IESVS·NAZARENVS·REX·IVDÆORVM*. In Christian art of the crucifixion it becomes "I.N.R.I.". Latin has no letter "J".

Crucifixion was used by the Romans to kill people because it was a long, drawn-out, and very painful process. Crucified victims could live for days before dying. After being whipped and stripped, Jesus was nailed and hung to a cross, where he died.

There are many things we do not know about crucifixion. It is mentioned in a number of ancient Roman writings but no descriptions are given. Christian art on crucifixion is useless because for the first few centuries Christians did not depict

Jesus on the cross. When Christians finally began producing images of Jesus on the cross, crucifixion had stopped as a practice.

There are several unanswered questions. Was the cross T-shaped or was it a single upright pole? Did the person to be crucified carry the entire cross or just the cross beam that was attached to an already standing pole? Was the victim nailed or tied to the cross, or both? Did the person typically die from asphyxiation, blood loss, or shock? Or a combination of these? Very likely there was no standard procedure on how crucifixion was done.

We do know that victims would be stripped naked; Christian art has always added a loincloth. To hasten a person's death, the Romans would break the legs of that person. All in all, crucifixion was very brutal.

The next part of the story about Jesus is where believers and nonbelievers disagree. Nonbelievers would say that after the death of Jesus his message and example so inspired his followers that they created a religious movement that would grow to become the largest religion in the world. Believers would say that Jesus rose from the dead and that his followers' experience of the risen Jesus led them to create the Christian Church.

This is the famous painting *The Crucifixion* by Matthias Grünewald (1470–1528), which is part of the Isenheim Altarpiece.[3] Who are the figures? The woman in white is Mary, the mother of Jesus. John, one of the disciples, is holding her. Mary Magdalene is kneeling.

The painting is filled with symbolism. On the right is John the Baptist. He was dead by the time of the crucifixion of Jesus, but in the gospels he pointed the way to Jesus—notice his hand. The lamb symbolizes Jesus. Lambs were slain as sacrifices for sin. Notice the blood of the lamb flowing into the cup. Catholics believe the cup of wine at mass becomes the blood of Jesus.

This is the famous painting *The Last Supper* by Leonardo da Vinci, who lived from 1452–1519.

FIGURE 6.1 Matthias Grünewald—The Crucifixion

---

3   It is on display at the Unterlinden Museum in Colmar, France.

FIGURE 6.2 Leonardo da Vinci—*The Last Supper*

B. SEVEN BASIC CHRISTIAN BELIEFS

Mainline Christians hold to these seven beliefs.[4] Mainline Christians are those who agree with the ideas of the Nicene Creed, which is quoted below.

1. Monotheism

Christians are monotheists. They believe in one God, though, as will be shown below, the Christian monotheist belief in one God is a bit complicated.

2. Messiah

Christians believe Jesus was the Messiah, the chosen one of God. Literally, the word means "anointed one." In the Old Testament/Hebrew Scriptures, kings were dedicated by anointing. Perfumed olive oil was poured on the head of a candidate to designate kingship. (In America, we designate a president with a swearing in.)

The term "messiah" has a long and complicated history. During the time of Jesus many people expected a messiah; however, many wanted a great political king or a military leader to lead a revolt against the Romans who occupied Judaea. Others expected a prophet in the model of Elijah. This is probably the reason why Jesus was reluctant to use the term messiah. Instead, he described himself as one who would suffer, be rejected by the religious leaders, and be killed.

---

4   This list is a somewhat artificial way to organize a description of these important beliefs. Other people might create a different list yet the key concepts would still be there.

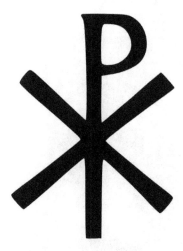

Later Christians removed all political connotations and redefined messiah as one who would suffer and die to redeem humans from their sins. Christians began using the Greek version of the word: Christ. In Greek it is pronounced "*Christos*" and written as "Χριστός."

In Greek, the first letter looks like an "X" and is called "chi." The second letter looks like a "P" and is called "rho." In Christian art these are combined in the symbol called the "chi-rho." In those churches that have art this symbol is very common. Have you seen it before?

Also, the "X" for the first letter of "Christ" in Greek is why you can abbreviate "Christmas" as "Xmas." The title of "Christ" for Jesus becomes so important it is almost used as a last name for Jesus. Also, Christians use the word to define themselves: Christians.

3. Resurrection

When Christians speak of the resurrection of Jesus they usually are considering several interrelated pieces.

a. Jesus died and rose.

Most mainline Christians believe that Jesus "really died on the cross and was really alive three days later." Most Christians reject the idea that Jesus went into a coma and came out of it in the tomb. Mainline Christians believe that he died on the cross but was seen alive three days later.

Christians explain this in slightly different terms. Some say the actual body of Jesus was raised up and brought back to life. Other Christians describe the body as somehow transformed; it was the same body, yet somehow different.

Also for mainline Christians, the meaning of "resurrection" is not that the followers of Jesus saw a ghost—Jesus had a physical body.

The Resurrection is not understood as merely symbolic, that "Jesus lives on our hearts." No, most mainline Christians believe that Jesus was alive three days later with a body.

b. The death and resurrection of Jesus brings salvation.

This is the core concept of Christianity. This point is often brought up in Protestant preachers' sermons. The logic runs like this: humans commit sin and separate themselves from God. The sin is so great that humans cannot overcome the gap between themselves and God.

Only Jesus by dying and rising can bridge the gap. Jesus pays the price for sin. Jesus redeems humans and brings salvation. Humans are saved from sin and the penalty of sin. The penalty of sin is to die and not go to heaven. According to Christians, Jesus saved his followers from sin and the penalty of sin. Hence, Jesus is their "Savior" and "Redeemer."

c. Christians expect to be resurrected themselves.
Christians expect to be resurrected after death, but not back to this life. Heck, you would still have to pay your house mortgage or student loans! Christians expect to be resurrected into heaven to live forever with God.

4. Incarnation
The word "incarnation" is based on the Latin word *carnis*, which means "flesh" or "meat," or "body." Notice the word for "meat-eater" is "carnivore." Incarnation is the belief that in Jesus, God has taken on human flesh. (Do not be confused. There is the Hindu term "reincarnation," but that is a very different idea.)

Mainline Christians believe that Jesus is both God and man; they believe he was truly God and truly man at the same time. Jesus was both human and divine. And as said before, "divine" means to be God. The traditional belief states that Jesus is one person with two natures: a divine nature and a human nature.

This may not be an easy concept to understand. If you say Jesus was just a good man, you are disagreeing with mainline Christian belief. If you say Jesus was God, but not man, you are disagreeing with mainline Christian belief. To say Jesus was an angel is to disagree with mainline Christians.

So the mainline Christian belief is that Jesus is both human and divine. According to mainline Christians, to deny that Jesus is God is a heresy called Arianism. To deny that Jesus is human is a heresy called Monophysitism. (Monophysitism means "one nature.")

For Christians, a key supporting belief of incarnation is the belief that Jesus was born of the Virgin Mary. Most Christians believe that when Jesus was born his mother Mary was still a virgin. Jesus was not conceived through the normal biological process. Instead, according to Christian belief, through a miracle God's power came over Mary and she became pregnant. This story is told in the Gospel of Luke, Chapter 1. The scene is called the Annunciation because the angel Gabriel announces to Mary that she will give birth to Jesus.

In her womb, Mary carried Jesus who was both human and divine. Christians go on to describe Mary giving birth to Jesus who was both human and divine. Because Jesus was born human and divine, some Christians call Mary the "Mother of God." Orthodox Christians refer to Mary as "Theotokos," the "bearer of God," or the "carrier of God." The point of this term is to insist that she carried in her womb Jesus who was both God and human.

Some Christians avoid the term "Mother of God" for Mary. They think it confuses people, but they agree with the concept that Mary gave birth to Jesus who was God and human.

Jesus is sometimes spoken of as the "Word." Sometimes he is called the "Word made flesh" or even the "Incarnate Word." Now you know what these titles mean.

5. Trinity

Trinity is the hardest Christian concept to understand. Many Christians are confused about it, but it is a key concept for Christians. Notice that the prefix of the word is "tri," which means "three" as in "tricycle" and "triceratops." This is an attempt to explain the Trinity, but some Christians may find this explanation unsatisfactory.

Christians are monotheists who believe in one God. But for mainline Christians this one God is made of three persons: Father, Son, and Holy Spirit. Jesus is the Son. These three are not human persons, they are divine persons. The traditional belief is that the Trinity is "One God, yet three divine persons."

To be a person is to have a separate awareness. You as a human have a separate awareness. You know you are you and not someone else. In a similar way, there are three separate "awarenesses" in the Trinity. The Father knows he is the Father and not the Son, and not the Holy Spirit. The Son knows he is the Son and not the Father, and not the Holy Spirit. The Holy Spirit knows it is the Holy Spirit and not the Father or the Son.[5]

To clarify the mainline Christian teaching on Trinity it is necessary to talk about two wrong ideas or heresies about Trinity. The belief in Trinity is not tritheism. It is not three separate gods.

"Trinity" is also not modalism. Modalism is the idea that there is one divine being playing three different roles. A mode is a role. A student may have three roles. He or she is a student. The same person may play a second role on a sports team and have a third role working at a job. The student has three roles and is in three modes: student mode, athlete mode, and employee mode—yet he or she is still one person.

According to modalism, there is one divine being who plays the first role as God the Father, then plays a second role as Jesus, then plays a third role as the Holy Spirit. Each role is played one at a time. But there is only one divine person.

---

5 Traditional gender pronouns are being used here to keep this as simple as possible.

The simplest argument against modalism is to notice in the gospels that Jesus prays to the Father. Unless Jesus is somehow praying to himself, Jesus and the Father would have to be separate beings.

Just to clarify: tritheism and modalism are heresies and considered wrong ideas by mainline Christians.

6. Normative Writings

The Christian Bible is made of two parts: the Old Testament and New Testament. A typical printed Bible is about 1,500 pages long. The Old Testament starts with the creation stories then moves through the history of ancient Israel up to the centuries before Jesus. The New Testament covers the life of Jesus and the activities of the first several generations of his followers.

All Christians believe the Bible is the guide for faith and belief. Christians agree on the importance of the Bible yet often disagree about what the Bible means, and how to understand it. For example, Christians who believe in the Bible disagree on many issues such as abortion, capital punishment, same-sex marriage, women ministers, and many other issues. Churches have been split over the Bible. Christians have even killed other Christians over what the Bible means, but they all agree that the Bible is the guide.

7. Continuous Community

Christians believe the Christian community started with the first followers of Jesus and that history has shaped the present Christian Church. Christianity is not reinvented each generation.

Also, Christianity is done in a group, in communities. As Jesus stated: "For where two or three are gathered together in my name, there am I in the midst of them" (Matthew 18:20). Although the hermit alone praying by himself is a part of Christian tradition, it is a very small part and most monks who pray by themselves are part of larger groups. Also, Christian communities have rituals. Two rituals are found in all Christian churches: baptism, and communion. These rituals are described below.

These seven basic Christian beliefs are held by mainline Christians. As stated above, these beliefs are based on the Nicene Creed. And, in fact, this is how you figure out who is a mainline Christian and who is not. Do they agree with these ideas?

Who are mainline Christians who agree with these ideas? Catholics; Orthodox Christians; and Protestants such as Lutherans, Reformed, Anglicans, Episcopalians, most Baptists, Methodists, and many Evangelicals are examples.

Who are the non-mainline Christians who would not agree with these ideas? Mormons, Christian Scientists, and Jehovah's Witnesses are the more prominent examples.

These beliefs are summarized in the Nicene Creed written in the year 325. Mainline Christians believe in the concepts of the Nicene Creed.

C. THE NICENE CREED

We believe in one God,
the Father, the Almighty,
maker of heaven and earth,
of all that is seen and unseen.

We believe in one Lord, Jesus Christ,
the only Son of God,
eternally begotten of the Father,
God from God, Light from Light,
true God from true God,
begotten, not made, one in Being with the Father.

Through him all things were made.

For us men and for our salvation
he came down from heaven:
by the power of the Holy Spirit
he was born of the Virgin Mary, and became man.

For our sake he was crucified under Pontius Pilate,
he suffered, died, and was buried.

On the third day he rose again
in fulfillment of the Scriptures;
he ascended into heaven
and is seated at the right hand of the Father.

He will come again in glory to judge the living and the dead,
and his kingdom will have no end.

We believe in the Holy Spirit, the Lord, the giver of life,
who proceeds from the Father and the Son.

"Nicene Creed," *Episcopal Book of Common Prayer*, pp. 326-327. 1979.

With the Father and the Son he is worshiped and glorified.
He has spoken through the Prophets.

We believe in one holy catholic and apostolic Church.

We acknowledge one baptism for the forgiveness of sins.

We look for the resurrection of the dead
and the life of the world to come. Amen.

D. THE CHRISTIAN BIBLE

When most people think of the Bible, they are thinking of the Christian Bible, which is made up of two parts: the Old Testament and New Testament. As said before, the Old Testament begins with the creation stories then moves through the history of ancient Israel up to the centuries before Jesus. The New Testament covers the life of Jesus and the activities of the first several generations of his followers. To put it simply, the Old Testament is before Jesus and the New Testament is Jesus and after.

The titles for these two sections—Old Testament and New Testament—are Christian labels. The world "testament" means an agreement, or contract, or covenant. According to these terms there was an old agreement between God and the ancient people of Israel. This old agreement was augmented or superseded by a new agreement between God and the Christian Church through Jesus.[6]

What Christians call the Old Testament is what Jews call the Bible. A Jewish Bible is the same writings as the Christian Old Testament.[7] Typically, Jews do not refer to their Bible as the Old Testament since "Old Testament" is a Christian label with a Christian meaning.

Among Christians there are two Old Testaments: the Catholic Old Testament and the Protestant Old Testament. The Catholic version has 46 books; the Protestant version has 39 books. The Catholic version was the standard up until the 1500s when the Protestant leader Martin Luther took out seven books: 1 Maccabees, 2 Maccabees, Judith, Tobit, Baruch, Sirach (also called Ecclesiasticus), and

---

6   Christians have different views and use different words to explain why the New Testament is "new" and the Old Testament is "old." Here the words "augmented" and "superseded" are used as possible words. Some Christians would have other explanations.

7   The Jewish Bible contains basically the same readings as the Protestant Old Testament.

Wisdom. One reason for excluding these books was that they were originally written in Greek. The rest of the Old Testament books were written in Hebrew.

If you are unfamiliar with the Bible, now is the time to get one and look at it. The word "book" may be confusing. If you hold the Bible in your hand it looks like one book, which it is. But the sections of the Bible are also called books. Look at the table of contents and you will see the list of the books (sections) of the Bible. Each book is divided into numbered chapters and the chapters are divided into numbered verses. These chapter and verse numbers make it easy to find a specific place in any Bible.

The New Testament, which can also be called the Christian Scriptures, has 27 books. The books are the four gospels, one Acts of the Apostles, 21 Letters (or Epistles), and one book called Revelation. The gospels are Matthew, Mark, Luke, and John. Because Matthew, Mark, and Luke have many similarities they are called the Synoptic Gospels. ("Synoptic" means "same view.") The Gospel of John is very different in style from the Synoptic Gospels.

E. HOW TO READ THE BIBLE

The big question about the Bible is how to read it. What kind of literature is the Bible and how do we read it? Two of the most common approaches to reading the Bible are the literalist view and the contextualist view.

1. The Literalist View of the Bible

Someone who insists on taking the Bible literally is called a "literalist." Literalists say the Bible is the "Word of God." What they believe is that God told the biblical writers what to put down, word for word. The Bible was somehow dictated by God and therefore there cannot be any mistakes. All the stories occurred exactly as they are told in the Bible.

The Bible describes the earth being created in six days about 6,000 years ago. Literalists think this is exactly what happened. The Bible says humans were created on Day Six, and there was no evolution. Literalists do not believe in evolution. Scientists estimate the earth is about 4.6 billion years old. Literalists say that science is wrong. Note the difference in numbers: 6,000 versus 4,600,000,000!

In the Bible there is the story of Jonah who lived in the belly of a fish for three days. Literalists believe this happened.

2. The Contextualist View of the Bible

The word "contextualist" is a new term to make this simpler. The older term for this view is the historical-critical method for reading the Bible. Someone who insists on the taking the Bible contextually is called a "contextualist."

The contextualist view holds that the Bible was written by humans. To understand any human writing or communication you have to understand the "context" or setting.

If someone says to me, "You are such a jerk!" I have to know the context to know how to interpret the remark. Is someone who does not like me calling me a jerk? Is a friend just teasing me? Is someone who really loves me just mad at me? If I am a boss, do I need to fire the employee who called me a jerk? Am I an actor in a play? How you would understand "You are such a jerk!" totally depends on the context.

According to contextualists, if humans wrote the Bible there could be historical mistakes. Or if four humans wrote the story of Jesus, there would be differences in how they tell the story.

Also, ancient people often told myths. So, contextualists think that some of the stories in the first part of the Book of Genesis (the first book of the Bible) are religious myths. So the Creation story is an ancient myth about religious ideas of the origin of humans. It is not science.

Contextualists believe the story of Jonah was meant to teach a lesson. Jonah did not actually live in the belly of a fish for three days. It turns out the book of Jonah is a very profound teaching story about religious hatred.

In the story, Jonah hates the Assyrians. He wants God to punish and destroy them. But God does not want to destroy the Assyrians. God wants Jonah to preach to them so they can be forgiven. After trying to run away from his assignment, sailing in the opposite direction, being swallowed by a fish (or whale), and then being spat out exactly where he started; Jonah winds up going to the Assyrian city of Nineveh and preaching. The people repent. Jonah is furious because he really wanted God to destroy his enemies. The profound message of the Jonah story is that God does not hate whom we hate.[8]

Contextualists believe you have to try to think like ancient people who had no science and very little written history and no archeology to know about what happened before them.

There are two kinds of Contextualists:

1.   Those who believe the Bible was written solely by humans. In this case, it is an ancient religious text, interesting but nothing more.

---

8   This is a Bible lesson apparently missed by many religious extremist groups.

2. Those who believe the Bible was written by humans, but inspired by God. The Bible is God's message written by humans in their own words. The Bible is God's Word but not God's words.

So, there are three basic views on how to read the Bible:
Literalist,
Contextualist—solely a human product,
Contextualist—a human product inspired by God.

Which view makes more sense to you?

Literalists are often called "fundamentalists." Some Christian fundamentalists are active in opposing theories about evolution and opposing the teaching of evolution in schools. Most fear that a non-literal reading of Genesis will undermine the Bible and Christian faith and morals. One of the reasons for the growth of the Christian homeschool movement is to set up schools that do not teach evolution.

Lastly, a famous song questions a literal interpretation of the Bible. It is called "It Ain't Necessarily So!" from the opera *Porgy and Bess,* written by George Gershwin. Check it out on YouTube.

F. APOCRYPHA

"Apocrypha" is an important word to know. The meaning of the word is "hidden." The general use of the word is reserved for writings or books that did not make it into the Bible. There are three main groups called Apocrypha. The first group is Old Testament Apocrypha, which are writings that did not wind up in anyone's bible, such as the Book of Enoch.

The second group are those seven books that are not in the Protestant Old Testament but appear in the Catholic Old Testament. These books, cited previously, are 1 Maccabees, 2 Maccabees, Judith, Tobit, Baruch, Sirach (also called Ecclesiasticus), and Wisdom. According to Protestants, the seven books are part of the Old Testament Apocrypha along with the Book of Enoch. Catholics do not consider these books Apocrypha because they see them as part of the Bible.

The third group is New Testament Apocrypha. Since most Christians agree on the list of the 27 books in the New Testament there is little dispute on this group. There are about two dozen writings that did not make it into the New Testament, such as the Gospel of Thomas and the Acts of Thomas. These are important writings for helping to fill in the complexity of the early Christian world. The Gospel of Thomas is particularly interesting.

The most important writing of the New Testament Apocrypha is the Gospel of Thomas. It is helpful to read it in comparison with the traditional four gospels.

It is easily found online and is very quick to read. It is made up of only 114 sayings or verses. The sayings can be divided into three categories: 1) Those sayings that are the same as in the gospels; 2) those sayings that are very close to sayings in the gospels; and 3) those sayings that are very different from sayings in the gospels. This third category is the most controversial. Are these actual sayings of Jesus that did not make it into the Gospels of Mathew, Mark, Luke, and John? If so, they fill out the picture of Jesus. If they are not actual sayings of Jesus, then they can be discarded. However, there is no agreed-upon way to prove that these are actual sayings of Jesus or to prove that they are not authentic sayings of Jesus.

G. CHRISTIAN BAPTISM AND COMMUNION

The two most important Christian rituals are baptism and communion. These are found in almost all Christian groups, yet different denominations have different views on these rituals. On baptism, keep in mind that in the gospel accounts in Matthew, Mark, and Luke, when Jesus is baptized, not much information is given on the details. (Jesus is not baptized in the Gospel of John.)

1. Christian Baptism

Regarding baptism, Christians disagree on three questions:

1. When should someone be baptized?
2. How much water should be used?
3. What does baptism mean?

Some Christians baptize babies to welcome them into the Christian community. Other Christians insist that baptism should wait until a child is a young adult and old enough to decide whether he or she believes the Christian faith.

Many Christians believe that only a small amount of water is needed for baptism. This has the practical advantage that baptisms can be done by pouring a small amount of water over the forehead of a child or an adult at a baptismal font, which is simply a bowl on a stand.

Other Christians insist that baptism should require full immersion: someone being baptized needs to go completely underwater. This

FIGURE 6.4 Baptismal font

requires churches to have baptismal tanks and changing rooms so people can get out of their street clothes and put on a gown or jumpsuit to be baptized. Maintaining facilities for full-immersion baptism involves extra effort and costs but many churches insist that this is how John the Baptist baptized people. Lastly, a few Christians even insist on doing baptism in an actual river.

The last issue is the meaning of baptism. For some Christians baptism takes away "original sin," which is the guilt passed down from the first human beings. Also in baptism, a person receives "grace," which is God's love and mercy given freely by God without being earned or deserved by humans.

Other issues about the meaning of baptism are important.

For some Christians a baptism is essential for salvation and going to heaven is impossible without it. Other Christians believe that baptism is the normal path for salvation but not absolutely essential. Still other Christians see baptism as not needed for salvation. For these Christians, salvation is dependent on one's acceptance of Jesus as Lord and Savior. In this case, baptism serves as a symbol of one's acceptance of Jesus.

It is important to say a little more on the idea of original sin. According to some Christians, the first people where Adam and Eve, and they disobeyed God. They committed the first sin and committed the original sin. Some Christians believe the guilt of Adam and Eve is passed on to all subsequent human beings. All humans are born with the guilt of original sin. For Christians who think this way, baptism takes away this guilt.

You could go ask your local minister to explain the meaning of baptism. Then go to the church up the road and ask the same question and see if the answers are close. The Wikipedia article on baptism offers a chart of various church positions that shows the complexity of the various views.

A final point on baptism is that for some Christians it serves as the birth ritual, and for other Christians it is the adulthood ritual. Those traditions that practice adult baptism often have dedication or naming ceremonies when a child is born. Sometimes this is called a "christening," a word that comes from the word "Christ." Christening is a tricky word since it is used in different ways. For some Christians a christening is the dedication of a child without baptism. For other Christians, christening is another name for baptism.

2. Christian Communion

Regarding communion, Christians disagree on four questions:

1. What is it called?
2. How often should it be done?

3.   What are the details?

4.   What is the meaning of Communion?

All Christians have some sort of Communion service but it goes by different names: Mass, the Lord's Supper, Eucharist, and Communion.

How often various Christian groups hold Communion services runs the gamut from once a year, to once a month, to twice a month, to every Sunday. For Catholics, going to Mass every Sunday is expected. But Catholics also have the option of going every day and many s follow this practice. If you drive by a Catholic church early on a weekday you will see people going to Mass.

The details of Communion vary widely. All involve bread and wine, or bread and grape juice. The bread can be an actual loaf from which pieces are torn off and handed to people. Many churches use flat wafers called hosts.

Some churches think that Christians should not drink wine in church, and so grape juice is used instead. Some churches use a common cup or chalice and everyone drinks from the chalice. Other churches pour the wine or grape juice into small, individual cups.

The last issue about Communion, and a very important one, is: What does it mean? Communion is based on the

FIGURE 6.5   Communion

example of Jesus at the Last Supper and the words he said over the bread, "This is my body," and the words he said over the wine, "This is my blood." For centuries Christians have argued over the meaning of these words. Three basic positions on the meaning of Communion have evolved.[9]

The first position is that in the Communion service, when the bread and wine (or grape juice) are blessed, the action is "merely symbolic." The bread is still bread, the wine (or grape juice) is still the wine (or grape juice). They are simply symbols that Jesus chose that remind Christians of what Jesus did by dying on the cross.

---

9   There are other positions but they are variations on these.

The second position is called "spiritual presence." In this view, when Christians come together to remember and reenact his Last Supper, Jesus is spiritually present in the community. Also Jesus's spiritual presence is different from a service without Communion. Furthermore, the bread and wine (or grape juice) are not changed in the process.

The third position is called "physical presence" or "real presence." In this view, the bread and wine really become the body and blood of Jesus. This view takes the words of Jesus, "This is my body," literally. Although the bread looks, tastes, and smells like bread and the wine looks, tastes, and smells like wine, somehow at the deepest level—at the essential level—they are changed into the body and blood of Jesus.

Several Christian groups adhere to this belief, including Roman Catholics, Orthodox Christians, Anglicans, Episcopalians and Lutherans, although they do not agree on how to explain what happens to the bread and wine in the Communion service.

H. MAJOR DIVISIONS IN CHRISTIANITY

There are many thousands of Christian denominations and groups, and it can be very confusing sorting them out. Many denominations, however, can be roughly grouped into five divisions. These divisions will cover most denominations but not all.

1. Orthodox Christians

These Christians represent the oldest Christian tradition. These are usually identified by national identity such as Greek Orthodox, Russian Orthodox, Rumanian Orthodox, and American Orthodox. (There are more groups out there.)

2. The Roman Catholic Church

The Roman Catholic Church represents by far the largest Christian denomination and is found throughout the world. The head of the Catholic Church is the pope, who lives in Rome.

3. Protestant Churches Coming from Europe

These are denominations that spilt off from the Catholic Church starting in the 1500s. Churches in this group would include the Lutherans, Presbyterians, Anglicans (and their American version, the Episcopalians), Baptists, Methodists, the Amish, and the Mennonites.

4. American-born Churches That Accept the Nicene Creed or Its Ideas

This group includes churches such as the United Church of Christ, which accept the Nicene Creed. This category also includes those churches that accept the Christian beliefs stated previously, even if they do not use the Nicene Creed itself.

5. American-born Churches That Reject the Nicene Creed

Churches in this category would include the Mormon Church, which is called The Church of Jesus Christ of Latter-day Saints, the Christian Science Church, and Jehovah's Witnesses.

DISCUSSION QUESTIONS

1. What are your thoughts on the life and teaching of Jesus?
2. If you are Christian, did you learn anything new in the Christian beliefs about Jesus? If you are not a Christian, what was the most interesting thing you learned about the seven basic Christian beliefs?
3. After reading about the different views on how to read the Bible, what is your thinking about how to understand the Bible?
4. What do you think about the Christian practices of baptism and Communion?
5. Are there different Christian churches where you live? What denominations do they represent?

Credits

- Fig. 6.1: Source: https://commons.wikimedia.org/wiki/File:Matthias_Gr%C3%BCnewald_-_The_Crucifixion_-_WGA10723.jpg.
- Fig. 6.2: Source: https://commons.wikimedia.org/wiki/File:Leonardo_da_Vinci_-_The_Last_Supper_high_res.jpg.
- Fig. 6.3: Source: https://commons.wikimedia.org/wiki/File:Simple_Labarum2.svg.
- Fig. 6.4: Source: https://commons.wikimedia.org/wiki/File:Hans_Egedes_Kirke_Copenhagen_font.jpg.
- Fig. 6.5: Copyright © DALIBRI (CC BY-SA 4.0) at https://commons.wikimedia.org/wiki/File:Fronleichnamsprozession_2017_Neumarkt_036.jpg.

CHAPTER 7

ISLAM

A. THE WORD 'ISLAM'

The religion is called "Islam," and a follower is a "Muslim." The word Islam means "submission"—submission to the will of Allah. Muslims are monotheists who believe in one god they call "Allah." Allah is the Arabic word for God. Islam also means "peace" and is based on the Arabic word for peace, *salaam*, which is related to the Hebrew word for peace, *shalom*. According to Muslims, one finds peace through submitting oneself to the will of God.

Some non-Muslims are surprised to learn that Islam means "peace." Often, Muslim extremists and terrorists appear in the news committing violent acts. What some non-Muslims do not understand is that Muslim extremists and terrorists are not typical Muslims and that most of the victims of such violence are other Muslims. The vast majority of Muslims want to live peaceful, nonviolent lives. These ordinary Muslims do not make the news.

B. MUHAMMAD[1]

The beginnings of Islam are traced to Muhammad, who was born around 570 into the Quraysh tribe that controlled the Ka'ba. The Ka'ba was the central shrine in the city of Mecca in what today is Saudia Arabia. At the time, several hundred gods were worshipped there, including Allah. The father of Muhammad died soon after his birth and his mother died when he was six, so he was raised by his uncle, Abu Talib.

At the time, Mecca was a busy place because of trading caravans. Long caravans of camels carried goods such as ivory, gold, incense, and silk. This trade brought prosperity to Mecca. Muhammad worked on such caravans. He encountered Christians and Jews in his travels. At age 25 Muhammad married Khadijah, age 40, a wealthy widow who gave birth to two sons who died in infancy and four girls who survived.

---

1   For a more thorough exploration of Islam, see Renard, *The Handy Religion Answer Book*, 121–182.

In the next years Muhammad would often go into the hills around Mecca to ponder and meditate. According to tradition, in the year 610, when he was 40, the angel Gabriel appeared to him as he prayed in a cave named Hira. Gabriel gave Muhammad messages to learn and then recite. Muhammad would continue to receive such revelations the rest of his life. He would memorize the messages and teach them to his later companions. After his death the messages would be written down as the Qur'an, the holy book of Islam.

From these messages Muhammad came to believe in only one god called Allah and to see that humans needed to submit themselves to Allah. He also believed he was the last of the line of prophets that included such figures as Adam, Abraham, Moses, and Jesus.

Muhammad began preaching that there was only one god, Allah, and that everyone was equal before God. Humans would be judged before God on how they lived. He preached against gambling, drinking alcohol, prostitution, and idolatry. Having female slaves or concubines for sexual purposes was wrong. He also preached against having great wealth when there was so much poverty.

His preaching was unpopular because many people wanted to continue the practices that he condemned. Yet no one could harm him because he was protected by his family clan; however, when key family members died, including his uncle, he no longer had protection.

In the year 622 he fled to the nearby city of Yathrib, where Muhammad had been asked to come to arbitrate disputes among various factions that included Arab tribes, Jewish tribes, and a community of Christians. This flight of Muhammad is called the "Hijrah." The year 622 AD/CE became Year 1 in the Muslim calendar. Yathrib would eventually be renamed Medina from *Medinat Al Nabi*, which means "the city of the prophet." Muhammad united the various tribes under the Constitution of Medina and he became the religious and political leader of Medina.

Next, the Muslims from Medina began raiding the caravans going into Mecca. Angry over the raids, Mecca sent a force of 10,000 in 627 to attack Medina, which defended itself by digging a defensive ditch around the city. Sometimes this battle is called the Battle of the Ditch. The army from Mecca failed to take the city.

In 630, Muhammad led his own force to Mecca. The city surrendered without a fight. Muhammad went into the Ka'ba and circled it seven times, then removed all the statues and idols. Muhammad dedicated the Ka'ba to the one god, Allah. This event is called the "hajj." (Ever since, Muslims have remembered this event by making their own hajj to Mecca.) Muhammad died in 632.

Muslims disagree on the question of how Muhammad can be depicted in art. Some Muslims avoid all images of Muhammad. Others allow images of Muhammad if his face is veiled. Some Muslims take great offense if they feel Muhammad is not portrayed respectfully.

C. THE QUR'AN

For Muslims the holy book is the Qur'an. (The older English spelling is "Koran.") The Qur'an is divided into chapters, with each chapter called a "sura." There are 114 suraat (the plural of sura) in the Qur'an. Although the first sura is short, the rest are organized by size from longest to shortest. Numerous figures from the Jewish and Christian scriptures are cited in the Qur'an, including Adam, Abraham, Moses, Gabriel, Joseph, Mary, and Jesus.

Muslims believe the true Qur'an is in Arabic. Thus, a translation of the Qur'an is not the true Qur'an. Muslims have followed a different path than Christians in spreading their faith. Christians have translated the Bible into almost every written language so people can read it in their own language. In spreading the faith, Muslims teach people Arabic so they can read the true Qur'an.

Muslims believe that Muhammad passed on exactly what the angel Gabriel told him, word for word, and that Muhammad added nothing to the messages, which were later written down by his followers as the Qur'an. The written Qur'an is called the "Created Qur'an" and is believed to be an exact copy of the "Uncreated Qur'an," which is in heaven.

The Qur'an is about the size of the Christian New Testament. The Qur'an does not have many stories, but it does have many words of exhortation. (Exhortation is encouragement.)

Muslims treat the Qur'an with great respect, and many Muslims are greatly offended by any mistreatment of a copy of it.

D. THE FIVE PILLARS

Key to Islam are the Five Pillars, which are the duties of being a faithful Muslim.

1. Shahada

Shahada means "profession," and here the word does not refer to one's occupation, but rather to the duty to profess or say one's belief. The first duty of a Muslim is to profess "There is no god but Allah, and Muhammad is his prophet."

A few points need to be made about this profession. Muslims are monotheists who believe in one God. Muslims, however, totally reject the Christian ideas of incarnation and Trinity. In the Qur'an, the idea that God would become human is called an "abomination" (something really terrible).

Muslims believe in the concept of "tawhid," which is the unity of God. God is one. There is no Trinity. Also, Muslims believe in Jesus as a human being who was a prophet, and was one in the line of prophets. Muslims believe Jesus was born of the Virgin Mary but that Jesus was not the Son of God, as Christians claim. Also, Muslims believe that although Jesus appeared to be crucified, he did not die. Muslims believe that Jesus ascended bodily into heaven.

When Muslims say that Muhammad is a prophet, they believe that he is a human being specially chosen to be the last of the line of prophets that include figures in both the Hebrew Scriptures and the Christian Scriptures. Muslims call Muhammad the "seal of the prophets," which in Arabic is "rasulullah." This means that Muhammad is the last prophet and prophecy is sealed after him.

2. Salat

Salat is the duty to pray five times daily, and there are many details involved. Muslims are to pray on a prayer mat facing Mecca. If one can go to a mosque and pray with others then that is best, but if not, one should pray by himself or herself.

A cycle of prayers is called a rakat or rak'ah. A rakat includes specific prayers and specific positions such as kneeling, bowing, and standing. It takes several minutes to complete a rakat. During salat a Muslim will complete two, three, or four rakat. Several short videos on how to perform salat can be found on YouTube.

FIGURE 7.1 Supplicating pilgrim at Masjid Al Haram, Mecca, Saudi Arabia.

3. Zaqat

This is a tax or religious contribution to help the poor. Typically, it is 2.5 percent of one's income and wealth, though it varies from place to place.

4. Sawm

Muslims are required to fast during the month of Ramadan: no food or drink during daylight hours. In Islam, months move around relative to the seasons, so the length of the days will vary from one year to the next.

5. Hajj

This is the duty to make a pilgrimage to Mecca in Saudi Arabia at least once in one's lifetime. The highpoint of the hajj is to go to the central shrine in Mecca and walk around the Ka'ba seven times. The Ka'ba is a black cubic building at the center of Mecca.

E. DETAILS OF THE HAJJ (THE PILGRIMAGE)

The Fifth Pillar of Islam requires that each Muslim make a pilgrimage to Mecca in Saudi Arabia at least once in a lifetime, provided one can afford it and that one is in good health. The pilgrimage, called the Hajj, takes place in the month of Dhu al-Hijjah, the last month of the Islamic year. In some cultures only male Muslims make the pilgrimage; in other cultures both women and men make the hajj to Mecca.

For the pilgrimage, women wear modest clothes; men wear a simple white robe made of two pieces of cloth. There are three reasons for this white robe. First, it is a symbol of purity. Second, it makes everyone look equal. (Often clothes are one of the ways we distinguish who is rich and who is poor.) And third, people remove all clothes that show ethnic or political differences. The hajj emphasizes the Ummah, which is the worldwide community of Muslims where all are equal before Allah.

Muslims begin the hajj in a state of holiness, known as Ihram. Pilgrims are to refrain from activities such as clipping their nails, shaving, covering their heads (for men), and having sexual relations.

A pilgrim then goes to the Ka'ba, the central shrine in Mecca. When one first sees the Ka'ba he or she says "Allahu Akbar" ("God is Great") three times, and then "La Ilaha Illallah" ("There is no god but God"). The pilgrim then performs tawaf, which is the ritual of walking around the Ka'ba seven times in a counterclockwise direction. One tries to get close enough to touch the black stone at the center. If a pilgrim cannot get close enough to it because of the crowds, the hand is pointed to the black stone.

FIGURE 7.2   The Ka'ba in Mecca

This next duty is called performing Sa'ay. In Islamic tradition, Hagar was the wife of the prophet Ibrahim (Abraham). She gave birth to Ishmael. Hagar was driven away by Ibrahim's other wife, Sarah. Hager found herself in the desert without water. She ran seven times between two hills searching for water. An angel appeared to her telling her that God would provide water. A spring of water appeared. Pilgrims reenact this by running or walking between the hills seven times. (The passage is now covered and air conditioned.) Pilgrims drink water from the spring, now called the well of Zamzam.

A number of steps are followed over the days that follow.

First Day
Pilgrims go to an area filled with tents called Mina. Here they spend a whole day in prayer.

Second Day
Pilgrims next go the plain at Arafat to pray, standing for the afternoon. After sunset, pilgrims go to Muzdalifah to spend the night in prayer. They sleep on the ground. Before leaving, each pilgrim gathers seven pebbles.

Third Day
Pilgrims return to Mina where they throw their pebbles at a wall that represents Satan. This is known as "stoning the devil." The next ritual is to sacrifice an animal such as a lamb or camel. A common practice is to buy a sacrifice voucher. A voucher represents an animal that is sacrificed, butchered, and then packaged to be shipped to feed the poor around the world.

Then men have their hair cut or shaved off. Women pilgrims cut off a lock of their hair. Then pilgrims return to Mecca for another tawaf.

Following Days
Over the following days pilgrims repeat the stoning of the devil once or twice. On the last day of their hajj, pilgrims perform a farewell tawaf of circling the Ka'ba seven times. After completing the hajj many pilgrims go on to the city of Medina to visit the tomb of Muhammad.

Although the hajj is a duty, many Muslims experience the making of hajj as the highpoint of their lives. One who has completed the pilgrimage is honored with the title "hajji."

F. DIVISIONS IN ISLAM

There are two main divisions in Islam: Sunni Islam and Shia Islam. Shia Muslims are often called Shi'ites and make up about 15 percent of Muslims and are mostly in Iran. Anyone following international news in the last 20 years should be familiar with these terms. Two issues divide these groups. One issue involves an old argument about who was the true leader of Islam after Muhammad died. The second issue is a disagreement over the final authorities for answering religious questions.

In some parts of the world there is much tension and conflict between Sunni Muslims and Shia Muslims. But keep in mind that while these conflicts include big religious differences, there are also historical, cultural, ethnic, national, and economic differences behind the conflicts.

G. JIHAD

Jihad is an important concept, but it is often misunderstood by non-Muslims. One meaning of jihad is "holy war," and in the long and complex history of Islam a numbers of wars have been fought as holy wars. Some Muslim terrorists have used the concept to justify their actions; however, most Muslims believe terrorist actions are not holy wars. Furthermore, most of the victims of such terrorists are Muslims. The vast majority of Muslims reject this kind of jihad. As do most people, most Muslims want to live their lives in peace.

Regarding warfare, the teaching for most Muslims is that only defensive wars are justified. This view is close to the common view among many people around the world and many Americans. (Note that after World War II the United States renamed the Department of War as the Department of Defense.)

Finally, it must be pointed out that for many Muslims the main meaning of the term jihad is "holy struggle." In Muslim thinking, the biggest struggle for humans is the inner spiritual struggle to submit one's self to the will of Allah. Some call this spiritual struggle the "greater jihad" and the struggle against the enemies of Islam the "lesser jihad."

DISCUSSION QUESTIONS

1. What did you learn about Islam?

2. Are the Five Pillars similar to practices in other religions?

3. Where is the nearest mosque to you? (You could do an online search.)

4. Go online and search for images of mosques around the world. Also look for images of Muslims making the hajj.

5. Can you find these countries on a map? These are the ten countries with the largest Muslim populations: Indonesia, India, Pakistan, Bangladesh, Nigeria, Egypt, Iran, Turkey, Algeria, and Morocco. Can you find Afghanistan? Why is Afghanistan important to Americans? Also, find the countries of Azerbaijan, Kazakhstan, Kyrgyzstan, Tajikistan, and Turkmenistan. In these countries the majority of the population is Muslim.

Credits

CHAPTER 8

EASTERN RELIGIONS

A. HINDUISM[1]

1. Origins

Hinduism is a very diverse religion that comes from India. In fact, the word "Hinduism" was created by Europeans to describe all the various religious activities and groups in India. However, a general and broad description is possible.

We start with a bit of history. Thousands of years ago, along the Indus River, which today is in Pakistan, early Indian society developed. This society had a strict social order called the caste system.

There were four main groups

> Brahmins—the families of the priests and intellectuals
>
> Kshatriyas—the families of the warriors and political leaders
>
> Vaisyas—the families of the merchants and farmers
>
> Shudras—the families of the servants

Another group was so low that they were off the caste system. Hence, they were called "outcasts" (the origin of the English word). The outcasts were also called the chandalas or untouchables or Dalits. In India, many people would not even touch them. Although this category is not legally recognizable, it still exists in many places in Hindu society and often Dalits experience prejudice, injustice, and sometimes violence.

For Hinduism, there are several important collections of religious writings:

> The Vedas—hymns to the Hindu gods
>
> The Brahmanas—writings on sacrifice

---

1 For a more thorough exploration of Eastern religions such as Hinduism, see Renard, *The Handy Religion Answer Book*.

Two Epic Poems:

the *Mahabharata*

the *Ramayana*

The Upanishads—writings on Hindu philosophy

2. Hindu Philosophy

When one first explores the philosophy of Hinduism it can seem confusing and impossible to understand. In fact, the concepts are not difficult, but for most people they require rethinking how they view reality. (Also, after studying Hinduism, if you are still confused, keep in mind that a Hindu guru might admit that the ultimate realities are beyond understanding.)

A key concept of Hinduism is reincarnation, the belief that all animals and humans have souls. When an animal or human body dies, the soul leaves that body and enters another body. When that later body dies, the soul goes into yet another body. A Hindu saying states: "Just as the body sheds worn-out clothes, so the soul sheds worn-out bodies."

The soul is caught in a cycle of birth, death, and rebirth; dying again, being born again, and on and on. This cycle is called "samsara." Samsara is a trap because in between each birth and death is suffering. The goal in Hinduism is for the soul to break free from the cycle of samsara. The release is called "moksha."

Reincarnation is guided by the concept of "karma." Some people talk about "good karma" and "bad karma," as if the term meant "good luck" and "bad luck." But that is not the Hindu understanding.

Karma is the law of responsibility. You are responsible for everything you do, think, or say. For every bad thing you do, think, or say, there will be a bad consequence—you will suffer for it. The consequences, however, may not occur during this lifetime; they may show up in future lifetimes. Karma covers multiple lives.

So if a person does evil and "gets away with it" in this life, he or she will suffer in future lives. If a person does good, then there will be good consequences in future lives.

But it is not just actions that matter. Thoughts and speech also count. A person who is filled with anger creates bad consequences even if the anger is kept inside and the person never acts on the anger.

Karma, as the law of responsibility, motivates us to be careful about what we do, think, or say so as to avoid suffering in a future life. It can also be used to explain suffering. If a person who has done nothing wrong in this life is suffering, then that person must have done something wrong in a previous life. Thus, some people can look at those in the lowest social classes suffering in poverty and, rather than feeling pity, could see them as being punished for wrong acts they did in a past life.

Besides karma, an additional problem for the soul is attachment. If the soul is attached to things of this world, then when the body dies, the soul needs to come back and get those things. If a person is attached to wealth, then when the body dies, the soul needs to come back into another body to get more wealth. If a person dies with physical desires such as lust, then the soul wants to get back into a body to satisfy that desire.

Also, notice that negative emotions are also attachments. If you have anger toward someone, you are <u>very</u> attached to that person even if you "hate his guts." Notice how much you think about the person you are angry with? Notice how sometimes you want to hurt that person. The desire to hurt the person is an attachment. If a soul dies with anger, it needs to come back in another life to express that anger.

Karma and attachment drive the cycle of samsara and determine the kind of life into which a person is reborn

3. What about the Gods?

In Hinduism there are thousands of gods. Three of the most important are Brahma, Vishnu, and Shiva. There are thousands of temples in India honoring the gods and millions of shrines to them in homes. Certain gods are honored by certain people. For example, soldiers are often devoted to the monkey god Hanuman. (Do an online image search for Hindu gods.)

On the surface, the religion resembles polytheism, a belief in many gods. But Hinduism is not polytheism, because all the gods in Hinduism are not separate beings but merely aspects or manifestations of a greater reality called "Brahman."

Brahman is ultimate reality, but Brahman is beyond understanding. Brahman is beyond space, time, and causality. Monotheists sometimes describe their God as having awareness, personhood, and memory. Monotheists sometimes describe having a "personal relationship with God." Hindus do not see Brahman as having such qualities.

As said previously, all the various gods are believed to be manifestations or aspects of Brahman. Since the concept of Brahman is so vague, Brahman is manifested in the various gods. In those various gods Hindus find figures to pray to and to worship.

If this is your first time studying Hinduism, then you might find it confusing. For example, notice that four key Hindu terms look the same: Brahma, Brahmins, Brahmanas, and Brahman. When you see these words, look closely at each one and double check that you have the right meaning. (Remember the baseball example of all the uses of the word "double": a double play, a double, and a doubleheader.)

The gods are Brahman but so is everything else: humans, animals, and plants. Even the physical world is Brahman. Everything is Brahman. Everything is one. Hinduism is monism. Everything is one. You are Brahman. Everyone else is Brahman. The Brahman that is you is called "atman."

If everything is one, then why do people treat one another so badly? Why do we hurt others if we are part of the same ultimate reality? The answer is that we humans are caught in an illusion that we are all separate beings. If we are separate, then I might benefit from your loss. If I take your money I have gained and you have lost. In Hinduism there is no such gain since we are all one. This illusion of separateness is called "maya." (The Hindu word "maya" looks similar to the word "Maya," the label for the Mayan people who lived in Mexico and Central America 800 years ago. Don't get them confused.)

Understanding maya is tricky. For Hindus, the idea that we are all separate is an illusion. An illusion is a wrong way of seeing. The correct way of seeing reality, according to Hinduism, is to see that we are all one. Most non-Hindus, however, see reality in the opposite way. Most non-Hindus believe we are all separate and also separate from other animals and physical things. And for non-Hindus who believe in God, God is a separate being. While Hindus think this is the wrong way to see things—that everything is separate—non-Hindus think it is the right way to see things: everything is separate.

4. Yogas—the Paths

Today, when many people use the word "yoga" they are referring to a series of physical movements and postures designed to improve physical health and emotional well-being. These practices come from India. But the word yoga has a much broader meaning. A yoga is a path. There are four paths in Hinduism to try to achieve moksha and release from the cycle of samsara. But it may take several lives to achieve moksha.

> Karma yoga
>
> Bhakti yoga
>
> Jnana yoga
>
> Raja yoga

Karma yoga is the path of doing one's duty but doing it with detachment. One's duty is determined by one's caste and one's stage in life. Bhakti yoga is the path of devotion. One devotes oneself to a particular god. Jnana yoga is the intellectual path, using meditation to overcome the illusion of maya. (The word "jnana" is pronounced like the second and third syllables of the Spanish word *mañana*.) Raja yoga is the royal path, the path often chosen by holy men, and it involves years of meditation and asceticism.

Also, in Hinduism there is a shortcut to achieving moksha and that is to die in the city of Benares. Many sick people go to Benares to die and be cremated on the banks of the Ganges River then have their ashes spread in the river.

The goal in Hinduism is to achieve moksha, to have one's soul absorbed into Brahman. This belief, however, is different from how monotheists think about heaven. Most monotheists believe that when they go to heaven they will take with them their sense of identity, their self-awareness, and their memory of who they are. In Hinduism, all such things are attachments that have to be let go of to achieve release.

To understand Hinduism you need two more words. "Puja" (also spelled "pooja") is the word for worship of a god. This can be prayers or offerings. "Guru" is the word for a teacher.

B. BUDDHISM[2]

1. The Life of Siddhartha Gautama

The next major religion is Buddhism, which begins with Siddhartha Gautama (c. 563–483 BC). According to Buddhist tradition, just after Siddhartha was born, his parents received a prophecy that he would become either a great king or a sage. A sage is a wise teacher. His parents wanted him to become a king, so they raised him in a palace of luxury with all his needs met. Siddhartha got married and had a son, but despite the luxury of his life he was deeply dissatisfied.

One day he went outside the palace and took in four sights: a decrepit old man, a sick man suffering in pain, a dead body being taken to be cremated, and an ascetic monk. ("Ascetic" means that the monk took on hardships such as fasting.) After seeing these four sights Siddhartha realized that humans suffer. He was deeply troubled. So he left everything to seek an answer to the questions "Why do we suffer?" and "What can be done to not suffer?" This period of his life is called the "Great Renunciation" when he renounced and gave up everything.

Siddhartha tried Hindu philosophy but found no answers. He became an ascetic monk and tried extreme fasting and denying the body's needs. But again he found no answers. Finally, after several years Siddhartha finally gave up and sat down under a Bodhi tree to wait for answers. He waited until he became enlightened.[3] Then he got the answers to his two questions on suffering. He became the "Enlightened

---

2   For a more thorough overview of Buddhism, see "Chapter 5, Buddhism" in Fisher, *Living Religions*.

3   There are different traditions as to how long he waited, from a few days to six weeks.

FIGURE 8.1 Buddha

One," the Buddha. His answers became the Four Noble Truths.

He spent the rest of his life gathering followers to listen to his teaching. He died when a friend mistakenly fed him poison mushrooms. The Buddha's last words were "Decay is inherent in all things; work out your salvation with diligence." What he meant was that nothing lasts and you are on your own to overcome suffering. Although the Buddha believed in the gods and that one might pray to them for a good harvest or for more rain, they were of no help in the key issue of overcoming suffering and breaking the cycle of birth, death, and rebirth. In the Buddha's teaching there is no being who is your savior.

2. The Four Noble Truths

The teaching of the Buddha is called The Four Noble Truths:

1. Life inevitably involves suffering.

2. The cause of suffering is desire.

3. To eliminate suffering, eliminate desire.

4. To eliminate desire, follow the Eightfold Path.

1. Life inevitably involves suffering. The word for suffering is "dukkha." To live is to suffer. We suffer physically, emotionally, and psychologically. Often suffering can be very intense. One reason for our emotional suffering is "anicca," or impermanence. We want good things to last but they do not. Friends and family go away or die. Our possessions grow old and we lose them. Health does not last. We grow old and die. Nothing is permanent, but we wish things would last and so we suffer. We also suffer because there is no permanent self. This last idea, called "anattā," will be discussed below.

2. The cause of suffering is desire. The word for desire is "tanha." Desire as the cause of suffering has several levels of meaning. First we desire things we do not get, so we are unhappy. Can you remember as a child being disappointed because you did not get the holiday gift you desperately desired? Or we desire something and we get it, yet we are disappointed by it.

Also, strong desires can cause suffering. Any kind of addiction can cause great suffering. Desperately wanting something we cannot have can be misery.

Buddhists believe in reincarnation. A further problem with desire is that it drives the cycle of birth, death, and rebirth. Sexual desire drives the cycle by causing humans to be born. Also, when we die our desires do not go away. They want to get into a new body so they can seek what is desired.

3. To eliminate suffering, eliminate desire. This third Noble Truth follows logically from the first two.

4. To eliminate desire, follow the Eightfold Path. Buddhism gives eight guides to overcome desire.

The Eightfold Path

Right view—have the right view of reality (as stated in the Four Noble Truths).

Right intention—dedicate oneself to pursuing enlightenment.

Right speech—avoid bad speech such as telling lies or gossiping.

Right action—avoid acts of violence and stealing.

Right livelihood—avoid any jobs that involve the killing of humans or animals.

Right effort—avoid negative states of mind.

Right mindfulness—be aware of what the mind is doing.

Right concentration—meditate.

The goal in Buddhism is to eliminate all desires and achieve a state of a bliss called "nirvana." One who has achieved this state is called an "arhat," a saint. Also, if one reaches nirvana there will be no reincarnation when one dies. (Buddhists often do not believe or speculate on the afterlife. Since there is no permanent self, there is no conscious awareness in the next life.)

The teaching of Buddhism is called "dharma." The Buddhist community is called the "sangha." An important Buddhist saying states, "I take refuge in the Buddha. I take refuge in the dharma. I take refuge in the sangha."

3. Four Important Buddhist Groups
Theravada Buddhism

To get a basic understanding of Buddhism one has to be aware of four groups. (There are many other groups.) The first two groups are the two major divisions of Buddhism: Theravada and Mahayana. Zen Buddhism and Tibetan Buddhism are smaller divisions, yet influential.

Theravada Buddhism is also called "The Way of the Elders." This version is closest to the example that the Buddha lived. In order to overcome desire one must leave ordinary life and become a monk. One must give up a career, having a family, having possessions or wealth. One goes to a monastery to give up everything.

At the monastery one's hair is shaved. This is a sign of giving up the outside world, but it also includes giving up one's identity. Our hair is one of the ways we express our individuality and identity. In military boot camp the heads of recruits are shaved for the same reason: to take away the recruit's sense of individual identity.

Buddhist monks spend their days in meditation trying to overcome all desire. But it is a difficult task. Monks support themselves by taking food offerings from the people who live near them.

In the Theravada Buddhist tradition, Siddhartha, who became the Buddha, was an enlightened man, but he was nothing more. He was an example to follow. Nirvana is difficult to achieve in this tradition.

Mahayana Buddhism

Mahayana Buddhism is called "the Great Boat" or "the Great Raft." Many people can achieve Nirvana because they can get help. In this branch of Buddhism the Buddha is a divine being. The Buddha who walked the earth was an incarnation of a divine Buddha essence. One can also get help from Bodhisattvas, people who lived in the past who achieved Buddhahood. They become beings to whom one can pray.

It is important to note that these two major branches of Buddhism disagree on a key point. In Theravada Buddhism the Buddha is man. In Mahayana Buddhism the Buddha is a divine being. This is a huge difference between these two branches of what is labeled as one religion.

Zen and Tibetan Buddhism

In addition to the two main branches, two smaller groups are important because of their influence: Zen Buddhism and Tibetan Buddhism. Zen Buddhism comes from Japan. The goal in Zen is to achieve enlightenment through extensive meditation. But Zen has no belief in any divine beings to help. There are Zen monasteries, but ordinary people also find Zen meditation helpful in coping with the stresses of life.

When Buddhism came to Tibet in the Himalayas it merged with the local religion to form a unique form of Buddhism. Tibetan monks are known for their unique clothes, their throat singing, and making of mandalas, which are sand paintings. Their leader, the Dalai Lama, is known worldwide as a voice calling for worldwide understanding and compassion.

4. Things to Think About

Desire

The Buddhist insight that desire is the cause of suffering is worth pondering by non-Buddhists. We live in a culture that seems to be working on the assumption that we will be happy and will end our sufferings when all our desires are met. We work hard to meet our desires, yet we are not that happy.

The advertising industry puts more and more ads in front of us with the illusion that if we can just meet our desires we will be happy. Start looking at the websites on your computer and start counting all the ads and pop-ups. Each logo is also an ad. It is not unusual to see a dozen or more ads within a few seconds on the Internet. Since you were born there has been a huge increase in the number of ads to which people are exposed.

It is important to clarify that if someone does not have enough money to meet his or her basic needs, such as food, shelter, and security, having more money will make him or her happier. But after basic needs are met, having more possessions and money do not make one happier.

Anattā (Optional Topic)

Anattā, the Buddhist view of "no self," is a difficult concept to understand; however, if one can understand it, anattā provides a very profound insight into the human condition and can change one's life. Anattā is the idea that we do not have a permanent self or identity. This is difficult to understand because most of us assume the opposite—that we have a permanent self.

Imagine yourself many years ago in kindergarten. You had a body that was much smaller and much different. Your mind had less knowledge and fewer experiences. But most of us believe in a "me" back there, that there was a "self" back there in kindergarten with that child's body, knowledge, and awareness, and since that time the permanent self, called "me," has traveled through the years. The body has grown and developed and the mind has learned new things and has had new experiences. Most of us assume there is a permanent "me" going through the years. We think that "I have a permanent self that has been with me since I was born and will be with me my entire life."

In Buddhism all of this thinking is illusion. An illusion is the wrong way to think or see. According to Buddhism, there is no permanent self or "me." What we think of as a permanent self is something we have imagined. We have an awareness of ourselves at each moment of our lives. We have connected those moments of awareness together to create a belief in a permanent "me." But this permanent self is a fiction. It is something we have created and we believe in.

For lots of people this fictitious sense of self creates all kinds of problems. Many of our emotional problems come from the belief in a permanent self. If something bad happened in the past the pain or resentment can last for many years. We carry the pain because we believe that "I" was injured in the past and "I" am here today with those memories. "I" am here today remembering the pain because someone hurt the same "I" many years ago.

In the Eightfold Path of Buddhism, the seventh piece is right mindfulness. The key to right mindfulness is to understand that there is no permanent self. An exercise in Buddhism is to walk a short distance very slowly and try to understand everything that is happening within one as one walks the short distance. An aware person can see the movements of the body, the thoughts in one's mind, sensations of the body, and the emotions in the mind. There is nothing more. There is no permanent self.

One can also notice that thoughts, body sensations, and emotions can change rapidly. The problem is that we humans think that some of these emotions and thoughts are permanent features of our selves. We think that these thoughts and emotions represent our permanent self. So a person can think, "I'm not good enough" and feel bad about himself or herself. According to Buddhism, this is just a thought with a feeling. Thoughts and feelings can be changed. The mistake the person makes is to turn these into a continuous belief with bad feelings about a permanent "me" that is not good enough.

As stated earlier, anattā is a very profound concept. But not everyone will get it. It is not difficult, but to understand it requires being able to revise the way one has viewed oneself for his or her entire life.

C. CHINESE RELIGION[4]

1. Overview

The religious picture of China is complicated and it continues to change. To understand the Chinese religious atmosphere today one needs to be aware of the nine major elements that have influenced Chinese religion:

> Native Chinese Religion
>
> Religious Taoism
>
> Philosophical Taoism
>
> Confucianism
>
> Imported Buddhism
>
> Importing Christianity

---

4   For a more thorough overview of Chinese religion, see "Chapter 6, Daoism and Confucianism" in Fisher, *Living Religions.*

Imported Islam

Communist Atheism

Western Materialism

The first element is ancient Chinese practices such as ancestor worship. The second element is a religious tradition that grows out of these ancient practices called religious Taoism. A third element is philosophical Taoism based on a small book, the *Tao Te Ching*.[5]

The fourth element is Confucianism, based on the ideas of Confucius. Since Confucianism is mostly a set of social and moral values it is not exactly a religion, but you cannot understand Chinese culture without knowing something about Confucianism. The fifth element is the imported religion of Buddhism. Mahayana Buddhism came to China and was influenced by Chinese culture. The sixth element is the next import: Christianity brought in by Europeans. There is also a significant population of Chinese who follow the imported religion of Islam, the seventh element.

The eighth element is atheism. This was promoted by Mao Zedong and the communist revolution starting in the 1940s. Under the communist government an official policy of atheism was followed and extensive efforts were made to rid the country of all religion. The efforts were not totally successful. Many religious elements still survive, but the general effect is that several generations of Chinese have been raised with no exposure to religion.

The ninth and final element is Western materialism. Since the opening of China, that nation has embraced such Western culture as its music, clothing, lifestyles, and a disinterest in religion common among many people in the West.

Chinese religious culture on the island of Taiwan is different. It was influenced by all of the elements listed previously except for atheist communism. Without a period that involved the repression of religion, religion on Taiwan has always flourished. Taiwan has a very rich and vibrant religious history.

2. Native Chinese Religion

Many ancient practices can still be found in China. One practice is ancestor worship. In Chinese thinking when an ancestor dies he or she becomes a spirit that

---

5   The distinctions between native Chinese religion, philosophical Taoism, and religious Taoism are not clear-cut. There is a tremendous overlap between these three elements. Also, generalizations about Taoism are difficult to make because there is such a diversity of practices and so many groups in Taoism. Separating out these elements—native Chinese religion, philosophical Taoism, and religious Taoism— is a helpful tool for one studying Chinese religion. These are the pieces one has to try to wrap his or her mind around to begin to understand Chinese religion.

can influence events among the living. It is important for the living to keep the ancestors happy. If the ancestors' spirits are offended they can create mischief for the living. On the other hand, ancestors can be benevolent and help the living. Duties to ancestors include such things as annual visits to the graves of ancestors and having a shrine in the house that lists the names of the ancestors.

An important concept is Shangdi (or Shang-ti), the deity of the sky. During the time of emperors the main duty of an emperor was to maintain harmony between heaven and earth with religious rituals. Shangdi is the spirit of heaven.

Another important concept is yin and yang. Everything is made of opposites. Yin represents qualities that are cold, dark, mysterious, and feminine. Yang represents qualities that are warm light, and masculine. The idea is not that one set of these qualities is good and the other is bad. Rather the goal is to balance yin and yang. In traditional Chinese thinking, illness is caused by too much of either yin or yang.

Below is the famous symbol of yin and yang.

In this symbol dark and light are balanced. But notice the two dots. Even within darkness there is light. At night the moon and stars shine. Even in light there is darkness, such as shadows on a sunny day.

Divination is another part of Chinese religion. The Chinese classic book the *I Ching* is one example. One tosses coins to select one of 64 symbols made of six lines. Each symbol has a fortune or prediction that goes with it.

Another important practice of divination is feng shui. The goal in feng shui is to find harmony between people and their physical environments. It is important when choosing a gravesite or building a house to make sure the site has good positive chi, which is energy. Feng shui is the practice of using physical space to enable the flow of good chi. Feng shui is used in designing houses and office spaces to create happy and prosperous environments.

FIGURE 8.2 Yin Yang

3. Philosophical Taoism

The term "Taoism" can also be spelled in English as "Daoism." The book the *Tao Te Ching* is also spelled as the *Daode Jing*. Philosophical Taoism is based on the *Tao Te Ching*. The word "Tao" means the "way," "Te" means "virtue," and "Ching" means the "book." The title can be translated as *The Book of the Way and of Virtue*. According to legend, the *Tao Te Ching* was written by Lao Tzu who lived around 600 BC.

The word "Tao" has three overlapping meanings. First, the Tao is ultimate reality. But this is beyond explanation or definition. "Those who know don't say; those who say don't know." Second, the Tao is the way of universe. Third, the Tao is the way to live life. The goal in Taoism is to live life in harmony with the way of the universe.

The image often used in Taoism is of a man floating in a stream. But instead of the man letting the water take him downstream he fights the current and is battered against the rocks. Taoism is about "going with the flow." According to Taoism, we are frustrated and unhappy because we fight the way of nature, which is the way of the universe. If we surrender to the way of the universe we will find peace, and we will find that what we need to do is easier.

FIGURE 8.3 Statue of Lao Tzu in Quanzhou.

4. Taoist Principles

In Taoism there are certain principles on how to live. These are worth understanding and thinking about. In many ways they represent the opposite of the values expressed in modern culture.

Non-being

This is not the idea that you should stop existing but rather the idea that you should stop promoting yourself as important. Have you ever met people with big egos? Everything has to be their way or has to be about them. They often make the people around them unhappy. Non-being is the opposite.

We are not important in the big picture. So why are we trying to "Make my mark" and "Leave a legacy"? Most of us will be completely forgotten once we have died and the people who knew us have also died. This view is not meant to be depressing but freeing.

Quietness

Quietness is more effective than being loud. Notice how much noise surrounds us. Many people have electronic devices around them making sound all the time. But notice that most noise is not very effective. For all the noise and volume of TV commercials, most people ignore most commercials.

If parents yell a lot at a child, often the child ignores what they say. Have you ever noticed that in an argument a person yells loudly to be listened to yet the person yelling back is not listening at all? In Taoism, being quiet is better and more effective. In the workplace, sometimes the person who does the most talking gets the least done. Often the people working quietly get more work completed.

Low position

The idea here is that being at the bottom is more effective and better than being at the top. In the physical world leverage is about getting below an object to move it. In martial arts a low center of gravity is a stronger position that a high center of gravity. Rivers flow to the valleys. They do not flow to the mountain tops.

Reversion

Anything taken to its extreme becomes the opposite. Sharpen a sword too much it will become dull. Many healthy and fit athletes wind up with health problems and lifelong injuries from practicing and playing too much.

Parents should be loving and show affection to their children. If parents show too much affection, however, it can stifle the growth of children and in the end turns out to not be loving.

Oneness with nature

The goal is to be in harmony with nature. This means not just the natural world, but also the very nature of things. So, for example, growing old is natural. Do not fight it. Find harmony with the natural order of things.

Spontaneity

Nature is spontaneous. It can rain in the morning then be sunny. The wind can blow this way then blow the other way. Be spontaneous. This point in Taoism was also a reaction to Confucianism, which developed detailed rituals.

Wu Wei

This term is sometimes translated as "nonaction." The idea is to do something so well it is easy. Be so skilled at something that is requires little effort.

5. Religious Taoism

It is not easy to explain religious Taoism since it has a long history, with a wide variety of practices, and numerous groups. The two most important groups are Temple Taoism and the Complete Perfection School. There are many Taoist temples and monasteries in China and Taiwan, some with elaborate rituals performed by priests in worship of numerous gods and goddesses.

Taoist practices include divination, exorcism, worship, and healing. In an attempt to live forever and achieve immortality, some religious Taoists have tried practices of special diets, alchemy, and breath control to extend life.

6. Confucianism

Confucianism is based on the teachings of Confucius (551–479 BC). "Kung Fu-tzu" is closer to the Chinese sound of his name, which means Kung the Master. His father died when he was young, so his mother sacrificed so he could become a scholar. He spent much of his career tutoring the sons of gentlemen and holding minor government positions. When he died, he was not well known and had only a few followers. But they spread his teaching and in time the ideas of Confucius would greatly influence Chinese culture and the entire Asian world. The book of his teachings is called the *Analects*. In one passage he stated, "What you do not wish for yourself, do not do to others." Later Confucian writings would include the *Great Learning*, the *Doctrine of the Mean*, and the book of *Mencius*.

Confucianism is a set of social practices based on properly understanding five relationships: ruler/subject, father/son, husband/wife, elder brother/younger brother, and elder friend/younger friend. The key is that although these are unequal relationships between a dominant and a subordinate, there are reciprocal duties going both ways. For example, although a subject must obey the ruler, rulers must take care of the subject. Confucian ideas shaped both family relationships and Chinese political culture.

Confucius taught the importance of "shu." Shu is reciprocity: treat others the way you want to be treated. Followers of Confucius also uphold five virtues: "ren" is compassion, the will to seek the good of others; "yi" is righteousness and benevolence; "li" is

FIGURE 8.4 Confucius

religious and moral behavior; "dhi" is wisdom; and "xin" is faithfulness. One who lives out the five relationships and upholds the virtues is considered a gentleman or an ideal man.

For Confucius, the key to a better society was not through tough laws and punishments but rather by teaching people how to live as good people. One of his political principles was that a ruler must guide the people by his own personal example of moral behavior.

DISCUSSION QUESTIONS

1. Do an online search for images of Hindu gods. Which gods are intriguing?

2. What do you think about reincarnation?

3. What did you find interesting in learning about Buddhism? What do you think about the relationship of suffering and desire?

4. Do an online search to find the nearest Hindu and Buddhist temples. Are there any near you?

5. Do any principles of philosophical Taoism appeal to you? How do Taoist principles compare with the values of typical Americans?

Credits

- Fig. 8.1: Copyright © Bernard Gagnon (CC BY-SA 3.0) at https://commons.wikimedia.org/wiki/File:Buddha_Statue,_Sanchi_01.jpg.
- Fig. 8.2: Source: https://commons.wikimedia.org/wiki/File:Yin_yang.svg.
- Fig. 8.3: Source: https://commons.wikimedia.org/wiki/File:Statue_of_Lao_Tzu_in_Quanzhou.jpg.
- Fig. 8.4: Source: https://commons.wikimedia.org/wiki/File:Konfuzius-1770.jpg.

CHAPTER 9

OTHER IMPORTANT RELIGIONS

A. THE SIKH RELIGION[1]

The Sikh religion could be grouped with either Western religions or Eastern religions because it has elements influenced by Islam and elements influenced by Hinduism. Sikhism is based on the teachings of Guru Nanak (1469–1539). He lived in the region called the Punjab, which today is in both India and Pakistan.

By the time of Guru Nanak, India had experienced a long and complicated history of having both Hindu rulers and Muslim rulers at various times. Hindus and Muslims lived side by side, often in tension. A teacher named Kabir (1440–1518) influenced Nanak with the concept that Hindus and Muslims worshiped the same divine reality. Kabir saw common ground between Hinduism and Islam and saw creeds and dogmas as irrelevant.

Nanak, just as the Buddha, left his home to seek answers to his religious questions. According to Sikhs, Nanak had a vision in which he was taken before God and told to preach "there is no Muslim and there is no Hindu." Nanak was to redeem the world by teaching prayer, charity, and clean living. Nanak took on the title of "Guru," which means teacher.

Nine other gurus followed Guru Nanak. The last of the ten, Guru Gobind Singh (1666–1708), declared he was the last human guru. Henceforth, the Adi Granth, the Sikh holy book, would become the Guru Granth Sahib. In a Sikh temple called a "Gurdwara," the Adi Granth is the center of worship. It is put atop a raised platform on cushions. A whisk is waved over it, which is an ancient sign of honor. When entering the Gurdwara, a Sikh bows to the holy book.

The Adi Granth consists of 1,430 pages and has nearly 6,000 verses. It begins with the most important text called the Japji. This is followed by 31 ragas, which are groups of hymns. Here are two samples from the Adi Granth:

> *Why do you go to the forest in search of God?*

> *He lives in all and is yet ever distinct;*

---

1   For a more thorough overview of Sikhism, see "Chapter 11, Sikhism" in Fisher, *Living Religions.*

FIGURE 9.1 The Guru Granth Sahib

> *He abides with you, too,*
>
> *As a fragrance dwells in a flower,*
>
> *And reflection in a mirror;*
>
> *So does God dwell inside everything;*
>
> *Seek Him, therefore, in your heart.[2]*

> *The quest of pleasure brings nothing but torment*
> *abounding; man thus makes of his evil desires only a*
> *shackle about the neck. Thou seeker of false delights,*
> *liberation comes only through the love of God.[3]*

According to some, the Sikh religion is monotheistic. Sikhs use several titles for the one God including "Ek Onkar," which means "One Creator." But according to other Sikhs, the category of monotheism does not adequately describe the Sikh tradition since as stated in the first line of the Adi Granth, God "cannot be reduced to thought." Thus, any category for the Sikh tradition does not adequately cover the diversity of religious belief in this tradition.

---

2 Adi Granth, Dhanasri, M.9.

3 Gauri Ashtpadi, M.1.

In the Sikh tradition, performing good actions is more important than carrying out religious rituals. According to Sikhs, one lives a good life by keeping God in one's heart and mind at all times. Devote Sikhs pray at least twice a day. Sikhs believe in hard work and living honestly. Sikhs also believe everyone is equal and thus they reject the Hindu caste system.

Sikh men do not cut their hair. They see their hair as a spiritual crown but it is to be only seen by God. Sikh men have beards and wear turbans to cover their hair.

B. OTHER RELIGIOUS TRADITIONS

There are dozens of religious traditions and thousands of religious groups that exist now and many more that have disappeared. It is impossible to discuss all of them. The following eight are important religions not treated in detail this book. Most of these have several millions followers each.

1. Jainism[4]

The Jain religion (also called Jainism) is an offshoot of Hinduism. The word "Jain" can be pronounced "jane" or "jen." There are more than four million Jains in the world. The Jain religion was founded by Mahavira, who lived in the 400s or 500s BC. He emphasized the importance of detachment. Three Jain principles are important: 1) nonviolence (Jains will not kill humans or animals and many Jains even avoid killing insects); 2) non-acquisitiveness (Jains avoid having possessions); and 3) relativity (Truth is relative. What is the truth depends on how you look at something).

2. Shinto[5]

Shinto is the traditional religion of Japan. It has greatly influenced Japanese culture and moral values. Although most Japanese participate in Shinto rituals, very few identify themselves as Shintoists. There are some 80,000 Shinto shrines in Japan. Shinto has no sacred scriptures and no founder.

The word Shinto means "the way of the gods." The gods are called "Kami." Three important Kami are Amaterasu, the sun goddess; and Izanagi and Izanami, the first man and woman. However, Shintoism sees a divine presence in all things.

---

4   For a more thorough overview of Jainism, see "Chapter 4, Jainism" in Fisher, *Living Religions*.

5   For a more thorough overview of Shinto, see "Chapter 7, Shinto" in Fisher, *Living Religions*.

FIGURE 9.2 A Shinto shrine

3. Tenrikyo

Tenrikyo is an offshoot of Shinto. It was started by Nakayama Miki, who lived in the 1800s. It is monotheistic, believing in Tenri-O-no-Mikoto as the Supreme Being. This religion promotes the joyous life through acts of charity and proper mindfulness.

4. Rastafarianism

This religion developed in the 1930s in Jamaica among the descendants of African slaves. Rastafarians (also called Rastas) believe that the Emperor of Ethiopia, Haile Selassie I (1892–1975), is the second coming of Christ or that he is God the Father. Haile Selassie is called the "Lion of Judah." Rastafarianism is influenced by Christianity (especially some passages in the Old Testament and the Book of Revelation), mysticism, and African culture.

Rastafari ceremonies use chanting, drumming, and meditation. Often marijuana is used to heighten spiritual experience. Reggae music grew out of this movement. Rastafarians do not cut their hair but instead grow dreadlocks, which represent the mane of a lion.

5. Cao Dai

The monotheistic religion of Cao Dai began in 1926 in Vietnam. "Cao Dai" means "high tower." It has more than four million followers. Cao Dai mixes elements from Confucianism and Taoism with organizational elements from Roman Catholicism such as a pope and bishops. In Cao Dai the symbol for God is an eye representing the Divine Eye.

6. Modern Paganism

This is a wide range of very diverse groups that are interested in the pre-Christian religions of Europe, ethnic religions, and folklore. For example, modern pagans might be interested in ancient Celtic Druidism or Norse (Viking) gods and mythology.

FIGURE 9.3 The Cao Dai symbol

The various modern pagan beliefs can be classified as polytheism, animism, or pantheism. Modern paganism often includes seasonal rituals at the summer and winter solstices and at the spring and fall equinoxes.

7. Bahá'í

The Bahá'í faith was founded in the 1800s by Bahá'u'lláh in Persia (modern-day Iran). The Bahá'í faith believes in the unity of all humankind and the unity of religion, and that God is the source of all religions. Bahá'í teachings emphasize principles such as the equality of men and women, world peace, and the importance of education.

8. Unitarians and Universalists

A group that split from mainline Christianity is called the Unitarians. Unitarians reject the idea that God is a Trinity. Instead, they insist God is one, a unity. Thus, they call themselves Unitarians. Another group that developed is called the Universalists, who believe that God would not send anyone to hell forever. They believe that in the next life God's love will ultimately transform everyone, even wicked people. In the end, everyone will go to heaven. Salvation is universal.

In America, these groups in 1961 joined to form the Unitarian Universalist Association. If someone wants a place that avoids the traditional religious doctrines, then checking

FIGURE 9.4 B'hai Temple, Wilmette, Ill.

out this church is a good idea. Unitarian Universalists hold a wide range of beliefs in their search for spiritual growth. They do not have any sort of creed defining what one is to believe.

THINGS TO EXPLORE

1. Have you ever listened to reggae music? If not, check out the music of Bob Marley.

2. Do an online search for images of Sikhs today. Find images of the Golden Temple and the ten gurus.

3. There is a beautiful Bahá'í temple outside of Chicago. Go online and find images of it.

4. Go online and look at Shinto temples in Japan.

5. Go online and find the nearest Unitarian Universalist church.

Credits

CHAPTER 10

RELIGIOUS WORDS

A. WRITINGS

Most religions have sacred texts or special writings. Here are some of the most important ones. Often within these religions much attention is given to how these books are to be translated, handled, and read. Also, within each religion there is often much debate, argument, and serious disagreement over how to interpret these texts and how to live out the requirements of the writings.

1. Hindu Writings

As described earlier, Hinduism is a religion of countless gods. Early hymns to the gods were collected along with other religious writings as the sacred texts called the Vedas, the most famous of which is the Rig Veda.

Early Hinduism involved many rituals involving priests. Religious devotion often consisted of making offerings, such as food, to the gods. The priests, called Brahmins, were at the center of this religion. The second important set of Hindu writings is the Brahmanas, which describe how to perform sacrifices and other rituals.

Two epic poems were written: the *Mahabharata* and the *Ramayana*.[1] The middle of the *Mahabharata* is a battle between two sets of brothers for control of the kingdom. Before the battle begins, Lord Krishna gives a long lecture to the warrior Arjuna about the meaning of life. The lecture is often printed as a separate book called the *Bhagavad Gita*.

Lord Krishna appears to be a human being, but he is actually the god Vishnu in human form. The appearance of a god in human form is called an "avatar." (The title of the 2009 movie *Avatar* came from Hinduism.) In the Ramayana, the god Vishnu appears as the avatar Rama. The story of the Ramayana follows Rama who rescues his wife Sita from the demon king Ravana.

---

1   One of my dreams in life is to be on the TV show *Wheel of Fortune* and the puzzle I have to solve is "MAHABHARATA AND RAMAYANA," and I would have bought an "A".

FIGURE 10.1   Arjuna (on left) listening to Lord Krishna.

Another set of Hindu writings are the Upanishads. These writings work out the philosophy of Hinduism, exploring concepts such as Brahman and Atman. The Upanishads are studied by the most advanced spiritual seekers.

2. Buddhist Texts

Buddhists of the Theravada tradition study an ancient set of texts called the Pali Canon, also called the "Tripitika," which means "Three Baskets." (Notice the prefix "tri" for three.) The three groups are:

Vinaya Piṭaka: texts that give the rules for being a monk.

Sutra Pitaka: sermons of the Buddha that were written down after his death.

Adhidharma Pitaka: philosophical writings that interpret Buddhist teaching.

In the Mahayana tradition, the sacred writings are the Sutras. The most famous is the Lotus Sutra, which contains the final teachings of the Buddha and how all beings can become like the Buddha.

3. The Christian Bible[2]

The Christian Bible is the most used religious text in history. It consists of the Old Testament and the New Testament. The Old Testament describes the religious history of ancient Israel. The New Testament describes the life of Jesus and the thoughts of the early followers of Jesus as they tried to live out their faith in Jesus.

Christian faith is based on the Bible. Christian services always include Bible readings. In some churches the minister is free to choose the Bible readings for each service.

In other churches the Bible readings for each Sunday are laid out in a book called the *Lectionary*. A *Lectionary* has a three-year cycle of Bible readings for services. In each Sunday service, four selections from the Bible are read aloud to the congregation in this order: an Old Testament reading, a psalm; and from the New Testament an Epistle reading and a gospel reading. The order cannot be changed. Although a lay person (someone from the congregation) can do the Old Testament or Epistle reading, and the psalm can be done as a song, typically the minister or priest always does the gospel reading. A common rule is that people can sit through the first readings, but stand up while the gospel is read. Although following the assigned *Lectionary* readings may seem restrictive, churches that follow the *Lectionary* often cover far more of the Bible over time than churches where the minister can choose the reading.

Many Christians have their own copy of the Bible to read, and many Christians bring their own Bible to church so they can follow along. For many Christians, individual or group Bible study is encouraged.

Generations ago the family Bible was often the most important book in many homes, and in some cases the only book in the house. Important family events—births, marriages, and deaths—were written on special pages in the family Bible.

The Christian Bible was described in more detail in Chapter 6 along with a discussion of different views on how to read the Bible.

4. The Jewish Bible

As explained in Chapter 5, the Jewish Bible is called the Bible, the Hebrew Scriptures, the Jewish Scriptures, or the Tanakh. The Jewish Bible is divided into three sections: the books of law called the Torah, the books of the prophets called the Neviim, and other writings called the Kethuvim. "Torah" means "law," "Neviim" means "prophets" and "Kethuvim" means "writings." A prophet is one called by God to speak for God. The first letter of the name of each section—T, N, and K—have been turned into the word "Tanakh," which is another name for the Jewish Scriptures.

---

2   For a more thorough exploration of the Bible see Jennifer R. Prince, *The Handy Bible Answer Book*. (Canton, MI: Visible Ink Press, 2014).

FIGURE 10.2 A Torah scroll

All synagogue services include readings from the scriptures. The bar mitzvah is the ceremony that recognizes that a Jewish boy is now an adult. The key moment in the service is when he reads aloud from the Torah scroll in Hebrew. Reform Jews and some conservative Jews have a similar service for girls called a bat mitzvah.

The Torah scrolls are treated with great reverence and kept in a special case in a synagogue called an "ark." Torah scrolls are written by hand and are proofread to make sure every single letter is correct. When reading from a scroll, a special pointer called a "yad" is used. This is to make sure the scroll is not touched so that no oil or dirt from the hand gets on the scroll.

During the annual Jewish celebration of Simchat Torah, the synagogue ark is opened and the scrolls taken out and carried into the congregation so that all can celebrate the gift of the law given by God.

Many Jewish children attend Hebrew school so they can read the scriptures in the original language. Private study of the Hebrew Scriptures is encouraged in Judaism. For many Jews becoming a scholar of the Torah is considered an honored calling.

5. The Qur'an

As explained in Chapter 7, the holy book for Muslims is the Qur'an. (The older English spelling is "Koran.") The Qur'an is divided into chapters. Each chapter is a called a "sura," and there are 114 "suraat" in the Qur'an. (Suraat is the plural of sura.) Although the first sura is short, the rest are organized by size from longest to shortest. Numerous figures from the Jewish and Christian scriptures are mentioned in the Qur'an, including Adam, Abraham, Moses, Gabriel, Joseph, Mary, and Jesus.

Muslims believe the true Qur'an is in Arabic. Thus, a translation of the Qur'an is not the true Qur'an. Muslims have followed a different path than Christians in spreading their faith. Christians have translated the Bible into almost every written language so people can read it in their own language. In spreading the faith, Muslims teach people Arabic so they can read the true Qur'an.

Muslims believe that Muhammad passed on exactly what the angel Gabriel told him, word for word. He added nothing to the messages, which were later written down by his followers as the Qur'an. The written Qur'an is called the "Created Qur'an" and is believed to be an exact copy of the "Uncreated Qur'an" that is in heaven.

The Qur'an is about the size of the Christian New Testament. The Qur'an does not have many stories. It does, however, have many words of exhortation. (Exhortation is encouragement.)

Muslims treat their holy book, the Qur'an, with great respect. Many Muslims are greatly offended by any mistreatment of the Qur'an.

6. The Sikh Text: The Adi Granth

As described in Chapter 9, in the Sikh tradition the holy book is the Adi Granth, which is also called the Guru Granth Sahib. "Guru" means "teacher" and "Sahib" means "master." In a Sikh temple called a "Gurdwara," the Adi Granth is the center of worship. It is put atop a raised platform on cushions. A whisk is waved over it, which is an ancient sign of honor. When entering the Gurdwara, a Sikh bows to the holy book.

The Adi Granth consists of 1,430 pages and has nearly 6,000 verses. It begins with the most important text called the Japji. This is followed by 31 ragas, which are groups of hymns. Here are two samples from the Adi Granth quoted in the previous chapter:

Why do you go to the forest in search of God?

He lives in all and is yet ever distinct;

He abides with you, too,

As a fragrance dwells in a flower,

And reflection in a mirror;

So does God dwell inside everything;

Seek Him, therefore, in your heart.[3]

3 Adi Granth, Dhanasri, M.9.

> *The quest of pleasure brings nothing but torment*
> *abounding; man thus makes of his evil desires only a*
> *shackle about the neck. Thou seeker of false delights,*
> *liberation comes only through the love of God.*[4]

7. Taoist Writings

The *Tao Te Ching* is an important little book. The word "Tao" means the "way," "Te" means "virtue," and "Ching" means the "book." The title can be translated as *The Book of the Way and of Virtue*. The title in English is sometimes written as *Daode Jing*. (The sound of the first Chinese character in the title sounds both like a "T" and a "D".)

This small book can be read in a half hour. It is made up of 81 short teachings. Some teachings are easy to figure out, others are more elusive. These writings are the basis of philosophical Taoism. According to the legend, the *Tao Te Ching* was written by Lao-Tzu who lived around 600 BC. Here is a sample from Chapter 11:

Emptiness

> *Thirty spokes surround the hub:*
>
> *In their nothingness consists the carriage's effectiveness.*
>
> *One hollows the clay and shapes it into pots:*
>
> *In its nothingness consists the pot's effectiveness.*
>
> *One cuts out doors and windows to make the chamber:*
>
> *In their nothingness consists the chamber's effectiveness.*
>
> *Therefore: what exists serves for possession.*
>
> *What does not exist serves for effectiveness.*[5]

Another important Taoist text is the *Zhuangzi* (also spelled Chuang Tzu), which contains stories and fables to illustrate the life of a Taoist sage

8. Confucian Writings

The *Analects* of Confucius is worth reading. This short book has twenty chapters, most of which are easy to figure out. These are examples of the lessons taught by

---

4   Gauri Ashtpadi, M.I.

5   Lao Tsu, *Tao Te Ching: The Richard Wilhelm Edition* (London: Arkana, 1985), 31.

Confucius that provide an overview of his ideas; however, as stated before, Confucianism is more of a set of social teachings than an actual religion. Other important Confucian writings are the *Great Learning* and the *Doctrine of the Mean*. The *Mencius* is another Confucian classic. It contains the teachings of Mencius who worked on the concepts of Confucius in more detail.

9. Non-Mainline Christian Writings

Mainline Christians—those who accept the Nicene Creed—believe that the Bible made up of the Old Testament and New Testament is the written revelation of God. Typically, they believe that such revelation ended when the New Testament was complete. There are, however, two important writings of non-mainline Christian groups: *The Book of Mormon* and *Science and Health*.

The Book of Mormon

Among groups that call themselves Christians are the Mormons, officially known as the Church of Jesus Christ of Latter-day Saints. Mormons have an additional book called *The Book of Mormon*. Mormons consider this book a new revelation equal to the Old Testament and New Testament. According to Mormons, in New York State in 1827 the angel Moroni appeared to Joseph Smith and showed him golden plates buried on a mountain. The plates had been left by descendants of the ancient tribes of Israel.[6] Smith translated the plates into English and produced, in English, *The Book of Mormon*.

Science and Health

A small but important group is the Christian Science Church. Do not confuse this church with the Church of Scientology. Scientology is totally different, though people often get Christian Science and Scientology confused. (See the Appendix on Scientology.)

The Christian Science Church, also known as the Church of Christ Science, is guided by the teaching of Mary Baker Eddy, who lived from 1821 to 1910. She wrote *Science and Health with Key to the Scriptures* (first published in 1875).

A key point of Christian Science belief is that illness is a mental error. People believe in sickness, so they get sick.[7] Stop believing in illness and it will go away. God does not want people to be sick.

---

6   Most historians do not believe that descendants of ancient Israel made it to the New World.

7   Christian Science teaches that only the spiritual is real and that the physical world is an illusion.

Christian Science services have readings from both the Bible and *Science and Health*. At services, no sermon or homily is allowed. No one else's ideas, such as might be brought up in a homily, are allowed.

B. STORIES

1. Religion Is Based on Stories

Religion is built on stories. The sacred writings of most traditions include many important stories. In many traditions the annual retellings of stories are important rituals. For ancient Babylonians, the New Year's celebration involved retelling or acting out the *Enuma Elish*, the Babylonian creation epic. For Jews, the Passover meal in spring includes telling or reading the story of the Exodus when Moses led the people of Israel out of Egypt. Around Christmas, Christian church services read the stories about the birth of Jesus from the Gospels of Matthew and Luke. Sometimes children act out this story in Christmas plays with Joseph, Mary, the baby Jesus, the shepherds, and the three kings.

Many people have personal stories of their testimony. In certain Christian churches it is common for people to tell their story and give their testimony of "How I came to Jesus."

Our own personal stories give us our identity. If you want someone to know who you really are, you tell stories about your life, especially meaningful stories. Stories give religions their identity.

2. Oral Traditions

Many groups have oral traditions that involve unwritten stories passed down from generation to generation. Many cultures had oral traditions because no one could read and write. In these cultures, unwritten myths were the core of their religion. Oral cultures have no books, and their religion can be very strong without them. In Christianity, Islam, Sikhism, and Judaism the "holy book" is central, so it is hard to imagine religion without a book. (But even these books are based on oral traditions that lasted for many years before being written down.)

Oral traditions survive in Native American culture, African traditional culture, and other traditional and tribal cultures. In many cases the oral stories have been written down; however, in many other places the stories have not been written down and are in danger of being lost. Elders who know the stories are dying off and young people are often not interested in learning the stories or learning the languages that tell the story.

Also, in the last several centuries, as more advanced cultures have conquered, overrun, or overwhelmed less advanced native cultures, much oral tradition has been lost. There is no good way to measure the scale of the loss, but it must be huge.

3. Myths and Mythology

What Is a Myth?

"Myth" is a difficult word to define even though it is an important concept. The word is used in several ways. The first use of the word myth is for a false belief. For example, it is a myth that if you do not wear your coat when the temperature drops you will catch a cold.

A second use of myth is for a story, often ancient, that supports religious belief and practice or that explains natural phenomena. In ancient cultures, myths served several purposes, such as giving meaning to life, explaining the origin of the cosmos and the human place in the cosmos, and enforcing moral and social values.

Creation myths fit this second use. Creation stories explain the origin of the earth and the human role within it. Because such stories are ancient, they often do not match scientific explanations. That should be no surprise. Ancient people created these stories thousands of years before the development of science.

A third use of the word myth is to refer to traditional or ancient stories that were meant as entertainment. Before electricity, storytelling was an important entertainment, perhaps the most popular form of entertainment. Storytellers and poets were important in many cultures. Often storytellers spent hours weaving their tales. Many of the Greek stories such as Jason and the Argonauts, the Perseus story, and the adventures of Hercules seem to be mostly for entertainment. Most of Norse or Viking mythology seems to be stories for entertainment with no profound meaning.

Mythology

The word "mythology" has several meanings. For studying religion the word refers to a collection of myths, such as "Greek mythology." Here is a list of some of the many cultures that have such mythologies: Aztec, Chinese, Hindu, Incan, Japanese, Mayan, Native American, Norse or Viking, and Pacific Island. Many of the stories of African traditional religion are often labeled as folktales.[8]

Did Ancients Believe These Stories?

Myths often have fantastical details that could never have occurred. In ancient times people may have believed some of these details such as the hero Perseus flying through the sky on winged shoes. But we do not know for sure how common people understood these stories. It is possible that some ancient people doubted that Perseus could fly in the same way modern people know that one cannot fly through the air like Superman or like Spiderman with his webs?

---

8   *The Handy Mythology Answer Book,* by David A. Leeming (Visible Ink Press, 2015), provides a comprehensive overview of the world's mythology.

A Controversial Story

The book of Genesis in the Bible begins with the creation story. This story is controversial. Literalists believe it is an accurate historical account of the creation of the earth in six days with God resting on the seventh day. Many literalists believe that each day in the story is meant to be an actual 24-hour day—not a long period of years—and that creation took place about 6,000 years ago.

Non-literalists (contextualists) believe the Genesis story is actually a myth, a made-up story. Yet this story provides profound insights: that the world was created in an orderly way by a caring God; that creation was good; and that humans—both men and women—were in the image of God. For non-literalists, the story is not accurate history or science but rather a profound story about humans and our place in the cosmos. The issue of how to read the Bible was covered in Chapter 6 where the terms "literalist" and "contextualist" were explained.

Mythology Is Alive and Well

The creating of myths is alive and well. But myths are no longer told orally. They are in books, TV shows, and movies. Modern myths are very popular, such as the *Star Trek* series in all its various forms, the *Star Wars* movies, the Harry Potter books and movies, and the *Lord of the Rings* books and movies. Modern mythology is more popular than ancient mythology. Hundreds of millions have seen *Star Wars*. The ancient Greeks who heard the Hercules stories would have numbered in the hundreds of thousands.

The Size of the Cosmos

A number of creation stories describe the origin of the cosmos or the universe. But keep in mind that ancients saw the universe as tiny compared with the modern scientific view. As explained before, science states that the universe is nearly 14 billion years old and is 92 billion light years across. A light year is six trillion miles. The universe is 92 billion x six trillion miles across! That is big!

Ancient people had only their eyes with which to view and try to understand the universe. Telescopes did not arrive until the 1600s. Many ancients believed the earth was flat and that the sun, moon, and stars were very small objects, perhaps just a few miles or less up in the air. They had no clue these were immense objects very far away. (The sun is 93 million miles away, the moon is 239,000 miles away, and the closest star is 25 trillion miles away!) If ancient people saw the sun as a small object, certain stories about the sun make more sense. Among the Native Americans of the Northwest coast there is the story of the raven that takes the sun from a box and flies it up into the sky. The story makes sense if you believe the sun is much smaller than we know it to be.

Not all ancients believed the world was flat. Some sailors in particular noticed how ships sailing away disappeared from the bottom, indicating the earth was curved. There was even an ancient Greek, Eratosthenes (c, 276 BC–c. 195 BC), who calculated the size of a spherical earth.

Theories about Mythology

The writer Carl Jung (1875–1961) held that ancient myths contain profound psychological insights into humans. Although myths come from different cultures, he believed they contained archetypes that hold universal meaning for all people. The writer Mircea Eliade (1907–1986) held that myths connect humans to sacred meanings beyond individual cultures. Other writers have seen myths as expressing power structures and sociological orders. In other words, myths helped the people on top to stay in power.

Joseph Campbell (1904–1987) studied and wrote extensively about mythology. Seeing common elements in many stories, he saw all the various myths as variations on one universal myth. George Lucas, the creator of *Star Wars*, was greatly influenced by Campbell's book *The Hero with a Thousand Faces.*

As an alternative view, however, is it possible that some of the common elements found in many myths are simply good storytelling techniques? For example, the hero has to leave home to go adventuring. In the imagination the listener leaves his or her own home place. Of course a great story would have to occur in a faraway mysterious place or the listener might typically think, "Nothing interesting happens in this boring village where I live." When Luke Skywalker pondered his destiny as he watched the two setting suns on the planet Tatooine, how many movie watchers ached to leave their own homes in the boring suburbs and travel to exciting and exotic places?

Lots of myths have trickster figures. Tricksters are needed in stories to create problems that have to be solved in the story.[9] Also, in many adventure stories the hero comes close to failing yet in the end succeeds in reaching his goal. This is good storytelling. A story in which the hero easily succeeds would be boring. Of course knights have to leave home and face dangers in their search for the Grail. Who would be interested in the story of knights staying home and polishing their armor?

---

9   For example, in the TV show *Seinfeld*, many of the plots revolved around problems created by George and Kramer. In the classic TV show *I Love Lucy*, Lucy often created her own problems that had to be solved, thereby creating plots for many episodes.

DISCUSSION QUESTIONS

1. If you have a religious background, what have you read of the writings of your own tradition?

2. What movies have you seen that were based on stories from the Bible?

3. Have you explored any writings of other religious traditions?

4. What are your favorite myths in movies, books, and television?

Optional Assignment: If you are interested, try writing your own myth.

Credits

- Fig. 10.1: Copyright © Arnab Dutta (CC BY-SA 3.0) at https://commons.wiki-media.org/wiki/File:Bhagavata_Gita_Bishnupur_Arnab_Dutta_2011.JPG.
- Fig. 10.2: Copyright © Lawrie Cate (CC by 2.0) at https://commons.wikimedia.org/wiki/File:Torah,_the_Jewish_Holy_Book.jpg.

CHAPTER 11

RELIGIOUS PLACES AND LEADERS

A. BUILDING AND SITES

Most religions have special sites or special buildings. Yet there is a great diversity of sites and buildings. And there are very different ideas about how these sites and buildings are understood.

1. Buildings

Most religions have buildings that allow believers to come together regardless of the weather. But there is a great range of buildings. At one extreme are the cathedrals in Europe built in the 1100s and 1200s. Go online and do an image search for "medieval cathedral" and take a look. These are beautiful, magnificent, and expensive buildings meant to last for centuries. And in some towns, such as Chartres in France, the cathedral is the center of the town and can be seen from miles away. At the opposite extreme are small storefront churches. Often found in America in poorer neighborhoods, old store buildings are used as churches.

Explore the buildings of other traditions by doing an image search with terms such as "mosque," "mosque interior," "synagogue," "synagogue interior," and "orthodox cathedral."

FIGURE 11.1 Chartres Cathedral in France.

Churches, mosques, temples, and synagogues come in all sizes from cathedrals and basilicas to rooms in someone's house and every size in between. Religious structures have been built in many architectural styles. Some buildings are dazzling with elaborate decoration; others are quite plain without any decoration.

Christian Churches

There are great differences among Christians regarding church buildings. Roman Catholic churches, especially older ones, tend to have decorations: statues, colorful stained glass windows, and candles. Often in a Roman Catholic church a spirit of reverence is desired. People are expected to be quiet in the church before and after services. Many Catholics genuflect as they take their seats in church. (To genuflect is to go down on one knee as a sign of respect for God.)

For Catholics, the church building is a unique place to encounter God. Catholics typically believe that God is present in the church in a special way.[1] Often Catholics feel that God is present in the church even if no one is in the building. Going into the church to pray by oneself is common. Because the church is a special place, Catholics avoid using the space for nonreligious events.

There are both practical and religious reasons for Catholic attitudes toward their churches. The practical one is that churches provide a quiet and inspiring place to pray. Even when other people are in the church and a service is not being conducted, one can pray quietly. There is a great need for such places, especially in the modern world were most public places are filled with much noise. (For example, think of all the TV sets in airports and restaurants.)

The religious reason for the atmosphere of Catholic churches is the belief that it shows a respectful attitude toward God. Implied is the idea that God is pleased by reverential attitudes in such places.

Other Christians have a different attitude toward church buildings. Many Baptist Christians and many Evangelical Christians, for example, believe God is not present in the building but in the people who come together to worship. So talking and conversing before and after the service is fine. In fact, often such conversations are encouraged as a way to build community. There is usually little need to maintain a reverent quiet atmosphere. And since God is present when the people are in worship, when the church is empty, it is empty.

One particular Christian group is the Quakers. Their full title is The Religious Society of Friends. Their buildings are called "meeting houses." The idea is that

---

1   Catholics believe that God is especially present when the Eucharist is being kept in the tabernacle, which is indicated by a lit red candle in the front of the church.

they want a regular place to meet indoors for religious services, but it is not a special place. It is not a "church." God is present in the believers, not in any building.

Mosques

The Muslim place of prayer is called a mosque. The word "mosque" means "Place of Prostration." Prostration means to bend down or lie down in prayer. (Do not be confused. To prostrate one's self is to bow down. There is another word "prostate," which refers to a gland in the male body.)

For Muslims there are strict rules about religious decoration in the mosque. Images of God or Muhammad are forbidden. Also, in a mosque there can be no images of humans or animals. So what is left? Two things are permitted: geometric designs and words from the Qur'an. Mosques, especially older ones, often have beautiful decorations using geometry and quotes from the Qur'an. Over the centuries elaborate and beautiful ways of using Arabic words as decoration have developed. This is called calligraphy.

Devout Muslims pray five times a day. They face the city of Mecca in Saudi Arabia. In each mosque there is niche or nook called the "mithrab" that tells members which way to face in prayer. Before modern times Muslims built mosques with four towers called "minarets." Five times a day a man, called a muezzin, would go up in the tower to call Muslims to prayer. Modern mosques often have only one symbolic tower.

Mosques have prayer mats on the floor but no chairs or pews. The prayer of salat involves standing, kneeling, and bowing. When the religious leader, called an "imam," gives a teaching the members sit on the floor. Women sit in the back of a mosque. This practice comes from the idea that men might be distracted during prayer if the women were in front of them.

Synagogues

Jewish synagogues come in all sizes and styles. The synagogue building often is the center of the local Jewish community. The word "synagogue" is a Greek word for "assembly." For Jews it is a place of prayer. In Orthodox synagogues women and men sit separately. Women are in the back or in the balcony.

There is a table in front called a "bimah" where the Torah is placed when it is read. Synagogues have a cabinet called Torah Ark where the Torah scrolls are kept. Synagogues are designed with the arc placed so that when the congregation is looking at the arc the people are facing Jerusalem. Synagogues typically have a continually lit lamp called the eternal light.

For many Jewish services a minimum of ten Jews is required. This is called a minyan. For Orthodox Jews it must be ten men.

Hindu Temples

There are many temples in India in all shapes and sizes. In America, as Hindu communities grow, a number of very large temples are being built in major cities across the country. Often the designs for temples are very elaborate with tall white pyramid shapes covered with statutes of various gods.[2] In the interior are colorful statues and shrines dedicated to various gods.

Buddhist Temples

There is a great variety of sizes and styles of Buddhist temples. Do an online image search for "Buddhist temple" to see some examples. Then search "Buddhist temple interior." Many Buddhist temples have statues of the Buddha prominently displayed. Buddhists also construct stupas, which are dome-shaped shrines that contain the relics of deceased Buddhist monks and nuns. Stupas are used as places of meditation. Do an online image search for "Buddhist stupa" to see some examples.

The Sikh Gurdwara

For Sikhs, the temple is called a Gurdwara. The focal point in the front of the Gurdwara is a platform with a canopy for the holy book, the Adi Granth. There are no chairs or pews in a Gurdwara; people sit directly on the floor. Do an online image search for "Sikh Gurdwara" to see some examples. Then search "Sikh Gurdwara interior."

No Shoes

In Buddhist, Hindu, and Sikh temples and in Islamic mosques people are required to remove their shoes before entering. In mosques people are also required to wash their hands, face, and feet. Mosques provide places to wash. In the Bible Book of Exodus where Moses encounters God in the burning bush, Moses is told to remove his sandals for he is standing on holy ground.

To modern people in the West the custom of removing shoes before entering a temple or mosque may seem strange. For many people to enter a religious building or someone's home barefoot would be a sign of disrespect. One would never go to a business meeting barefoot or wearing flip-flops. So why are shoes removed in certain religious traditions?

The custom goes back to a time of unpaved muddy streets, when livestock such as chicken and pigs lived next to houses. Horses and oxen in the streets left manure. In such conditions it made perfect sense to leave your outdoor shoes at the door when

---

2   Some of the Hindu temples in America are built with spaces on the exterior for statues to be added later when more money is raised.

you entered a home or a religious place. Many Asian families still have the custom of leaving outdoor shoes at the door and putting on indoor shoes or house slippers. This custom simply had the practical benefit of keeping the house or temple much cleaner. In time the custom also became a sign of respect.

No Pews

Christian churches and synagogues have pews or chairs to sit on during services. Catholic churches also have kneelers that fold down when the congregation is kneeling and then fold up when not needed.

Many religious buildings do not have seating. Mosques have prayer matts. In Hindu, Buddhist, and Sikh temples the people either stand or sit on the floor.

2. Historic Sites

Many religions have special sites where something occurred in the history of that religion. For Muslims the most important special sites are Mecca, where Muhammad made the first pilgrimage, and the Dome of Rock in Jerusalem, where Muhammad is believed to have ascended to heaven to speak with God during his night journey.

For Christians, the site where Jesus was born in Bethlehem and where he was crucified in Jerusalem are special places. Churches mark the spots and many thousands of believers visit the sites ever year, although it is impossible to prove these were the exact spots were Jesus was born and crucified. The route in Jerusalem that Jesus walked as he carried his cross to be crucified is called the Via Dolorosa (the Way of Sorrows). Many Christians on pilgrimage retrace the steps of Jesus. The Garden of Gethsemane and the Mount of Olives are also visited.

Catholics have many historical sites because of the Catholic belief in saints. Saints are holy people whose lives serve as models for Christians. There are thousands of Catholic saints and many have sites marking key moments in their lives. The town of Assisi in Italy is filled with special locations from the life of Saint Francis and is a very popular pilgrimage and tourist site. In medieval times the shrine of Thomas Becket was a popular pilgrimage destination, as in the *Canterbury Tales* written by Geoffrey Chaucer (1343–1400). Also, the Basilica of Saint Peter in Vatican City in Rome is an important site for Catholics.

In Buddhism there are four significant sites related to the life of the Buddha. Many Buddhists make pilgrimages to these places. The most important is the Deer Park in Bodh Gaya, India, where Buddha found enlightenment. Lumbini in Nepal is the birthplace of the Buddha. Sarnath, India, is the site of his first sermon; and Kushinara, India, is where he died.

For Sikhs the holiest site is the Golden Temple in Amritsar, India. The formal name of the building is Harmandir Sahib. 100,000 people visit it each day.

FIGURE 11.2 The Golden Temple

For Jews, the Temple Mount in Jerusalem is an important site because the Jewish Temple stood there until destroyed by the Romans in 70 AD. However, many Jews will not go to the area where the Temple stood. The Temple had a room called the "Holy of Holies" that people were not allowed to enter. Since no one knows where that room would have been, many Jews avoid the entire area. Instead, Jews visit the Wailing Wall, the Western Wall of the Temple Mount area, to pray. "To wail" means to cry or lament. Over the centuries many Jews have lamented events in their history. Also, important for Jews are sites that remember the Holocaust.

One of the most famous religious buildings in the world is the Hagia Sophia in Istanbul, Turkey. (This city was called Constantinople when it was built.) "Hagia Sophia" is Greek for "Holy Wisdom." The Hagia Sophia was built in the 500s AD by Roman Emperor Justinian as a Christian church. It has a massive dome. It later became a mosque and four minarets were added. Now it is a museum.

Tombs of Holy People

In many religious traditions the practice of visiting holy people's graves is important. For Catholics, visiting the tombs of saints is part of their tradition with a long history.

For Muslims, the Tomb of Muhammad in the city of Medina is a holy site. When Mohammed first entered the city it was called Yathrib, then later renamed after him as *Madinat al-Nabi*, the "City of the Prophet."

FIGURE 11.3   The Hagia Sophia in Istanbul, Turkey, with its four minarets.

For Jews, the Tomb of Abraham in Hebron is a special place. It is also believed to be the burial site of Sarah, Abraham's wife; Isaac his son; and Rebekah, the wife of Isaac.

Honoring tombs is less significant in Hinduism and Buddhism because of the practice of cremation. Bodies are burned in a fire (called a funeral pyre) and the ashes are scattered, or dumped into a river such as the Ganges. Thus, for Mahatma Gandhi, who led India to independence in 1947, the site where he was killed is honored.

The grave of Confucius is in his home town of Qufu, in Shandong Province, China.

Perhaps, the most famous tomb in the world is the Taj Mahal in India, built by King Shah Jahan for his wife, Mumtaz Mahal. This tomb, however, is primarily not a religious site.

An Aside

Many people find it interesting to visit the graves of famous people. The website Findagrave.com lets you do a "Famous Grave Search." Think of a famous dead person and look up where he or she is buried.

One of the most popular graves in America is the tomb of the singer Elvis Presley (1935–1977) at his home Graceland in Memphis, Tennessee. Hundreds of thousands of people visit Graceland each year. On the eve of the anniversary of his death tens

FIGURE 11.4 Elvis Presley grave, Graceland.

of thousands stand in line for hours for a candlelight procession to remember Elvis. He died August 16, 1977.

Ancient Temples and Pyramids

Ancient peoples constructed many magnificent religious buildings. Many no longer exist but a surprising number survive, though many are in ruins. Remnants of ancient temples are found in Greece and Italy and around the Mediterranean Sea. The Parthenon in Athens, Greece, is the most famous. In Rome, the Pantheon, the "Temple to All the Gods," has been preserved through the centuries and looks much as it did when it was built more than 2,000 years ago.

The Egyptians built about 100 pyramids as tombs for their pharaoh kings. The biggest and most famous are the three pyramids at Giza. Near each pyramid the Egyptians built a mortuary temple where people could go to worship the dead king.

The Egyptians built numerous temples such as those at Karnak and Luxor.

The ruins of many Hindu and Buddhist temples and monasteries still stand in Asia. Angkor Wat in Cambodia was originally built as a Hindu shrine, but later became a Buddhist shrine. It is the largest religious monument in existence.

In Central America stand the ruins of a number of Mayan cities such as Palenque, Copan, and Tikal. The Mayans built stepped pyramids. (A camera shot of the pyramids at Tikal was used in the movie *Star Wars: A New Hope* as the site of the rebel base on the moon of Yavin 4.)

Figure 11.5 The pryamids at Giza.

Figure 11.6   Buddhist monks in front of the Angkor Wat.

The ruins of Aztec pyramids can be found in the center of Mexico City. Mayan and Aztec pyramids were used for religious ceremonies, including human sacrifice. A live victim was dragged up the stairs and then cut open with a flint knife. The still-beating heart of the victim would be pulled out as an offering to the god of the sun.

Mythic and Natural Places

There are also mythic places where events described in myths were supposed to have happened. For example, in Greece there are many places connected to stories in Greek mythology. In southern England, the Castle of Tintagel is connected to the legends of King Arthur.

There are also many natural places believed to be sacred such as Mount Fuji in Japan. It is considered sacred in the Japanese religion of Shinto. The Black Hills in South Dakota are considered sacred by Native Americans. In fact, for some all of nature is sacred.

Native American Structures

Native Americans have been in the New World for more than 20,000 years. Much of their ceremonial activity took place outside. Large archaeological sites have ceremonial plazas the size of football fields. Over the millennia Native Americans also built ceremonial buildings, lodges, plank houses, mortuary houses for the dead, and other structures used for religious purposes. These structures, however, were made of wood, bark, thatch, and mud and have disappeared over time. But the ruins of buildings built of stone such as those in the Southwest have survived and show the importance of religious structures. Also, a number of earthen mounds have survived.

There are many groups of Native Americans. In the Southwest (Arizona and New Mexico) there are several groups called the Pueblo people, including the Hopi and Zuni. "Pueblo" is the Spanish word for town. There are also ancient people, such as the Anasazi, whose ruins dot the landscape. For both current Pueblo peoples and the ancient peoples, the key sacred building was and is the kiva.

The kiva is a round building typically about 12 to 30 feet in diameter. The kiva is often partially in the ground and partially above ground, and topped with a dome made of wood covered with mud. The kiva is entered from the top of the dome. At the countless archeological sites in the Southwest, most have kivas. At Mesa Verde in Colorado the Anasazi built large villages in cliffs, and each village contains numerous kivas.

On the floor of the kiva is a small pit called the "sipapu" (pronounced see'-pa-poo). It is the navel of the world. In Pueblo origin stories humans and animals, led by Spider Grandmother, came from below the earth and emerged onto the surface. They came out at the "place of emergence," which the sipapu represents. In some villages the people believe the sipapu in their kiva is the actual site where humans emerged.

Many rituals are performed in the kiva. Most important are the kachina dances. Kachinas are spirits that bring rain. Kachina dancers wear elaborate costumes

FIGURE 11.7 Cliff Palace Village at Mesa Verde in Colorado. Note the numerous kivas.

and represent the kachina spirits. Children are taught about the spirits with kachina dolls.

Each kiva in a pueblo belongs to a particular religious society. To enter a kiva and participate in the rituals a person has to be initiated into the society. In contrast, many churches encourage visitors and welcome people who want to check out a particular denomination. But kivas are not open to the public. This, in part, reflects a long and complicated history that saw Spanish and Mexican missionaries and governments attempt to destroy these religions. There is also an attitude that kivas are sacred places where sacred ceremonies take place. To open these places and ceremonies to outsiders as spectators, especially with their cameras, would violate the sacred space.

Another important Native American group in America would be the Mound Builders, who reached their peak about 1,000 years ago but who had been building mounds 1,000 years before that. When Europeans arrived in America, about 200,000 Indian mounds existed along the Mississippi and Ohio River valleys. Many of these mounds were burial mounds; many were ceremonial mounds. Most have been destroyed by white Americans eager for land.

One of the surviving mounds is Monks Mound at the Cahokia Mounds site in Illinois, a few miles east of the city of St. Louis, Missouri. This mound rises 100 feet above what would have been a great ceremonial plaza. The city had a population of perhaps 20,000. At the time it was bigger than the city of London. The city declined after about 1200 AD.

B. LEADERSHIP

1. Many Kinds of Leaders

Most religious groups have some sort of leader. But there is a wide range of types of leaders and their roles. For Jews, the leader of a local synagogue or congregation is called a "rabbi."

In Sunni Islam, a local leader of a mosque is called an "imam." An imam runs the local mosque, leads services, and teaches at some services. In Shia Islam the word "imam" is used differently. Here the word refers to special figures in the past whose teachings guide later generations of Muslims.[3]

Most Christian churches have a minister who is the spiritual guide for the community. Typically, the minister leads the services, preaches at the services, and is

---

3   The role of imams in Shi'a Islam is a complex topic and beyond the scope of this book.

in charge of the administration of the church. Ministers have different labels in different denominations such as "pastor," "reverend," or "priest."

Ministers become ministers in different ways. In some denominations each local church has a board of elders that selects ministers. Often such a board makes all the important administrative decisions about a church.

Sometimes ministers set up their own churches. They get a building and attract a congregation. Sometimes these congregations can get quite large, and sometimes services are broadcast on radio or cable TV.

Some Christian denominations have regional bishops who oversee the churches in their area and assign ministers to each church. Some denominations have regional governing boards that assign ministers and oversee local churches or work with local congregations as they hire ministers.

The elaborate structure of the Roman Catholic Church involves six layers: the laity; the religious; deacons; priests; bishops/archbishops/cardinals; and the pope.

In the Orthodox Church there are local priests, bishops, and special bishops called "patriarchs."

2. Who Becomes a Leader?

Since there is a wide range of leadership types, there is a wide range of requirements to become a leader. In many traditions becoming a religious leader requires extensive education and training, and approval by an authority such as a bishop or governing board.

There are also groups in which the leader is believed to have some special gift or revelation. Sometimes a leader is believed to be specially chosen by God. In a few cases such leaders have led their followers to disastrous ends. (See Chapter 20 for examples.)

3. Women in Leadership

One of the changes in religion over the past decades is the increasing number of woman in leadership roles in some traditions. Some Christian denominations have women pastors. Women rabbis are allowed in Reform and Conservative Judaism. Other traditions, however, exclude women from leadership such as in Orthodox Judaism and in a number of Christian denominations.

Historically, a number of important women have started their own religions, including Mother Ann Lee, founder of the Shakers; Mary Baker Eddy, founder of the Church of Christ Science; Ellen. G. White, founder of the Seventh-day Adventist Church, and Nakayama Miki, whose teachings became the religion of Tenrikyo in Japan.

1. What are some of the church buildings near where you live?
2. Have you ever visited famous and impressive religious buildings?
3. Have you ever visited the tombs of famous people? Who were they?
4. Should religious buildings have religious art and statues, or not?
5. What do you think of women as religious leaders?

Credits

CHAPTER 12

RELIGIOUS RITUAL AND RELIGIOUS TIME

A. RITUALS

All religions have important ceremonies or rituals. The dictionary defines a ritual as "the established form for a ceremony."[1] In the simplest meaning of the word, a ritual is a repeated way of doing something that gives meaning. A religious ritual can be simple or elaborate. Often rituals have no practical benefit. For example, the practical thing on a Sunday morning would be to stay home and clean house rather than go to church.

Rituals are also found outside of religion such as singing the national anthem before a baseball game, an annual town parade, or Halloween decorations and trick-or-treating. Rituals can be formal or informal. There is a joke among some Jews that since they do not celebrate the birth of Jesus at Christmas, the Jewish ritual for celebrating December 25 is to go out for Chinese food and go see a movie.

Religious rituals can be local or international. Around the world, countless small shrines exist that are only used for prayer by the people who live nearby. At the other extreme is the Catholic Mass, which is celebrated around the world. Although Mass is done in the local language, the structure of the Mass is the same all across the globe.

The most frequently practiced ritual ever in human history is salat, the Islamic prayer. There are more than a billion Muslims in the world, many of whom are faithful in praying salat five times a day.

1. Types of Rituals

There are five types of religious rituals: daily rituals, weekly rituals, seasonal rituals, special events, and rituals to mark life stages.

Examples of Daily Rituals
Many Christians pray every day. Many do daily Bible study. Some Catholics go to Mass daily.

---

1 Merriam-Webster's Dictionary

Praying salat five times a day is one of the duties of Islam. Praying in groups, especially at a mosque, is preferred. When that is not possible Muslims pray privately on small prayer rugs.

Many Hindus and Buddhists pray or meditate daily and have small shrines in their homes or workplaces. Many visit temples every day.

Daily prayer is important for many Jews. Daily Torah study is also important for some Jews, and some Jews visit the synagogue each day.

In the Sikh religion, praying several times a day is required. Sikh men are required to comb their uncut hair twice a day with a comb called a kangha as part of their prayer.

Many Native Americans have daily rituals. One example is going out before sunrise, facing east, and chanting for the sun to rise.

Examples of Weekly Rituals

Most active Christians go to church each Sunday. But one group of Christians, the Seventh-day Adventist Church, follows the Jewish definition of the Sabbath as Saturday. Seventh-day Adventists go to church on Saturday.

The Jewish Sabbath starts on Friday at sundown and continues to Saturday at sundown. Active Jews hold a Sabbath meal with prayers and blessings on Friday evening at their homes. Many Jews go to synagogue on the Sabbath, either on Friday evening or Saturday morning.

Devout Muslims go to a mosque on Friday for prayer. Many Hindus and Buddhists visit temples on a weekly basis. In America, Sunday is the popular day to go to temples because many people do not work on Sundays.

Examples of Seasonal Rituals

Jewish seasonal celebrations were described in Chapter 5. Christian seasonal rituals will be discussed below.

Muslims have three important yearly celebrations. Ras Al-Sana is the New Year's celebration on 1 Muharram. (Muharram is the first month in the Islamic calendar.) Two important months in the Islamic calendar are Ramadan and Dhu al-Hijjah. During the month of Ramadan, Muslims are required to fast with no food or drink during daylight hours. At the end of Ramadan there is a feast to celebrate the breaking of the fast: Eid al-Fitr. This takes place on the first day of the month after Ramadan. The tradition is to wait for the crescent moon of the next moon month to appear before feasting. This is why the crescent moon is an important symbol in Islamic art. Also, because months move around on the Islamic calendar relative to the seasons, the lengths of the days of Ramadan can vary from one year to the next.

The other important month is Dhu al-Hijjah during which millions of Muslims travel to Mecca to make the pilgrimage required by the Fifth Pillar of Islam. The pilgrimage ends with a feast called Aid al-Adha. This feast is celebrated both by Muslims on pilgrimage and those who remain at home.

Two important festivals for Hindus are Holi in spring and Diwali in November or December. Holi is a festive celebration that includes throwing packets of colored powder on one another. Diwali is the festival of lights and it remembers the story of the return of Lord Rama after defeating the evil king Ravana. It also honors the annual visit of Lakshmi, goddess of prosperity and good luck.

Buddhists celebrate three important festivals each year: 1) Hanamatsuri, the flower festival remembers the birth of the Buddha; 2) Bohdi Day celebrates the day the Buddha received enlightenment; and 3) Nirvana Day, a solemn remembrance of the death of Buddha's body and his entrance into Nirvana.

Among Native Americans there are countless seasonal festivals. Some are linked to the winter solstice, the spring equinox, the summer solstice, and the fall equinox. Hundreds of ancient Native American archaeological sites indicate where the sun will rise on the horizon on significant days. Native Americans often held celebrations for planting; when crops reached maturity, such as Green Corn dances; and for harvest. The Pueblo people of the Southwest have a whole sequence of dances to bring the seasonal rain. Kachina dancers represent kachina spirits who are the rain spirits that bring rain.

Examples of Special Events Rituals
Many religions have rituals that are only used for special events. Some examples would be ceremonies to install a new leader such as a minister or a bishop, or ceremonies to dedicate a new building. Special ceremonies can mark tragic events, such as 9/11 memorial services.

2. Rites of Passage[2]

Most cultures mark four transition times in life: birth, adulthood, marriage, and death. These are known as the "rites of passage." "Rite" means a ritual or ceremony. These four rites mark four transitions or "passages" from one stage of life to another: 1) being born into life, 2) going from childhood to adulthood, 3) going from being single to being married, and 4) going from this life to the next.

Most religious traditions mark these moments in life. For example, Sikhs have Naam Karan, a naming ceremony in which an infant is named by opening at random

---

2   For a more detailed explanation of rites of passage, see Lawrence S. Cunningham and John Kelsay, *The Sacred Quest: An Invitation to the Study of Religion*, (Boston: Prentice Hall, 2010), 74–76.

the holy book, the Adi Granth. The first letter on the page becomes the first initial of the child's name. Many Jews hold a b'rit bat, which is a blessing ceremony for a new-born girl. All Jews hold a bris, which is the circumcision ceremony for a male baby on the eighth day after birth. Many Christians baptize infants.

For many Christians, the adulthood ritual is confirmation; for other Christians the ceremony is adult baptism. In the Sikh religion, baptism is the adulthood ritual. In Judaism, it is the bar mitzvah for boys and, for some groups, the bah mitzvah for girls. Hindus hold upanayana, the Sacred Thread ceremony.

Most religions have marriage ceremonies. In most traditions marriage is seen as something more than a legal agreement between two people. Many monotheists see marriage as an agreement taking place before God.

All religions have ceremonies for death. There is a wide range of practices as to how the body is treated and how death rituals are to be performed. There is also a wide range of beliefs about what happens, if anything, after death. These beliefs will be explored in Chapter 13.

3. A Basic Religious Service

There are four elements to a basic religious service: prayer, readings, preaching, and music. Most religious services include them. Prayer can take many forms. It can be quiet or aloud. Prayer can be said by the minister or the congregation. Prayer can be spontaneous or written or memorized. The Our Father is a common Christian prayer known by most Christians. Meditation and reflection are alternatives to prayer.

Religious services almost always include readings from the sacred writings such as the Qur'an, the Hebrew Scriptures, the Christian Bible, or the Adi Granth. Sometimes other readings such as poetry are used.

Most religious services include some sort of preaching or teaching. This part is sometimes called a sermon or homily.[3] In some religious groups—such as some Christian evangelicals—the preaching is the most important and longest part of the service. In many groups only the minister or leader can do this part of the service.

Music can take many forms such as hymns sung by the congregation or performance pieces done by soloists or groups of musicians. Organs have been very popular in churches going back hundreds of years because organs in the pre-electric days were able to produce much sound with only one musician. An organ can fill a cathedral. In many people's minds, organ music sounds like church music. Some

---

3 Some Christian groups see a homily as an application of the scriptures to the congregation's daily lives, and see a sermon as a broader and more theoretical discussion of the scriptures and religious doctrine. Most people use the words interchangeably.

churches have a choir or group of musicians. Some evangelical Christians even have rock bands.[4] Music can also be as simple as drumming or using cymbals.

There are often strict rules in various religious groups on what music is allowed. For example, in many Orthodox Jewish synagogues the only singing is done by a male cantor without any instruments. In some Christian churches only religious songs are allowed at weddings; popular love songs are not permitted. Some churches only allow traditional hymns and frown on anything that sounds like popular music.

Islam is an exception regarding music because most Islamic services do not include music; however, the one group of Muslims that regularly includes music are the Sufi mystics.

These elements—prayer, readings, preaching, and music—are even found in nonreligious services. For example, a funeral service for a nonreligious person could include a quiet reflection on the dead person's life, poetry readings, a eulogy in which a friend talks about the deceased, and nonreligious music.

B. TIME

1. Religion and Calendars[5]

Many religions view time as special or sacred. Marking time, knowing how the year and its seasons change, has always been important for humans. For hunters and gatherers, it was vital to follow the migrations of animals and know when various plants could be eaten. For farmers, knowing when to plant is crucial. In northern locales the trick is to plant the seeds late enough so that a late frost does not kill the young plants but not too late so that the plants dry out in the hot summer. In other places the key is planting at the right time to catch the seasonal rains. Calendars help farmers to know when to plant. But at some point in human development calendars went beyond such practical needs.

Religious priests probably did the work of developing more advanced calendars. Creating calendars required studying the stars and planets. It required mathematics and writing. In many ancient societies only the priests had such skills and the time to devote to studying time.

---

4   Not everyone agrees that rock music is appropriate for a church or appropriate for spreading the Christian message. On the TV show *King of the Hill*, Hank Hill stated regarding Christian rock: "You're not helping Christianity and you're hurting rock 'n' roll."

5   For an excellent explanation of calendars and various religious celebrations, see Margo Westrheim, *Celebrate! A Look at Calendars and the Ways We Celebrate* (Oxford: One World, 1999).

Calendars began to be used to set religious holidays such as New Year's festivals. In some cultures the priests used calendars to determine good luck days and bad luck days. Very likely the esoteric knowledge that priests had of time and calendars gave them a mysterious aura that reinforced their authority in religious matters. To the ordinary peasant it might have appeared that the priests had mysterious or secret knowledge of time, and so the priests should be obeyed. As a result, most of the calendars around today either have roots in religion or are connected to religion. As you will see, even the calendar you use every day has months and days named after ancient gods.

2. Mythical Vestiges in Our Calendar

Most of the details of our calendar were worked out by the Romans. Called the Julian calendar for Julius Caesar, it went into effect in the year 45 BC. The calendar had a leap day added every four years to the end of February.

Months

The Romans gave us our month names. The month *Januarius* was named after Janus, the god of beginnings and endings—often shown with two faces. This month became January. *Februa*, a religious ritual of purification, became *Februarius*, which became February. The Romans named the next month *Martius* after Mars, the god of war. It became March.

The origin of the month name "April" is a little unclear. It might be based on the word "aperire," which in Latin means "to open," as in the opening of flower buds. "Maia," a Roman fertility goddess, became *Maius*, which became May. Juno, the wife of Jupiter, had a terrible marriage. Jupiter had many affairs, yet Juno became the goddess of marriage. The Romans called the next month *Junius*, which became June. Even today we talk about a "June bride." Romans also had the custom of the bride and groom feeding each other cake.

The Romans named the next months after numbers: *Quintilis* (fifth month), *Sextilis* (sixth), *Septembris* (seventh), *Octobris* (eighth), *Novembris* (ninth), and *Decembris* (tenth). Several English words also are based on numbers: "quintuplets" (five babies); "octagon" (eight-sided shape); "novena" (nine days for prayer); and "decade" (ten years). But by now you should be confused. If "oct" means "eight" then why is October the tenth month? If "dec" means "ten" then why is December the 12th month? The answer is that when these month names were first used, March was the first month of the year. Later, when January became the first month, the number names were not changed.

The Romans renamed *Quintilis* as *Julius* for Julius Caesar, and renamed *Sextilis* as *Augustus* for Augustus Caesar, and so named the months of July and August. Also, the Romans decided the lengths of the months, which requires a poem to remember:

> *Thirty days have September,*
>
> *April, June, and November;*
>
> *Thirty-one the others date,*
>
> *Except in February, twenty-eight;*
>
> *But in leap year we assign*
>
> *February, twenty-nine.*

The Romans worked out the nuts and bolts of our current calendar with the Julian calendar. But the calendar was 11 minutes off each year from the true solar year (the time it takes the earth to make one revolution around the sun). In 1582, Pope Gregory XIII tweaked the calendar to fix the 11-minute problem and reset the calendar. Our current calendar is named after him: the Gregorian Calendar. It is also sometimes called the "secular calendar" to differentiate it from religious calendars such as the Jewish calendar.

Days of the Week
The seven-day week came from the ancient Israelites who got it from the ancient Babylonians. The Romans took the seven days and named them after the seven planets they could see: *Dies Solis, Dies Lunae, Dies Martis, Dies Mercurii, Dies Jovis, Dies Veneris,* and *Dies Saturni.* These would be the day of the sun, the day of the moon, and the days of Mars, Mercury, Jupiter, Venus, and Saturn. Notice the word "solar" is used for things related to the sun, and "lunar" is used for things related to the moon.

By now you are probably thinking, "I thought there were nine planets. What about planet earth? What about Uranus, Neptune, and Pluto? And the sun and moon aren't planets!" The Romans defined a planet as a "wanderer" that moved in relation to the stars. So that definition included the sun and the moon. Also, the Romans thought everything revolved around the earth so they did not call earth a planet. The Romans could not see Uranus and Neptune without telescopes. They also could not see Pluto. (Today the debate on whether Pluto is a planet or not continues. Poor Pluto!)

Look at the Spanish days of the week, starting with Sunday: *Domingo, Lunes, Martes, Miercoles, Jueves, Viernes,* and *Sábado.* Tuesday through Friday match planets. "Domingo" is the Lord's Day, and "Sábado" means the Sabbath.

Our English weekdays start with the "Sun's day." Monday is the "Moon's day." The next five days were named after German gods. The god of war was Tew. So we get "Tew's day" or Tuesday. Woden (also called Odin) got the next day. "Woden's day" became Wednesday. (Note that it is not spelled the way we say it: "wendsday.") Thor was the god of thunder and lightening so "Thor's day" became Thursday. Freya was the goddess of fertility as was Venus. "Freya's day" became Friday. The last day, "Saturn's day," became Saturday.

3. How We Label Years

Why was that year called "2010"? From where do the year numbers come? What year were you born?

Many people know that our system for numbering years has something to do with Jesus, since our years are labeled AD. Most people also know that BC means "Before Christ" and that BC is used for years long ago. Many people think AD means "After Death" and think our years are numbered starting with the death of Jesus. But if AD means "After Death" and BC means "Before Christ," what do you call the 30 some odd years when Jesus lived: DC for "During Christ"? (I suppose you could change AD to AC for "After Christ." Then you would have AC and DC as year labels, which would match the electrical systems and you could use them as a band name.)

It turns out that AD is not "After Death" but really means *Anno Domini,* which is Latin for "Year of our Lord." *Anno* means "year" and it became the English word "annual." *Domini* means to "Lord over" or "rule" and it became the English word "dominate" and the Spanish name for Sunday: *Domingo*—the Lord's day. So, AD counts from the birth of Jesus. The church with the 2010 cornerstone was built 2,010 years after the birth of Jesus. But there is a complication.

The system of counting everything from the birth of Jesus comes from a Christian monk named Dionysius Exiguus, who lived around the year we call 500 AD in what today is Syria. (At that time Christianity was the main religion in that region of the world.) In his time, years were dated using the old system of counting from the year the city of Rome began. Year 1 of the Roman calendar was the year we call 753 BC. (Romans labeled their years "AUC," which is Latin for *ab urbe condita,* meaning "from the founding of the city.")

As a Christian monk, Dionysius thought the most important event in history was the coming of Jesus and so he put year 1 as the birth of Jesus. Dionysius, however, was probably off by a few years. More likely Jesus was born anywhere from four to six years earlier. So a common range for the birth of Jesus is 6–4 BC.[6] But keep in mind that this range is a best guess.

The problem with the year labels AD and BC is that they are based on Christian titles for Jesus. The labels are not "Before Jesus" and "After Jesus," which would be based on the name of Jesus. Rather, these terms are based on titles for Jesus: the Christ and the Lord. Only Christians, however, believe that "Jesus is the Christ and the Lord." So many non-Christians and nonreligious people prefer an alternative system that uses the same year numbers but nonreligious labels. So the AD label becomes CE for "Common Era," and BC becomes BCE for "Before the Common Era." "Era" means a long period of time.

If you are not familiar with BC/BCE dates notice that the numbers go down as time passes. The Buddha lived from 563 to 483 BC/BCE. For AD/CE dates the numbers go up as time passes. Martin Luther lived 1483–1546 AD/CE.

Also, the year before 1 AD is 1 BC. There is no year 0. Now this is a tiny point and may not bother most people but it affects different views on when centuries start and when millennia start. Did the twentieth century begin with the year 1900 or 1901? Technically, if there is no "Year 0" then the century began with 1901 and ended with 2000. Most people, however, counted the century from 1900 to 1999.

A thousand years is a millennium. We are now in the third millennium, according to the system set up by Dionysius Exiguus. But did the third millennium begin with 2000 or 2001? Technically, if there was no "Year 0" the millennium began on January 1, 2001. But in the minds of many people it began on January 1, 2000. Smart people went to two millennium parties and did not worry about it.

As for Jesus, if the range for his birth is 6–4 BC/BCE, then when was he crucified? No one can pin this down for certain. The range of 27–33 AD/CE seems likely. The Gospel of Luke says that Jesus began his public ministry when he was "about 30 years of age" (Luke, 3:23). In the Gospel of John there are three references to the yearly Jewish Passover. A traditional view developed that Jesus started his public ministry at 30 and that it lasted three years, with Jesus crucified at age 33. But scholars have been unable to neither prove these ages as definitely correct nor pin down the exact years of his birth and crucifixion.[7]

One last point is that when a date for some event is not known for certain, a little "c." is put before it. This is an abbreviation for the Latin word *circa*, which means

6   This puts one in the strange position of saying, "Jesus was born four to six years 'Before Christ.'"

7   One problem with counting the Passovers in John's gospels as a true reflection of the time frame of the public ministry of Jesus is that the Gospel of John contains so many symbolic elements that it is hard to know whether the Passover references are symbolic or true accounts of what happened in the life of Jesus.

"around or about." (Notice the Spanish word *cerca* means "about.") For example, the years when Confucius lived are uncertain so they can be given as c. 551–c. 479 BC.

4. The Jewish Calendar

The Jewish calendar is extremely complicated because it combines the lunar calendar with the solar calendar. Some years have 12 months, some have 13. And the length of the year can be 353, 354, 355, 383, 384, or 385 days.

An important Jewish seasonal ritual is Passover, which is usually celebrated on the first full moon of spring. Spring begins with the spring equinox, which can fall on March 19, 20 or 21. Passover is usually the first full moon after the spring equinox, which is why Passover moves around. Jewish seasonal rituals were covered in more detail in Chapter 5.

5. The Islamic Calendar.

Our everyday calendar is based on a solar year. A solar year is the time it takes for the earth to make one revolution around the sun, which is roughly 365 1/4 days. An alternative calendar is the lunar calendar, which follows the moon. The moon goes through phases starting with the new moon. A new moon is when you cannot see the moon because you are looking at the dark side of it. In the next days the moon grows from a crescent moon to a half moon then to a full moon. Then the moon decreases in size down to a half moon then a crescent moon and then you cannot see it because you are again looking at the dark side. (Go online and look at a chart of the phases of the moon.)

The Islamic calendar follows the moon. Each month matches the phases of the moon with a full moon in the middle of the month. If you see a full moon you know it is the middle of the month. The lunar cycle from one new moon to the next new moon takes roughly 29 1/2 days. To allow for the lunar cycle, the Islamic calendar alternates 29-day months with 30-day months. A lunar calendar is based on 12 lunar cycles. The problem is that 12 lunar cycles makes a year of 354 days, which is 11 days short of the solar year. So the Islamic calendar does not match our regular calendar. To know the date for a specific day one needs to own an Islamic calendar or simply go online and look it up.

One result of the shorter year is that Islamic months creep forward 11 days each year relative to the solar calendar. In the standard calendar in the Northern Hemisphere, August stays put in the summer and January is in the winter. But Islamic months move around. The month of Ramadan moves relative to the seasons. When Ramadan is in winter the days are shorter so the Ramadan fast is easier. When Ramadan is in the summer the days are longer and the fast is harder.

6. The Christian Liturgical Calendar

Many Christians follow a liturgical calendar that is used for deciding when to celebrate various religious events. Christmas celebrates the birth of Jesus on December 25. The Gospels of Matthew and Luke describe the birth of Jesus but offer no indication what time of year this occurred. About 300 years after the birth of Jesus, as Christianity spread throughout the Roman world, Christians took an existing feast of the sun celebrated on December 25 and turned it into a celebration of the birth of Jesus.

Many Christians celebrate the four Sundays before Christmas as Advent, which anticipates the coming birth of Jesus. Many Christians have an Advent wreath in their home or in their church, with the wreath's four candles (three purple candles and one pink candle) marking the four Sundays. The last week of Advent is usually less than seven days, depending on which day of the week Christmas falls.

Also, the first day of Advent marks the beginning of the Christian liturgical year. The Sunday before Advent is called "Christ the King Sunday" and marks the end of the previous liturgical year.

FIGURE 12.1 Advent candles

Easter falls in spring, and on Easter Christians celebrate that Jesus rose from the dead. But Easter moves around on the regular calendar. In the gospels, Jesus had his "Last Supper" on a Thursday night. Jesus was celebrating the Jewish Passover, although he changed the meaning of it. The Jewish Passover is on the first full moon in spring. Jesus was crucified the next day, Friday. Christians believe Jesus rose from the dead on Sunday. So Christians have followed the custom of celebrating Easter on the first Sunday after the first full moon after the first day of spring (the spring equinox). Go online and find out the spring equinox for the current year. It will be March 19, 20, or 21. Then look up the dates of the full moons in March and April. Find the first full moon after the equinox. Then find the Sunday after it. That should be Easter.[8]

---

8   This simplified explanation ignores several complications. For example, in the Gospel of John the Jewish Passover meal was on Friday night. Also, Christians argued for many centuries over when to celebrate

The week before Easter is called Holy Week, starting with Palm Sunday to recall when Jesus entered Jerusalem and was greeted by people waving palms. The later days of the week are Holy Thursday (night of the Last Supper), Good Friday (the day Jesus was crucified), Holy Saturday, and then Easter.

Before Jesus started his public ministry he spent 40 days in the desert in prayer. Christians remember this by the period called Lent, the 40 days before Easter—not counting Sundays—when Christians are supposed to devote more time to prayer and repentance. (Repentance is being aware of one's sinfulness and asking God for forgiveness.)

It is a custom for some Christians to not eat meat on Fridays in Lent. Fish is the usual alternative. Many churches hold fish fry's on the Fridays in Lent. A fish fry is a chance to get a good fish dinner and visit with friends. They are often fund-raisers for churches. If you have never been to a church fish fry, check one out. You do not have to be a member of the church to attend. Just bring your appetite.

Lent begins on Ash Wednesday. Many Christians celebrate Ash Wednesday by going to church, where a priest or minister makes a cross on the person's forehead with ashes and says, "Remember that you are dust and unto dust you shall return."[9] This passage from Genesis is a reminder of one's death so that one should make spiritual things a priority.

After Easter two important religious celebrations follow. In the gospels Jesus ascended into heaven 40 days after he rose from the dead, so many Christians celebrate Ascension Thursday after Easter. (In counting the 40 days of Lent, Sundays are skipped. In counting the 40 days between Easter and Ascension Thursday, the Sundays are counted.)

In the Jewish tradition, Pentecost, called Shavuot, is celebrated 50 days after Passover. Christians have their own Pentecost. In the New Testament book Acts of the Apostles, after Jesus ascended into heaven his followers were gathered together on the Jewish feast of Pentecost. According to the story, they received the Holy Spirit and then went out preaching boldly. Christians recall this event on Pentecost Sunday, which is 50 days after Easter.

There also two less important feasts not celebrated by all Christians. In the Gospel of Luke, the angel Gabriel appeared to Mary and told her that she would have a child named Jesus. This scene, called the Annunciation, has shown up in many paintings, especially in the Renaissance. Many Christians celebrate this event as the Annunciation on March 25, nine months before Christmas. After the

---

Easter before settling on the Sunday celebration.

9   A priest can also say, "Turn away from sin and be faithful to the gospel" or "Repent, and believe in the Gospel."

FIGURE 12.2   The Annunciation by Fra Angelico.

appearance of Gabriel, Mary visited her cousin Elizabeth who was six months pregnant with John the Baptist. Christian tradition designated June 24—three months after the Annunciation—as the feast of the birth of John the Baptist.

In the liturgical calendar, there are blocks of time that are not part of Advent, Lent, or the weeks after Easter. These weeks are called "Ordinary Time." For those traditions that honor saints, each saint is given a feast day on the calendar. October 4 is the Feast of Saint Francis of Assisi. Since Francis is the patron of animals, some churches have a pet blessing on that day.

Mardi Gras

Mardi Gras is the nonreligious celebration on the last day before Lent. Hundreds of years ago, Christians did not eat meat during the 40 days of Lent. So people would eat up all the meat in their homes before Lent. "Mardi Gras" is French for "Fat Tuesday," not because you ate so much you got fat but rather because you ate meat and the fat with it. Up until recent times, people ate the fat with the meat. This in part makes the meat taste better, but also because people needed more fat in their diet. This is different than the modern problem where people have too much fat in their diet.

In some Christian cultures, theater and performances were banned during Lent. From this developed the idea of special celebrations before Lent. Mardi Gras in some places such as Brazil is known by the name Carnival. The word probably came from the Latin words *carne* for meat and *levare* to take away. Over the centuries Mardi Gras or Carnival has evolved and lost any connection to religion. In Rio de Janeiro, Brazil, there are parades with massive floats and thousands of people in elaborate costumes. For some people, Mardi Gras provides an excuse for reckless excessive drinking and immoral behavior.

7. Other Calendars

Many other calendars also exist such as the Hindu and Bahá'í calendars. For many people these calendars are used only for determining religious festivals while the regular secular calendar is used for business. There is also the very ancient Chinese calendar. The Chinese New Year is an important celebration. The Chinese also have a zodiac, which is the cycle of 12 years designated by animals: rat, ox, tiger, rabbit (hare), dragon, snake, horse, sheep (goat), monkey, rooster, dog, and pig. Go online and look up the current Chinese year. In which Chinese year were you born?

DISCUSSION QUESTIONS

1. What are some interesting religious rituals you have attended? If you have never attended such rituals, see what you can find on YouTube.

2. How does your family mark the four life stages: birth, adulthood, marriage, and death?

3. What are important nonreligious days that you celebrate?

4. Do you celebrate any religious holidays? Which ones?

5. Check out the moon tonight to see what phase it is in. Look up when the next full moon appears.

Credits

- Fig. 12.1: Copyright © Jonathunder (CC BY-SA 3.0) at https://commons. wikimedia.org/wiki/File:AdventCandles.jpg.
- Fig. 12.2: Source: https://commons.wikimedia.org/wiki/File:ANGELICO,_ Fra_Annunciation,_1437-46_(2236990916).jpg.

CHAPTER 13

ISSUES IN RELIGION

A. DEATH AND THE AFTERLIFE

1. Reincarnation.

Hindus and Buddhists believe in reincarnation. As described in Chapter 8, reincarnation is the belief that all animals and humans have souls. When an animal or human body dies, the soul leaves that body and enters another body. When that later body dies, the soul goes into yet another body. A Hindu saying states: "Just as the body sheds worn-out clothes, so the soul sheds worn-out bodies."

The soul is caught in a cycle of birth, death, and rebirth: dying again, being born again, and on and on. This cycle is called "samsara."

2. Heaven and Hell

Most religious people believe there is life after death. For many believers, such as Christians, if you do good and obey God's commandments, you will go to heaven. If you fail to follow God's commandments, then you will go to hell to be punished. A person will stay in heaven or hell forever. For other believers, the key is faith in God. True faith leads to heaven, the wrong faith, or inadequate faith, leads to hell. For many religious people heaven is the ultimate reward for living morally and hell is the ultimate punishment for not living morally.

Speculation about heaven and hell has a long history in religion. It is part of literature, such as the famous *Divine Comedy* by Dante, and many movies, such as a clever look at the afterlife in the movie *Bill and Ted's Bogus Journey*. Through the centuries artists have used their imagination to depict heaven and hell.

"Fire and brimstone" is an expression used several times in the Bible. Brimstone is sulfur. "Fire and brimstone" might have originally been a volcanic image since volcanoes often have the unpleasant smell of sulfur. For many Christians, the expression became an image for hell: hell was filled with fire and brimstone. The term also is used for "fire and brimstone preaching" in which a minister talks frequently about hell and damnation as God's punishment for sinners who do not change their ways.

3. Heaven without Hell

There are also many religious people who believe in heaven but no hell. Many Jews hold this view. Jehovah's Witnesses do not believe in hell. For many people the idea that God could send people to hell to be punished forever is inconsistent with the idea of a loving God. So what happens to bad people when they die? One answer is that they cease to exist. Jehovah's Witnesses, for example, have this belief.

Another answer that some people have given is that hell is not eternal. Rather, it is punishment that does not last forever. Sometimes this belief is called universalism. The idea is that God's love will eventually transform everything so that every person eventually goes to heaven. Universalism was described in Chapter 9.[1]

4. The Underworld

In ancient times many cultures believed in an underworld as the abode of the dead. Many ancient people believed that it was literally below them in the earth. In many cultures, such as in ancient Egypt, when the sun set at night it entered the underworld and then traveled through the underworld at night to emerge at dawn.

The ancient Greeks believed in the place of the dead often called Hades, named after the God of the dead: Hades. Over time the concept evolved and some Greeks believed in the Elysian Fields, which was a nice place in the underworld for good people.[2]

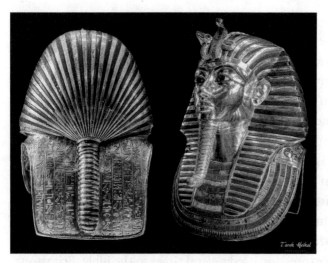

FIGURE 13.1 Mask of King Tutankhamun

Ancient Mesopotamians believed in an abode of the dead, a dusty, dry place. For ancient Mesopotamians it was important to make offerings of food and wine for the dead so they would have some nourishment in the underworld.

The ancient Egyptians went to elaborate lengths to provide for people in the underworld. They saw the underworld as a duplication

---

1   This belief is religious universalism. There is also philosophical universalism, which is a different concept.

2   In the famous play by Tennessee Williams *A Streetcar Named Desire*, Blanche Dubois comes to the Elysian Fields neighborhood in New Orleans hoping to find heaven, and instead she finds a hell that drives her to insanity.

of the present life. In burials, especially royal burials, great expense and effort were expended to provide for the needs of the deceased in the next life. The treasure from the tomb of King Tutankhamun is the best known example of Egyptian efforts to provide for the dead king in the afterlife.

In the Hebrew Scriptures/Old Testament the ideas of heaven and hell were not developed. Rather, the belief was that people died and went to an underworld called Sheol, the place of the dead. Good and bad went to the same place. According to Psalm 6, "For in death there is no remembrance of you [the Lord]. Who praises you in Sheol?"

The Zoroastrian religion played a key role in introducing the concepts of heaven and hell to Judaism and Christianity and these traditions influenced Islam. More will be said on Zoroastrianism in the Appendix.

5. Purgatory

Purgatory is a concept that shows up in Roman Catholic teaching. Belief in purgatory solves a problem. When good people of faith die, they go to heaven. When extremely bad people die, if they have never asked God to forgive their sins, they go to hell. But what happens to those who are not good enough for heaven and not bad enough for hell? The answer to this question, developed in the 600s, is that such people go to purgatory where they have to suffer or pay for their unforgiven sins. Then they can go to heaven.

Notice that the word "purgatory" is based on the word "purge," which means to clean out. It is also close to the word "purify." In purgatory, one is cleansed or purified of his or her sins so he or she can go to heaven.

In the Middle Ages, purgatory was seen as a place of great suffering where people spent a long time before getting to heaven.

The custom of praying for "the poor souls in purgatory" was developed to shorten their time. Next

FIGURE 13.2 Ludovico Carracci painting (c. 1610) An Angel Frees the Souls of Purgatory.

came the selling of "indulgences." An indulgence was a document that freed someone from purgatory.

In the 1500s, Martin Luther, who began the Protestant movement, rejected both
the sale of indulgences and the concept of purgatory because they went against the
basic Christian idea of being saved by having faith in what Jesus did. He also rejected
these concepts because he could not find either "purgatory" or "indulgences" in the
Bible. The Catholic Church stopped selling indulgences but still holds to the belief
in purgatory as a place or process of purification for those who die with unforgiven
sins. Once purified, they go to heaven.

6. Who Gets to Heaven?

Among many monotheists an important question is "Who gets to heaven?" A related
question is "What are the requirements to get to heaven?" For Christians, there are
three basic positions on this question: exclusivist, inclusivist, and pluralist.

The exclusivist position holds that Christian faith is the only way to get to
heaven. Those who do not have such faith will not go to heaven. Some Christian
exclusivists say that even those who never had the chance to hear the teachings of
Christianity about Jesus will go to hell. Many exclusivists believe the vast majority
of people who have lived and who now live will not go heaven, and therefore will
go to hell.

One example of the Christian exclusivist view is the teaching of John Calvin
(1509–1564), who lived in Switzerland. He taught the concept of "predestination,"
that God has already determined who will go to heaven and who will go hell.
Furthermore, nothing a person can do in this life can alter his or her destiny for
heaven or hell.

The Christian inclusivist position is that although faith in Jesus is the normal
path to salvation, others, such as non-Christians who are moral people, will also
go to heaven. Inclusivist Christians cannot imagine a God who would send the
majority of people to hell.

Christian pluralists hold that there is more than one path to heaven. Other religions are valid paths to get to heaven.

7. Jewish Views on the Afterlife

As said before, there is a great diversity of belief in Judaism. In general, Judaism
focuses on this life, so although most Jews believe in an afterlife, there is not much
teaching about it. The Jewish term for the afterlife is *Olam Ha-Ba,* which means
"The World to Come."

Among Jews, many believe in a resurrection of the dead in an afterlife. Also, some
Jews believe in reincarnation. Some Jews believe there is some kind of punishment
for wicked people in the afterlife; however, most Jews do not believe in an eternal

hell. Those Jews who believe in a heavenly afterlife typically do not hold the exclusivist position that the Jewish faith is the only path to heaven.

If one reads the Hebrew Scriptures/Old Testament one may be surprised about how little is said about the afterlife.

8. The Afterlife in Islam

Muslims believe in a paradise after death called "Jannah," which has several levels. The criterion for getting to paradise is good deeds and holding to Islamic beliefs such as the belief that Mohammed is the final prophet. Muslims typically believe that after people die they stay in the grave until a "final judgment." Those who are faithful and have lived a good life will go to Jannah. Those who did not live a good life will go to hell, called "Jahannam" or "Nar." In Islam, Jews and Christians are called "people of the book" and the Qur'an states that some Jews and Christians will go to heaven. Other than these two exceptions, the typical Muslim view is that "infidels," non-believers, will not go to heaven.

9. The Final Judgment

A key concept that came from Zoroastrianism is the belief in a final judgment that will decide who goes to heaven and who goes to hell. This concept has worked its way into Judaism, Christianity, and Islam. There are two ways of thinking about the concept. One is of an individual judgment when a person dies: soon after death one is judged and sent either to heaven or hell. Another view is that there is a collective final judgment of all people at the end of time. Often people's views on this are not so clear. Some believe in a final judgment yet at the same time may say at a funeral, "She is in heaven now."[3]

B. SIN

In religious thinking a sin is doing something morally wrong. For monotheists, a sin is often explained as breaking one of God's rules.

In several religions the big problem is that humans disobey God and God's rules. The Hebrew Scriptures/Old Testament are filled with stories of the ancient Israelites continually sinning by stubbornly refusing to obey God. The Jewish yearly celebration of Yom Kippur is a chance to look back and see how one has done wrong in the past year.

---

3   One way around the contradiction of a final judgment at the end of time and an individual judgment when a person dies is to recognize that the issue is a question of time. Many people, however, think that heaven is eternal and beyond time; so the problem of the different times for an individual judgment and a final judgment may not even exist.

In Islam, the goal is to submit oneself to the will of God. This is hard because the human tendency is to sin and not follow the will of God. In Christianity, Jesus died on the cross to pay the price for human sin. But people have continued to sin.

When talking about sin, two complicated questions arise. The first: "How do you know what are God's rules?" Religious books such as the Bible and the Qur'an do not address all the important moral issues. Over the centuries Jewish, Christian, and Islamic scholars have thought and written extensively trying to figure out which human actions are sins.

The second question: "What are the punishments for breaking God's rules?" Some sins seem minor and not too serious, other sins seem quite serious. Shoplifting a pack of gum is minor compared with embezzling $100,000. Having a brief, flirtatious conversation with a married woman is minor compared with having a sexual affair with a married woman. Again, scholars in the three major monotheistic traditions have spent a lot of time and effort exploring the seriousness of different sins and what God's punishments might be for the various sins.

The Catholic tradition has made a distinction between venial sins and mortal sins. Venial sins are the less serious sins and mortal sins the serious ones. Mortal sins are also called deadly sins. According to Catholic teaching, if one dies having committed a mortal sin and that sin has not been forgiven by going to confession, then that person will not go to heaven.

A list developed in the 300s among Christian writers naming the "seven deadly sins": lust, gluttony, greed, sloth (laziness), wrath (anger), envy, and pride. These things often lead people to do bad things. They might be better labeled as the "seven deadly vices." A vice is the quality one has that leads one to commit sinful actions. Sins are specific actions. Greed is a vice but it is not a sin. However, if a greedy person steals money then a sin has been committed.

The opposite of vice is a virtue. A virtue is a quality that leads one to do good actions. For example, honesty is a virtue that leads one to make truthful statements.

Repentance happens when one realizes that he or she has done wrong and expresses regret and sorrow for his or her action. Repentance might include apologizing to a person or admitting one's sorrow to God. True repentance also implies the corollary that one will try to avoid doing this wrong action again in the future.

C. SACRIFICE

1. Animal Sacrifice

For modern people it is hard to understand the practice or purpose of animal sacrifice. In the ancient world, such sacrifices could be offered in thanksgiving to a god for some blessing or to honor a god or show devotion to a god. Sacrifices could also be offered if someone had angered a god. If a person offended a god by doing something wrong, the god had to be appeased. Something valuable had to be offered such as a sheep, goat, or an ox. Only by an offering of blood could the god be appeased. But keep in mind that usually the meat of the animal was eaten.

Animal sacrifice stills exists. In Islam at the end of the pilgrimage, an animal is sacrificed on the religious holiday of Aid al-adha. The sacrifice is a symbol of Abraham's willingness to sacrifice his son. The animal can be a cow, camel, sheep, or goat.

Muslims on pilgrimage celebrate Aid al-adha in Mecca. In Mecca there are immense refrigeration facilities to store all the meat so that it can be sent to needy people around the world. Muslims who are not on pilgrimage celebrate Aid al-adha at home. The meat is divided into three parts. One part is kept for the family; another is given to relatives, friends, and neighbors; and a third is given to the poor and needy.

Animal sacrifice is practiced by some Hindus, particularly in the Shakti school of Hinduism. Animal sacrifice is still part of some tribal African religions. It also is part of voodoo and Santeria. These are two religions that developed in the Caribbean yet have African roots. Two groups that do not conduct animal sacrifice, yet are sometimes falsely accused of it, are Wiccans and Satanists.

Animal sacrifice played a very significant role in ancient religion. Ancient temples had altars for sacrifice. The stories of Greek and Roman mythology are filled with references to sacrificing animals. A small group of ancient Romans practiced the custom of the taurobolium in which a bull would be sacrificed on a metal grate while a person stood underneath. When the bull was killed the initiate would be doused in blood.

The Hebrew Scriptures/Old Testament are filled with many references to animal sacrifice including rules on how and when to do it. With the destruction of the Jewish Temple in 70 AD/CE, animal sacrifice stopped for Jews.

In the gospels, in a famous scene, Jesus went into the Temple area to drive out the animals used for sacrifice and the moneychangers who exchanged money used to buy the animals for sacrifice. Christians have argued over the meaning of the scene but one possible meaning is that Jesus totally rejected the system of animal sacrifice for forgiveness of sins. Instead, Jesus spoke of God directly forgiving sins.

It is hard for modern people to understand, "Why if I had committed a sin in the ancient world would an innocent sheep have had to die so my god would not have been angry at me?" (What is ironic about this modern attitude is that far more cows die in one year to make hamburgers than were every sacrificed to the gods.)

2. Human Sacrifice

If we look at the history of religions we know that there was human sacrifice. In the Bible, human sacrifice is condemned. If there is a rule against something, it is assumed the practice must have been going on. There are stories in Greek mythology, such as the story of the Greek Goddess Demeter holding a young boy in the fire to burn away his mortality, that seem to hint at older practices of human sacrifice. But by the time of the classical age of ancient Greece, human sacrifice was long gone. Very likely, the ancient Carthaginians in North Africa did child sacrifice. The Vikings sacrificed captive enemies. The Mayans frequently conducted human sacrifice. The Aztecs conducted human sacrifice on an immense scale, killing thousands of people in single ceremonies. Both the Mayans and Aztecs believed that human sacrifice was necessary to bring order to the cosmos.

3. Abraham

One of the most important sacrifice stories appears in the Bible, in Genesis, where God tests Abraham by asking him to sacrifice his only son, Isaac. If you have never read the story, go to an online Bible and read the story at the beginning of Genesis, Chapter 22.

People have argued over the story and what lesson can be learned from it. Some have even argued over the question, "What would you do if God asked you to sacrifice your son?" Since Abraham's time, however, there have been no credible cases of someone being asked by God to sacrifice a child.

The big question in the story is, "Did Abraham think that he was going to sacrifice his son?" Or, "Did Abraham know that he was not going to sacrifice his son?" The simplest reading of the story is that Abraham knew he was not going to sacrifice Isaac. The "test" was not whether Abraham was willing to do what God asked—even sacrificing his Isaac—but rather the test was whether Abraham knew that his God would not in the end ask him to sacrifice his son. Abraham passed the test.

Two details illustrate that Abraham knew he would not sacrifice Isaac. When Abraham, Isaac, and two servants arrived at the designated place, Abraham said to the servants, "Both of you stay here with the donkey, while the boy and I go on over yonder. We will worship and then come back to you." Then, while Abraham and Isaac walked to the place of sacrifice, Isaac asked, "Where is the sheep for the sacrifice?" Abraham answered, "God himself will provide a sheep for the sacrifice." These two statements show that Abraham knew he would not be sacrificing his son.

The other interpretation—that Abraham thought he was actually going to sacrifice Isaac—would mean that Abraham twice lied so as to not panic Isaac, and that in the end God tricked Abraham.

You can make up your own mind about the meaning of this story. As stated previously, the simplest reading of the story is that Abraham knew that his God was not going to ask to him to sacrifice his son.

The story of Abraham being asked to sacrifice his son is also an important part of the Islamic tradition. Many Muslims, however, understand the son to be Ishmael and not Isaac. Also, in the Islamic telling of the story, Abraham told Ishmael and Ishmael willingly consented to be offered as a sacrifice.

FIGURE 13.3 Abraham sacrificing Isaac

4. The Term 'Sacrifice' Today

For Christians, the theme of sacrifice is still very important. Christians believe all animal sacrifice is unnecessary because the final sacrifice was Jesus offering himself on the cross as payment for human sin.

For some Christians the theme of sacrifice shows up in remembering what Jesus has done. In Catholic thinking, the Mass, sometimes called the "sacrifice of the Mass," recalls the sacrifice of Jesus.

The word "sacrifice" commonly shows up with a very different meaning. The term can be used when one makes a personal sacrifice to give up something for a greater good. So, for instance, someone giving up time to work at a soup kitchen is making a sacrifice. Sometimes people make large sacrifices in response to a religious call such as giving up careers, wealth, and even family attachments.

DISCUSSION QUESTIONS

1. What are your views on the afterlife?
2. If you believe in the afterlife do you hold to an inclusivist, exclusivist, or pluralist view?

3. What do you know about ancient mythology? What do you know about the preparations that ancient Egyptians made for the afterlife?

4. What do you think about the list of "seven deadly sins" or "seven deadly vices"? Would you add anything to the list?

5. What are your thoughts on the story of Abraham being asked to sacrifice Isaac?

Credits

- Fig. 13.1: Copyright © Tarekheikal (CC BY-SA 4.0) at https://commons. wikimedia.org/wiki/File:King_Tut_Mask_front_and_back.jpg.
- Fig. 13.2: Source: https://commons.wikimedia.org/wiki/File:Carracci-Purgatory.jpg.
- Fig. 13.3: Copyright © Phillip Medhurst (CC BY-SA 3.0) at https://commons. wikimedia.org/wiki/File:The_Phillip_Medhurst_Picture_Torah_116._ Abraham_sacrificing_Isaac._Genesis_cap_22_vv_10._Brun.jpg.

CHAPTER 14

RELIGION AND MORALITY

A. MORALITY AND RELIGION

For many people a belief in God is central to a person's moral beliefs. God is the basis of any moral system. In this view, a belief in God adds three things: 1) the moral rules, 2) rewards and punishments in this life, and 3) rewards and punishments after death in the next life.

In the opinion of many believers, God gave them their moral rules. The best-known set of rules in the Western world is the Ten Commandments. (More detail on the Ten Commandments was given in Chapter 5.) There are different versions of the Ten Commandments. Here is one example:

1. I am the Lord your God, you shall have no other gods.

2. You shall have no graven images or likenesses.

3. You shall not take the Lord's name in vain.

4. Keep the Sabbath holy.

5. Honor your father and mother.

6. You shall not kill.

7. You shall not commit adultery.

8. You shall not steal.

9. You shall not bear false witness.

10. You shall not covet your neighbor's wife or possessions.

Many religious groups and religions have over time worked out detailed teaching on a wide range of moral issues. In Judaism, there is a long history of Talmud study, much of which revolves around how a faithful Jew should live. As stated before, there is great diversity in Judaism and, hence, a diversity of views on moral issues.

In Islam, there is a long tradition of developing answers to moral questions. One source would be "ijma," which are agreements among scholars of the past on important issues. Buddhists are guided by the Eightfold Path and much has been written about how to understand and apply the eight principles.

In Christianity, different denominations have developed teaching on a wide range of issues. The Catholic body of moral teaching is the probably the most extensive. Some Christian groups, such as some Baptists, leave it up to the individual studying the Bible to decide moral questions.

1. The Divine Command Theory

The belief that God gives the moral rules of what is right and wrong is called the "divine command theory." Under the theory, God gives the rules and enforces them with rewards and punishments. This is why many religious people fear a lack of religion. They feel that if people are not religious then they will not fear the punishments of God and will do bad things. (Chapter 16 explores how nonreligious people answer this objection.)

In the divine command theory, God enforces morality with rewards and punishments. Religious people often speak of the rewards and punishments both in this life and after death. For many religious people, God rewards with heaven those people who are good and have faith. In heaven, people will live with God forever in happiness. Many religious people also believe that bad people will be punished in hell forever. Among Roman Catholics there is also a belief in purgatory, where people who are not good enough for heaven nor bad enough for hell will go until they are purified of their sin and can go to heaven. Some ideas of purgatory include the idea of being punished for unforgiven sins.

Besides the rewards or punishments after death, many religious people believe that God also rewards and punishes people while they are still living. For example, the Bible contains a number of passages stating that God rewards those who are faithful to his laws. In Christian churches, when someone gives a testimony you might hear, "I was on the wrong path, my life was misery, until I found Jesus."[1]

There are three difficulties with the divine command theory. First, it does not work with people who do not believe in God. Second, how do believers figure out what God wants? For example, the Bible does not directly address a number moral issues such as abortion and the removal of medical life support for a terminal patient. Third, believers disagree on what are God's rules. On every moral issue—e.g. capital punishments, homosexuality, and war—religious people hold very different views from one another.

---

1 Common Sense could also weigh in that many behaviors have natural punishments built into them. For example, irresponsible sexual behaviors have all kinds of unwanted consequences.

2. The Language of Morality

It is important to clarify a few terms. Something that is moral is something that is right and good. Something that is the opposite is immoral. Respecting other people's property is moral; stealing other people's property is immoral.

A system of values on what is right and wrong would be a system of morals. Do not get the word "moral" confused with the word "morale." Morale means having a positive spirit. Someone might say, "The morale of our football team is high going in today's game."

Morality is a noun, such as, "She has a high standard of morality."

"Ethics" is another word for morality.[2] An action that is moral is "ethical." An immoral action is "unethical."

B. RELIGION AND SEX

1. Teachings on Sex

Most religions have teachings about sexuality. In a number of religions, the traditional view has been that the only moral sex is between a married man and woman. Many religions have seen homosexuality as immoral. Some religions make a distinction between being homosexual and homosexual acts, and judge homosexual acts as being sinful. Some religions have even seen masturbation as immoral. Traditional religions also view premarital sex and adultery as being wrong. Adultery can be a married person having sex with someone who is not his or her spouse or it can be an unmarried person having sex with someone who is married.

In many cultures in recent decades attitudes about sexuality have changed dramatically. In general, attitudes have been more open about which sexual activities are acceptable. In particular, attitudes on homosexuality have totally changed in many places. Some religions are rethinking their teachings on sexuality and some are not.

2. Celibacy and Chastity

Some religions promote the importance of celibacy. Celibacy is the idea of choosing to not marry and to not have sex. For Catholic priests, brothers, monks, nuns, and sisters it is required. Such people take vows of celibacy. For Buddhist monks the requirement is to give up marriage and sex and to live in a monastery.

---

2   Some people see a difference in the use of the words "morality" and "ethics." Most people do not make a distinction.

For women, often the word "chastity" is used instead of celibacy but it means the same thing: giving up marriage and sex. Large numbers of Catholic women have become sisters or nuns and taken the vow of chastity.

It is sometimes hard for modern people to understand celibacy. Today contraception is readily available and effective, making it possible for one to be sexually active and not have children. But this is a fairly recent development. In decades past very little contraception was available. So if person was sexually active there could very likely be children, and perhaps lots of them. And raising children typically required a huge commitment of time and effort.

In such an environment celibacy would make more sense. If one wanted to dedicate one's life to God and not be caught up in the responsibilities of raising a family, giving up sex and children would make perfect sense. One was not just giving up sex but also the likelihood of having children and all the responsibilities that would entail. However, because of the availability of modern contraception, a dichotomy seems to have evolved in some people's minds, who now think of sex without the obvious connection to having children.

The Shakers were an interesting American example of celibacy. The Shakers lived in a community but practiced celibacy with separate dorms for men and women. In their church services, the men and women would enter by different doors and sit separately. If a married couple joined the Shakers the couple would live separately and practice celibacy. The Shakers often took in orphans, which made up for the fact that their members were not producing children.

3. Sex in Religion—Temple Prostitution

Often people are surprised to learn that some ancient religious practices involved sex. In the ancient city of Corinth, the Greeks built a temple to the goddess Aphrodite. Under the Romans it became the Temple of Venus. A thousand women worked there as temple prostitutes. Corinth was a seaport and many sailors stopped there, and apparently the sailors were religious. Going to the Temple of Venus was a religious act and obviously a sexual act.

The New Testament includes two letters written by Paul to the early Christian community in Corinth. In the first he encourages his followers to be sexually moral. "Do you not know that your bodies are members of Christ? Shall I then take Christ's members and make them the members of a prostitute? ... Do you not know that your body is a temple of the holy Spirit within you, whom you have from God, and that you are not your own?" (1 Corinthians 6:15, 29.) To fully understand the importance of these passages one has to know that some members of Paul's congregation were tempted to visit the Temple of Venus up on the hill.

In the religion of Baal, the god Baal was male and his female counterpoint was Astarte (also called Asherah). The Canaanites believed that when Baal and Astarte had sex the world became fertile. So temples to Astarte had temple harlots who would provide sex as a religious act. Temples to the Mesopotamian goddess Ishtar also included temple harlotry. One can make a distinction between the term "prostitute" who sells sex for economic reasons and a "harlot" who sells sex for religious and economic reasons.

The Hebrew Scriptures/Old Testament has a number of metaphoric references to harlotry as an image for Israel's worship of false gods such as Baal and Asherah. But as a metaphor it has several layers of meaning. On one level it is about unfaithfulness, as in the case of a married man who goes to a prostitute. But it also has the other meaning of harlots in the employ of shrines to false gods and goddesses such as Baal and Asherah.

Also, the Hebrew Scriptures/Old Testament contains assessments of the various kings of Israel. Most of the kings fell short in terms of living up to the requirements of God's laws. Often the kings were accused of failing to get rid of the "high places and sacred poles." The high places were shrines to the god Baal and the sacred poles were phallic symbols. (A phallic symbol represents the penis.)

C. MARRIAGE

1. Monogamy

> *Marriage. Marriage is what brings us together, today. Marriage, that blessed arrangement. That dream within a dream. Then love, true love will follow you forever. So treasure your love.*
>
> —*The Impressive Clergyman, The Princess Bride*

The word "monogamy" comes from Greek. "Monos" means one, as in "monotheism." "Gamos" means marriage. "Monogamy" means marriage of only two people.

Almost all religions have rituals for marriage. Sometimes the ceremony is quite elaborate. Some couples insist on a "big church wedding" even if they are not regular churchgoers.

For most of human history most religions have promoted marriage as being between a man and a woman. Many religions still hold this view. Most societies, up until very recently, had laws that only allowed for marriage between a man and a woman.

In the past several decades in America and Europe, attitudes on marriage have changed radically. Fifty years ago very few people were open to the idea of same-sex marriage. Now many people are open to it and in some places the majority of people support that option. Many countries have now legalized same-sex marriage.

Some religious groups and churches have long supported same-sex marriage. Other religious groups and churches have stayed with the traditional definition of marriage that they have held for hundreds or thousands of years. Often those who oppose same-sex marriage believe that traditional marriage of a man and woman is part of God's plan for humans and not subject to change.

For many people the principle of freedom is important so that adults of the same sex should be free to get married and have the legal privileges that go along with marriage. The principle of freedom, however, also means that certain church groups should be allowed to follow their tradition and not support same-sex marriage.

Some churches have gone through upheaval, loss of members, and even division over this issue. Some members want to accept and bless same-sex marriages and other members want to hold to the traditional view that marriage is between a man and woman.

2. Polygamy

Polygamy is the practice of one man having more than one wife. Remember that "poly" means "many." Polyandry is the rarer practice of one woman having more than one husband. Polygamy has shown up at various times in religious history. In the Bible, Jacob had two wives and two maid servants with whom he had children.

In the early rules of Islam, Muhammad allowed men to have up to four wives, provided the husband treated them all equally. Muhammad was trying to stop the practice of men owning slaves for sex. Believe it or not, this was a step forward for women.

This rule is still on the books in Islam, but except for a few places, the majority of Muslims practice monogamy. Polygamy does, however, exist in traditional African culture.

Among Mormons, polygamy is part of their history. Called "plural marriage, it was practiced by a minority of Mormons as early as the 1830s. It was practiced publicly from 1852 until 1890 when it was stopped, but there are fringe groups of Mormons who still practice it today.

D. RELIGION AND ALCOHOL

Many religious traditions oppose the drinking of alcohol. It is, for instance, forbidden for Muslims, Buddhists monks, and Mormons. Many mainline Christian denominations such as the Baptists, Pentecostals, the Salvation Army, many Methodists, and many evangelicals also oppose drinking.

Some groups see drinking as fundamentally wrong. This position is called "prohibitionism." Others groups take the view that drinking is not inherently wrong but because so many people cannot drink responsibly it is best to not drink. This position is called "abstentionism" from the word "abstain," which means to "avoid something."

Other groups take the position known as "moderationism," that drinking in moderation (drinking responsibly) is acceptable. For some denominations in this group liquor is even served at functions such as church picnics, church fund-raisers, and wedding receptions in a church hall.

However, within the groups that hold the moderationist position, there are often many leaders and members who are very aware of the problems created by the misuse of alcohol and are active in fighting alcoholism and the abuse of liquor. For instance, often in domestic abuse incidences, alcohol is involved. Sometimes religious groups let Alcoholics Anonymous or other recovery groups hold meetings in their buildings.

The Bible has many references to wine. It was part of Jewish religion and culture. From biblical times to the present, many Jewish celebrations, especially Passover and Purim, call for the drinking of wine.

In the Christian Scriptures/New Testament, Jesus did not preach against drinking liquor. At the wedding of Cana, Jesus turned water into wine. At his Last Supper, Jesus took wine and blessed it along with bread. The bread and wine then become important symbols for Christians. As discussed in Chapter 6, some Christian groups use wine at Mass, some use grape juice, and some give members of the congregation a choice of wine or grape juice.

In the history of religion there were rituals that included alcohol and sometimes drunkenness. Here are a few examples. Ancient Egyptians drank wine and beer to the gods and made offerings of the same to the gods. In ancient Greece drinking wine was an important part of the Cult of Dionysus, the god of wine. Getting drunk was seen as being possessed by Dionysus. In ancient Mexico and Meso-America there were rituals involving an alcoholic drink called "pulque," a drink made from the sap of the maguey plant.

E. RELIGION AND WEALTH

Religions have had a long and complicated history dealing with money. Religions have many views on money. On one side are those who see wealth and prosperity as a sign of God's blessing. To support this position some cite passages in the Bible that God will bless those who are faithful and follow God's laws. This view also takes the form of a movement that preaches the prosperity gospel. In this movement wealth is seen as a sign that one is right with God.

On the other side is a long tradition of rejecting wealth. The Christian Saint Francis of Assisi (1181–1226) was famous for rejecting wealth and insisting that his followers live a life of poverty with no money and no possessions. This emphasis on poverty also shows up among Buddhist monks who give up all possessions and support themselves by taking offerings of food from the people who live near the monastery. In Hinduism, holy men called "sadhus" often give up all money and possessions to follow a life of meditation to achieve moksha.

Among the Jains there is a rejection of possessions. Ironically, many Jains work hard and do not spend their money on possessions so they wind up quite wealthy. In particular, there are a number of Jains in the diamond trade.

In Islam, one of the Five Pillars is zaqat, which is a tax or contribution to help the poor. The tax varies from country to country but it is typically 2.5 percent of one's wealth and income.

Among Christians there is a wide range of views. Jesus, especially in the Gospel of Luke, seems to speak against wealth. Jesus rejected the common notion that the wealthy were blessed by God, stating, "Blessed are the poor." Jesus told a rich man to "Sell your possessions and give to the poor, and you will have treasure in heaven. Then come, follow me." (Mark, 10:21.) Yet many Christians are very wealthy and either do not consider or explain away such teachings of Jesus about wealth.

Some Christians hold the view that wealth is not a problem unless one makes an idol of it. Having wealth is fine unless it controls one too much. It is interesting to note that no scripture passage makes this distinction.

Among Jews poverty is not seen as virtuous. Many see wealth as a sign of God's blessings; however, charity and philanthropy are important practices for many Jews.

One complication in religion is that often religions desire to have special buildings and special people dedicated to religion and sometimes special schools. All of these cost money and in some cases a lot of money. Great cathedrals or magnificent churches cost money. A full-time minister with support staff costs money. An elaborate church organization of bishops or even a pope costs money. Schools costs money. Having a school system of grade schools, high schools, colleges, and universities costs money. Even charity services to help the poor cost money. So in many religious groups raising money is important and ongoing. But do not assume that a religious group that has impressive buildings always has a lot of money in the bank. Such buildings can be a big cash drain.

One last point to consider is that many religious groups have done much to help the poor and needy. Many charity programs are supported by religious groups. For example, many orphanages and hospitals have been set up by religious groups.

DISCUSSION QUESTIONS

1. What do you think about the "divine command theory"?

2. What are your views on same-sex marriage?

3. Have you attended weddings that were religious ceremonies? What were the religious elements and symbols in the wedding?

4. What are your views on the proper use of alcohol? Or should people not drink? If you are college student, have you seen the misuse of alcohol by other students?

5. What are you views on religion and wealth?

RELIGION AND ART, SCIENCE, AND TECHNOLOGY

A. RELIGION AND ART

1. The Debate over Images

Religions have different views on the use of art and images. Some religions, such as Hinduism, have lots of religious art, statues, and images. In Islam, however, religious statues and images are forbidden.

Christians disagree on the use of images. Religious decoration is abundant in Roman Catholic churches—especially older ones—and in Greek Orthodox churches. Presbyterian and Baptist churches have no images and art except perhaps a simple wooden cross.

One view sees art and images as a doorway to the sacred. Art and images allow the emotions and the imagination to stop focusing on the world around one and instead focus on the sacred. The opposite view sees art and images as a distraction, or worse—idolatry.

2. The Second Commandment?

Churches or religions that ban statues and images often see them as false gods or idols. Some groups cite the Bible commandments, "You shall have no false gods before me" and "You shall have no graven images before me," to argue against any kind of images. ("Graven" means "carved," such as statues carved out of wood or stone.) These commandments required worship of only the one God of Israel, Yahweh, and forbad worship of other gods such as Baal, Dagon, and Marduk. The people surrounding the ancient Israelites worshipped these other gods as statues made of wood, fired clay, and stone. Very likely these statues were seen as representations of the gods, through which the gods could be approached and worshipped. The Bible commands were twofold: the Israelites were not to worship other gods, nor have their statues. And the Israelites did not make statues of the God they worshipped.

The commandments quoted above are from the well-known Ten Commandments; however, religions disagree on how to number them. Some label the rule against "graven images" as the Second Commandment. Other groups, especially those with statues and art in their buildings, drop this commandment that prohibits images.

It is important to point out that religious groups with images and statues do not believe that the images or statues are somehow divine. Hindus who pray before statues of the gods typically do not believe that the statues are in fact the gods. Roman Catholic churches have statues. But Catholics typically do not think that a statue of Jesus really is Jesus. It is just a statue that represents Jesus.

3. Religious Art

Historically, religious art makes up a significant proportion of all the art that has been created. A college art history course covers much religious art. Here are just a few examples, but the reader should explore other examples of religious art by doing an online image search on topics such as Hindu gods, statues of Buddha, Christian saint paintings, religious icons, the religious paintings of Caravaggio, Islamic art, Inuit masks, Iroquois false faces, and African tribal masks.

Some famous renaissance examples of religious art include Botticelli's paintings *Birth of Venus* and *Primavera*; Leonardo da Vinci's painting *The Last Supper*; Michelangelo's *Pietà*, which is a statue of Mary holding the dead Jesus; and Michelangelo's paintings on the Sistine Chapel ceiling.

FIGURE 15.1 Michelangelo's Pietà, Saint Peter's Basilica, Vatican City.

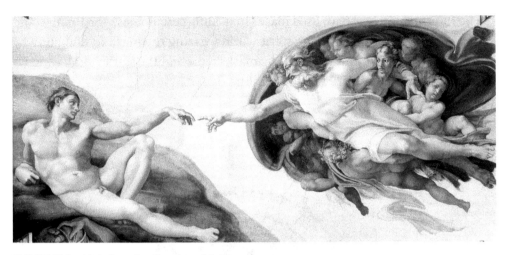

FIGURE 15.2 Michelangelo—Creation of Adam

Among all Christians two common symbols are the cross and the crucifix. What is the difference? A cross is just that. Most Christian churches have a cross displayed. A crucifix is a cross with a statue attached of Jesus either dying or dead. Only some Christian churches display the cross with the statue affixed.

In the Christian Orthodox tradition, a specific type of religious image called an "icon" is important. An icon is a painting—often on a wood panel—of Jesus or of a saint. Typically painted in a stylized way to represent that which is holy, icons are not meant to be natural looking such as in the style of Renaissance religious art. Icons are used in churches and for personal devotion and veneration of the figure in the icon. Often candles are lit before icons.

Islam bans most religious images. In a mosque you will see no images of God, holy people, humans, or even animals. Instead, the walls inside many mosques are decorated with elaborate geometric designs and beautiful calligraphy quoting the Qur'an.

In a Jewish synagogue the use of art and imagery is limited. Images of God and images of holy people such as Abraham or Moses are avoided. Instead, one sees symbolic images of scrolls, the Ten Commandments on tablets, the Jewish star, or the menorah.

Hindus fill their temples with colorful statues of gods and cover the exterior of some temples with statues. To see examples, do an online image search of "Hindu gods" and "Hindu statues."

Native Americans make extensive use of art for ceremonial purposes. For example, the kachina dancers of the Southwest Pueblo people wear elaborate costumes designed to represent the various kachina spirits. Kachina dolls teach children about the various kachina spirits. (Do an online search to see examples of kachina dolls.)

The Inuits (Eskimoes) have used masks in healing ceremonies. A shaman would go into a trance and travel to the spirit world wearing the mask to find out why someone was ill. The unnatural looking masks represent the spirit world, which is very different from the natural world around us.

FIGURE 15.3 Eskimo mask

The "False Face" masks of the Iroquois were used in healing services.

In African tribal religion masks play important roles. For many centuries Europeans looked down on this art as primitive until in the twentieth century when artists began to appreciate the sophistication of this art.

FIGURE 15.4 Iroquois mask

FIGURE 15.5 African tribal mask

Pablo Picasso included images of African masks in his 1907 painting *Les Demoiselles d'Avignon* (*The Women of Avignon*).

FIGURE 15.6 Les Demoiselles d'Avignon

B. RELIGION AND SCIENCE

Many people believe there is a fundamental conflict between religion and science, but this is more myth than anything. In fact, the myth was created by two writers in the 1800s, John William Draper (1811–1882) and Andrew Dickson White (1832–1918), who compared the "rationality of science" with the "ignorance of religion."

Admittedly, for some people there actually is a conflict. Biblical literalists believe the earth is only 6,000 years old and there was no evolution. For them a serious conflict exists between biblical literalism and science. For people who do not read everything in the Bible literally, the problem disappears.

A problem also exists when scientific technology raises moral issues. This is not a fundamental conflict between science and religion but rather a set of religious and moral questions about the use of technology. Some examples of this problem are seen in the debates over using human embryos for stem cell research; cloning

FIGURE 15.7 Galileo

of humans; advance genetic testing of fetuses, which can sometimes lead to abortions; or technologies that keep terminally ill patients alive with a very low quality of life.

And then there is the Galileo affair.[1] For many people this provides the best example of the conflict between science and religion. Galileo Galilei (1564–1642) was convicted and put under house arrest for upholding the views of Copernicus that the sun was the center of our solar system.

Several points need to be made about the Galileo affair. First, the Catholic Church in 1992 admitted that the treatment of Galileo was wrong. Second, the treatment of Galileo was not a witch hunt against science. It was a very complicated affair made worse by Galileo needlessly antagonizing a number of his opponents. Third, Galileo did not go to prison but had to stay on his estate. Fourth, if Galileo was part of a plan to fight science then who was the next victim? There was none.

In reality, throughout Europe most of the scientific thinkers held religious beliefs, including Nicholas Copernicus (1473–1543), Sir Francis Bacon (1561–1626), Johannes Kepler (1571–1630), René Descartes (1596–1650), Blaise Pascal (1623–1662), Isaac Newton (1642–1727), Robert Boyle (1627–1691), and Michael Faraday (1791–1867).

The Catholic priest Saint Albert the Great (1193–1280) wrote extensively on theology but also on astronomy, botany, geography, mineralogy, and zoology. Gregor Mendel (1822–1884), a Catholic priest and monk, did important studies on genetics. Finally, the pope in Rome has a Pontifical Academy of Sciences to advise him on science questions. Pope Francis has spoken about the problems of global climate change and damage to the environment. So it turns out the so-called "fundamental conflict between religion and science" does not exist.

C. RELIGION AND TECHNOLOGY IN SERVICES

In religious services today one finds a wide range of practices regarding the use technology. Some services have very little technology; some use the latest cutting-edge technology. But keep in mind that electricity and plumbing have only

---

1   A detailed overview of Galileo's life and his trial can be found on Wikipedia, s.v. "Galileo Galilei."

been available for a little more than a hundred years. Your not-so-distant ancestors went to churches that had no lighting once the sun went down, other than candles and kerosene lamps, and had outhouses in back. There were no microphones. In large churches and synagogues anyone talking to the congregation had to speak loud enough to be heard.

If you visit Europe, check out the famous cathedrals such as Notre Dame in Paris and the Cathedral of Chartres, outside of Paris. When you visit, notice that these cathedrals do not have heating or air conditioning. Originally, they had no electric lights and no chairs or pews to sit on during the several-hour services. Bathrooms were not part of the original design.

Today, most religious buildings in America and Europe have heating, air conditioning, electricity, and restrooms. In fact, building codes in many places require these things. Sound systems for microphones and speakers are standard in a church of any size.

Some churches today go further and have video cameras that not only record the service but also project the service on a big screen in the church. The congregation can see a close-up shot of the preacher. Video projectors display song lyrics, making songbooks unnecessary. Some churches resemble studios with cameras broadcasting the service on cable TV. Some evangelical churches have bands that play with great sound systems and soundboards that make a would-be rock band jealous.

But many congregations do not want video cameras and projectors in their services. Such technology is seen as distracting from the sacredness of the building and the service. Also, many people would like church to be a place to escape from technology. Notice how we are surrounded by video monitors in airports, in restaurants, in bars, and even on gas pumps. A religious building should be different.

DISCUSSION QUESTIONS

1. If you are part of a religious tradition, what do you think about the question, "Should statues and images be allowed in religious buildings?" If you are not religious, what do think about religious statues and images?

2. What is your favorite religious art? If you do not know any examples of religious art, go online and find some examples. You could do an online search for such topics as "saint statues," "paintings of saints," "religious icons," "Jewish religious art," or "Hindu gods."

3. Do an online image search of Native American art for such topics as "kachina dolls," "Iroquois masks," "Eskimo masks," "Northwest coast masks," and "African tribal masks." What do you find interesting?

4. Do you see areas where conflicts exist between the conclusions of science and your own religious beliefs, or not? What are your thoughts on the relationship of religion and science?

5. Have you ever been to a religious service with big video screens and the latest sound technology? Did you like the atmosphere or not? What makes for a proper religious environment?

Credits

- Fig. 15.1: Source: https://commons.wikimedia.org/wiki/File:Michelangelo%27s_Piet%C3%A0_Saint_Peter%27s_Basilica_Vatican_City.jpg.
- Fig. 15.2: Source: https://commons.wikimedia.org/wiki/File:Michelangelo_-_Creation_of_Adam_(cropped).jpg.
- Fig. 15.3: Source: https://commons.wikimedia.org/wiki/File:Mask,_Alaska,_Nunivak_Island,_Eskimo,_Cup%27ik,_c._1880,_wood,_cormorant_feathers,_sinew,_pigment,_fur,_linseed_oil,_with_later_addition_of_shellac_-_De_Young_Museum_-_DSC00294.JPG.
- Fig. 15.4: Copyright © Wellcome Images (CC by 4.0) at https://commons.wikimedia.org/wiki/File:Mask_of_the_false-face_society,_Iroquois,_North_America._Wellcome_M0012692.jpg.
- Fig. 15.5: Copyright © Roman Bonnefoy (CC BY-SA 4.0) at https://commons.wikimedia.org/wiki/File:African_mask2-romanceor.jpg.
- Fig. 15.6: Source: https://en.wikipedia.org/wiki/File:Les_Demoiselles_d%27Avignon.jpg.
- Fig 15.7: Source: https://commons.wikimedia.org/wiki/File:Justus_Sustermans_-_Portrait_of_Galileo_Galilei,_1636.jpg.

CHAPTER 16

OTHER SYSTEMS OF BELIEF AND NONBELIEF

A. MORE ON ATHEISM

Atheism is the view that there is no God or gods. (Atheism can also be described as the lack of belief in God or gods.) Most atheists also do not believe in an afterlife or reincarnation. Atheists typically believe that when we die everything comes to an end: our identity, our sense of self, and even our memory.

There are a lot of atheists, perhaps 13 percent of the world's population. There are many types of atheists with different ideas on how to live life. In addition, many people are atheists in their thinking but do not label themselves as atheists.

It is difficult for religious people to understand atheists. For religious people, their religion gives the meaning of life, the moral rules to live by, and a belief in heaven after death. The hope of heaven gives the reason to live morally. To religious people, atheism seems to take away all meaning to life.

There are some atheists who agree. Without religion life is meaningless. Some atheists insist on this point: life is absurd and meaningless. Notable atheist writers, such as Jean Paul Sartre (1905–1980) and Albert Camus (1913–1960), have made this point. However, many atheists insist that life without a belief in God can have lots of meaning.

Here are five typical approaches to how atheists live. There are more.

1. Enjoy life while you can. Pursue pleasure.

2. Try to make life better for yourself and others since this is the only life we have.

3. Try to make the world better.

4. Just get by as best you can.

5. Do whatever the heck you want—good or bad. Pursue self-interest and only care about others if they have an effect on you.

For atheists in categories two and three, morality and ethics are very important. These types of atheists often hold high standards of ethics. The difference is they do not base their ethics on the "divine command theory."

For ethical atheists, moral values have to be based on reason. Moral rules have to make sense on their own terms. "Do not steal," for example, is a good rule because it makes sense. Also, the motivation for being moral should be the goodness of being moral and the good effects of being moral. Many parents raising children try to get them to move beyond doing the right thing for fear of punishment, in contrast with children doing the right thing because it is the right thing. Ethical atheists want to get people to move away from the childlike motivation of punishment from God as the reason to be moral, and to move toward a more mature understanding of acting morally because it is a good way to behave.[1]

Lastly, there are also some atheists who are active in trying to discredit religion. The most famous is Richard Dawkins (born 1941) who wrote the book *The God Delusion*.

B. HEDONISM

Another approach to life is called "hedonism." In hedonism, the point in life is to have as much pleasure as possible and to avoid pain. The goal is to <u>maximize pleasure and minimize pain</u>.

Typically, hedonists, those who follow hedonism, do not believe in God (or gods) or an afterlife. Or God and the afterlife are concepts they do not think about. So if there is no God or afterlife, there is no punishment for doing bad and no reward for doing good.[2] "All you have is this life. You might as well have a good time. You are going to die anyway. So during this life you want to get as much pleasure as possible and avoid pain."

But there is a problem with pleasure. It often brings pain because pleasures have costs. Drink too much beer and you get sick! Often, the more intense the pleasure, the more intense the pain that follows. For example, illegal narcotics; the drugs that give the biggest rush often create the biggest pains: addiction, financial disaster, damage to the body, legal problems, and death. Sex can bring pleasure but it can bring all kinds of pain. (One important argument for sexual responsibility is that it avoids many unwanted negative and painful consequences.)

---

1   This book is using the words "moral" and "ethical" interchangeably.

2   There were some ancient Greek hedonists who believed that the gods existed, but they did not believe that perfect beings such as gods could be bothered about human beings. A perfect god would not be sad about human suffering or sin, nor would a perfect god need human prayer, devotion, and sacrifice to be happy.

But despite the problem that pleasures can cause pain, some hedonists become party animals, living the wild life, trying to always keep the pleasure ahead of the pain. There are many people today living a hedonist lifestyle.

Nevertheless, there is a very different way to understand hedonism. It could be called "classical hedonism," since it is based on the ideas of the ancient Greek philosopher Epicurus (341–270 BC). He thought that the simplest way to have pleasure and avoid pain was to live a simple life. If one can be satisfied with simple things, in the end one will have more pleasure and avoid all the pain that trying to pursue more intense pleasures can bring.

C. DEISM

In studying religion it is important to know about a movement called deism. It is not exactly a religion, though it has religious beliefs. Deism honors Jesus, but deism denies the key beliefs about Jesus. It is not Christianity, though deism has been very influential. Many important figures in American history were deists.

Deism came out of the Enlightenment in France and England in the 1700s. It was an attempt to base religion on reason, not tradition or authority. Believers of deism in particular rejected the Roman Catholic Church.

"Deism" is from the Latin word *Deus*, which is "God." Deists (believers in deism) believed one could get religious truth through reason. One did not need God to reveal truth. Using reason one could figure out that God existed, and that he created the universe. One could figure out the moral law of the universe, just like one could figure out the natural laws of science, using reason. You do not need God to reveal "Thou shall not kill" since you could figure this out on your own.

Deists did <u>not</u> believe God acted in history. God created the world and then left it alone. Deists believed that the man Jesus did exist, but he was simply an enlightened man. Deists threw out all basic Christian beliefs about Jesus: that Jesus was born of the Virgin Mary, that Jesus was the Son of God, that Jesus rose from the dead, and

FIGURE 16.1   George Washington as a Mason.

FIGURE 16.2 Symbol of the Masons

that God is a Trinity of Father, Son, and Holy Spirit. Deists thought these beliefs were unreasonable. Jesus was a great teacher and nothing else.

Many of the founding fathers of this country were deists: Thomas Jefferson, Benjamin Franklin, George Washington, Thomas Paine, and Ethan Allen. They were not traditional Christians.

Deists organized themselves as the Masons (also called the Freemasons.). Some of the founding fathers became Masons.

Many famous and powerful figures have been members of the Masons. Many American presidents have been Freemasons, 14 to 16, depending on how you count them.

The word "mason" originally meant someone who worked with stone. The Masons claimed they had descended from the stone masons who built the great cathedrals of Europe. The tools of a real stone mason were a square and a compass, and these tools became symbols of the Masons. "G" stands for God.

Another key Mason symbol is the obelisk. It was originally an Egyptian symbol. It is no accident that the Washington Monument is an obelisk.

Because many famous and powerful people have been Masons, the Masons are often included in conspiracy theories claiming that Masons control the world. Such theories are nonsense. Masons are a secret society. They developed as a secret society because in some places their key ideas were considered dangerous: equality, brotherhood, and democracy.[3]

FIGURE 16.3 The Washington Monument

---

3 *The Simpsons,* of course, has poked fun at Masons. In a classic episode, Homer joins the "Stonecutters."

Here is another Mason symbol. Do you recognize it?

FIGURE 16.4 The Great Seal.

D. THE ZODIAC AND HOROSCOPES

There are many star constellations in the night sky. Twelve can be seen along the path the sun follows. These are the zodiac constellations.

TABLE 16.1 Zodiac Constellations

Aries	The Ram	Mar. 21–Apr. 19
Taurus	The Bull	Apr. 20–May 20
Gemini	The Twins	May 21–June 21
Cancer	The Crab	June 22–July 22
Leo	The Lion	July 23–Aug. 22
Virgo	The Virgin	Aug. 23–Sept. 22
Libra	The Balance	Sept. 23–Oct. 23
Scorpio	The Scorpion	Oct. 24–Nov. 21

TABLE 16.1 *Continued...*

Sagittarius	The Archer	Nov. 22–Dec. 21
Capricorn	The Goat	Dec. 22–Jan. 19
Aquarius	The Water Bearer	Jan. 20–Feb. 18
Pisces	The Fishes	Feb. 19–Mar. 20

The dates given represent when the sun can be seen against each constellation, which means you cannot see that constellation at that time. So when the sun is in the constellation of Taurus from April 20 to May 20, that means that you cannot see Taurus because the sun is blocking the view. (If you can imagine the sun turning off for a moment, you can imagine seeing Taurus in the now dark sky with the now dark sun in front of it.) The word "zodiac" originally meant "circle of animals" since seven of the constellations represent animals.

Going back to at least ancient Babylonian times, people have believed in astrology. In the ancient world, astronomy and astrology were combined; for modern people, however, astronomy is the scientific study of the stars, and astrology is the nonscientific practice of trying to predict the future based on the position of the sun relative to the constellations. Astrology also looks at the positions of planets.

Astrology is the belief that somehow the stars either control events in life or they predict what will happen. Astrology is an example of divination. We still have expressions such as "It's in his stars." Horoscopes are an example of using astrology to predict the future; you just need to know your sign. Find your birthdate in the list above. That is your sign.

Throughout history there has been much interest in astrology. Quite a few people believe in its accuracy. Many others, however, are quite skeptical of the claims of astrology.

E. WITCHCRAFT

Witchcraft is an important part of religion with a very long history and prehistory. In fact, some argue that witchcraft is the religion with the longest continuous history of being practiced. The basic idea of witchcraft involves trying to find harmony with the natural forces of nature. Keep in mind that effective medical science is only about a hundred years old. In a prescientific world without real medicines, witchcraft often tried to heal illness using beliefs about the workings of nature.

In many ways people have totally incorrect images of witchcraft. Images of witches have been shaped by Halloween costumes and movies such as *The Wizard of Oz.* Yet many such images of witches show a total lack of any real knowledge of what witchcraft is about.

To make it more complicated, witches have been harassed and persecuted throughout much of their history. Many of the charges labeled against them have been exaggerations or outright falsehoods. This has added to the confusion and misinformation. Some people make the distinction between "black witchcraft"—what you see in the movies—and "white witchcraft," which is what modern witchcraft is about. In black witchcraft, spells are used to hurt people. White witches do not use spells that way.

The word "witchcraft" can apply to a wide variety of practices and to modern witchcraft. The main impulse of witchcraft is to find the natural energies and movements of nature and to live one's life in accordance with nature. Witchcraft in its various forms can involve healing, spells, sorcery, esoteric knowledge (secret knowledge), magic, and shamanism.

Some groups call themselves "covens." Some have secret societies and some have priests with extensive rituals. One important group is Wicca, also called "pagan witchcraft." Many Wiccans worship both a Great Horned God and Great Moon Goddess.

In witchcraft the cycles of the sun and moon are important as are seasonal celebrations (with Celtic names) such as Samhain in the fall and Beltane in spring. Winter and summer solstices and spring and fall equinoxes are also important.

F. NECROMANCY, SPIRITUALISM, AND SPIRITISM

Necromancy is the practice of calling up the spirits of the dead. Necromancy is an example of divination that claims to contact the dead to get answers. This practice is often called "spiritualism." When people get together to contact the dead it is called a séance. Someone who practices spiritualism is a "spiritualist."

Sometimes spiritualists use the Ouija board. ("Ouija" is pronounced "wee-gee.") The Ouija board has the alphabet printed on in it. Several people sit around a table and put their hands on a "planchette," a piece of wood or plastic. The planchette moves over the board indicating different letters and supposedly spelling out messages. Over the years Quija boards have even been marketed as a board game.

Interest in spiritualism has its ups and downs. In the history of spiritualism there are and have been many sincere people who believe they can communicate

FIGURE 16.5 Ouija board and planchette.

with the dead. It was popular in England during World War I when so many young men died and for so many soldiers there were no marked graves. (Many soldiers died from explosions, leaving nothing to bury; many soldiers never got buried; and many bodies had no identification so they were buried in unknown graves.) Some grief-stricken families turned to spiritualists to contact their lost sons.

There also have been quite a few people who used tricks to convince people that they were communicating with the dead. Often people were tricked to get their money. The famous magician Harry Houdini (1874–1926) spent much time debunking fake spiritualists. ("Debunk" means to prove something wrong.) Houdini did his magic using tricks, and so it was easy for him to figure out the tricks that fake spiritualists were using.

"Spiritism" is similar to spiritualism, but in spiritism there in an emphasis on reincarnation.

1. Contacting the Dead

Although spiritualists try to contact the dead, most other religious traditions think it is wrong to try to contact those who have died. Many people point out that contacting the dead does not work. Once people are dead they do not communicate with the living. That is one of the effects of being dead. Some traditional Christians even think that Ouija boards are dangerous and the work of the devil.

Other traditions think that contacting the dead is possible but that it is a bad thing to do. The problem is that when the spirits of the dead are called up they may not go away. They may stick around and cause problems. Thus, it is not good for the living and it is not good for the dead, who should continue their journey to the next life.

In Native American traditions there are many customs to encourage the spirits of the dead to leave. For example, in some groups the name of the deceased cannot be mentioned for a year, lest the saying of the name might call back the spirit of the dead person. Some tribes have the tradition that before burial the body is held in the air and torches are waved under the body to cut any ties between the dead and the world of the living.

In the Bible, contacting the spirits of the dead was prohibited (e.g., Lev 19:31, 20:6). King Saul violated the rule when he asked the witch of Endor to call up the dead prophet Samuel (1 Samuel 28: 8–25).

G. SEEKERS

An important category of people are religious seekers. These are people trying to find religious meaning. Sometimes they do find it, but often they spend their entire lives never finding the final answers to their questions. Even prominent religious figures such as the monk Thomas Merton (1915–1968) and Mother Teresa (1910–1997) died still searching for answers.

Sometimes seekers feel inadequate, especially around people who are certain about their religious faith and beliefs. In certain religious traditions people with doubts, uncertainties, or questions are looked down upon. Seekers should take comfort, however, in knowing there are many fellow seekers out there. They are in good company. Some seekers even get philosophical and say, "It's the journey that's important, not reaching a destination." Perhaps you are reading this book because you are seeker.

DISCUSSION QUESTIONS

1. According to atheists you do not need a belief in God to create a moral system. What do you think? Do moral values have to come from God?

2. What do you think about Hedonism? What are the risks and costs of pursuing pleasures?

3. What do you know about Wiccans? Do an online image search for Wiccan ceremonies. What looks interesting?

4. What are your thoughts on deism? Do an online image search for Masonic temples. Are there any near where you live?

5. Do you know anyone who is a religious seeker?

Credits

- Fig. 16.1: Source: https://commons.wikimedia.org/wiki/File:Washington,_the_Mason.PNG.
- Fig. 16.2: Copyright © MesserWoland (CC BY-SA 3.0) at https://commons.wikimedia.org/wiki/File:Square_compasses.svg.
- Fig. 16.3: Copyright © David Bjorgen (CC BY-SA 2.5) at https://commons.wikimedia.org/wiki/File:Washington_Monument_Above_Trees.jpg.
- Fig. 16.4: Copyright © 2015 Depositphotos/stillfx.
- Fig. 16.5: Copyright © Marcelo Braga (CC by 2.0) at https://commons.wikimedia.org/wiki/File:Tabuleiro_Ouija.jpg.

CHAPTER 17

THE HUMAN PLACE
IN THE COSMOS

A. FREEDOM AND FATE

One of the mysteries of life is the question of how much of our life is guided by our free choice and how much is controlled by factors outside of our choice. A common idea in human thinking down through the centuries is that there is some force that guides our destiny.

For some people this force is God who has a plan and direction for our lives. Sometimes the guidance of God is called Providence. (This word is used as the name for the capital of the state of Rhode Island.) Some people have argued, however, over how to balance the concept of God's guidance of human lives with the concept of free will.

For others, a vague principle known as fate guides human lives. Fate can be seen as a beneficial force that guides our lives in the right direction. Fate can also be seen as a malevolent force trying to destroy us. Or fate can be seen as capricious and unpredictable.

The ancient Greeks believed in the concept of fate that determined our destiny but they never clearly defined it. It was called Moira and in the Greek myths sometimes fate even controls the gods. The famous play *Oedipus Rex* by Sophocles is a story of people trying to escape a terrible fate yet in the end their efforts to avoid their fate makes it happen.

The musical piece *Carmina Burana* by Carl Orff (1895–1982) dramatically explores the issue of fate in the first two movements: "O Fortuna" and "Fortune plango vulnera." Find the music online to listen to and find an English translation of the Latin words. For example: "Fate—monstrous and empty, you whirling wheel, you are malevolent, well-being is vain and always fades to nothing, shadowed and veiled you plague me too; now through the game I bring my bare back to your villainy."[1]

The *Star Wars* movies include the concepts of destiny and "The Force" guiding events. But these fun and exciting movies also show the contradiction in this type

---

1   Wikipedia, "O Fortuna."

of thinking. If events are destined to turn out some way, such as the Emperor will be defeated, then why do the Rebels have to work so hard to make that happen?

The question of fate versus freedom is something everyone should think about. How much is in our control in life and how much is out of our control? Life turns out to be a strange mix of both.

B. DIVINATION

Humans have to make decisions all the time. Whom should I marry? Should I take this job? What career should I chose? (What horse should I bet on in the fifth race?)

What makes decisions difficult is that they have to be made in the face of uncertainty. When we marry it is uncertain what a potential spouse will be like in five years. It is uncertain what you will be like in five years. It is uncertain how I will feel about my spouse in five years. If I take this job will I like it in five years? How will the company be doing in five years? If I buy a particular stock will it go up or down?

We wish there were a way to get some extra information. Throughout history humans have turned to divination to get answers to help make decisions. Divination is any attempt to get answers by doing such things as asking the spirits, the dead, or the gods for answers; or examining the stars, natural forces, natural signs, or natural energies. The word comes from the idea of "divining what the gods have to say." The word, however, covers a wide range of practices.

In ancient religions people would ask the gods for answers. In ancient Greece many people would travel to the popular shrine of Apollo in the town of Delphi. At the shrine was the Oracle of Apollo. The oracle was a woman who would go into a trance after chewing hallucinogenic leaves. She would give answers to questions. Often the messages were garbled, and the priests of the shrine would rework them before giving the answers to the questioner. Greek literature has many stories about the Oracle of Apollo such as the play *Oedipus Rex* by Sophocles and the *Apology* of Plato about the trial of Socrates.

The Greeks would also interpret the action of birds as guidance. The ancient stories the *Iliad* and the *Odyssey* offer several examples. In the *Iliad* Book 12, the Trojans believe they are on the verge of defeating the invading Greeks. But an eagle flies across with a snake in its talons. The eagle seems victorious over the snake but the snake bites the eagle near the throat and the eagle drops the snake and the snake survives. The sign is a warning to the Trojans that they will not defeat the Greeks. The Trojans ignore the warning.

In ancient Mesopotamia, priests would sacrifice goats and sheep and then examine the livers or lungs for signs to predict the future. Priests were trained on how to read livers. This is called extispacy. In the Bible, the Book of Ezekiel describes

FIGURE 17.1 Ruins of the Temple of Apollo in Delphi.

the Babylonian King Nebuchadnezzar deciding to attack Jerusalem: "For the king of Babylon stands at the parting of the way, at the fork in the two roads, to use divination; he shakes the arrows ... he inspects the liver." (Ezekiel 21:21.)

Ancient Chinese religion has many examples of divination such as reading the cracks on turtle shells burnt in a fire or the book the *I Ching*. Fortune cookies are another example but they originated not in China but perhaps in Japan or Los Angeles or San Francisco.

These are just a few examples of the countless types of divination that have been used through the centuries. Divination is still being used today and shows up in many tribal cultures. Some have even used it to figure out where to dig a well to find water, using a stick called a "divining rod." Popular modern versions of divination include horoscopes, fortune telling, palm reading, and talking to psychics. Many people use psychic hotlines. Although some people use divination for entertainment, many others are seriously trying to find guidance for life decisions.

The question about divination is this: "Does divination provide better information than normal human judgment?" Most people are skeptical that it provides good information. In fact, most people believe it is a bad way to make decisions. If divination really worked then wouldn't there be many people using it to make millions in the stock market?

Also, many predictions, such as those found in horoscopes or given by psychics, are vague. This means the receiver can put his or her own spin or interpretation on the predictions. And because the predictions are vague, it is hard to prove that a prediction is wrong. A fortune-teller or psychic could answer that the prediction was misunderstood. Typically, predictions are not as specific as "Move to New Jersey in May. You will meet your spouse on the second Tuesday morning on a bench in Elysian Park in Hoboken." Such a prediction would be easy to prove or disprove.

C. FERTILITY

Fertility plays a significant role in the history of religion, especially in the ancient world. Countless gods and goddesses were dedicated to fertility. Here are a handful of names from various religions: Aphrodite, Astarte, Baal, Brigid, Demeter, Dionysus, Freya, Ishtar, Isis, Shiva, Tepoztēcatl, and Venus.

FIGURE 17.2   The Venus of Willendorf.

For modern people, fertility as part of religion is very hard to understand. Although we are totally dependent on farm produce and farm animals for food, most people are unaware of how food is processed. We are totally dependent on the fertility of fields and livestock even when that means using massive quantities of chemical fertilizers on fields and extensive use of artificial insemination for animals. Yet most of us are unaware of the origins of our food. Most people have never visited a farm. Most people are also totally unaware of the processing that occurs once crops and animals leave the field.[2]

Also, today most people want to limit their family size. Many people want to be sexually active but either have no children or have a limited number of children. Most modern people try to limit their own fertility. On the other hand, if a couple wants to conceive but cannot, it is usually treated as a medical problem rather than a religious problem.

In the ancient world things were quite different. Humans needed fertility to survive. Humans needed their fields to be fertile so they could grow grain and not starve. They needed their livestock—sheep, goats, and cattle—to be fertile. They wanted to have lots of healthy livestock. Although many modern people eat meat several times a day, in many ancient cultures people only ate meat on special occasions. Ancient people raised sheep and goats for wool and milk. Cows were raised for their milk and oxen were used to plow fields.

Also, in the ancient world livestock, especially cattle, were seen as a measure of wealth. (This idea still exists in African tribal society.) Ancients measured wealth by something physical that could be seen and touched. Modern people measure

---

2   The movie *Food, Inc.* provides insights into the food production process.

wealth with tiny charges of energy in a computer that represent money deposited in a bank.

Ancient people needed their fields to be fertile and they turned to the gods for help. They made prayers, offerings, and even sacrifices to the gods to ensure fertility.

Related to fertility was the importance of rain. In a number of ancient cultures and tribal cultures, a significant part of religion was devoted to rain. Among the Pueblo people—the Native Americans found in Arizona and New Mexico—rain dances were and still are an important part of the religious culture.

Up until recently most men wanted their wives to be fertile so they would have lots of children. But ancient people did not know biology, or that for conception to occur the male sperm has to join with the egg produced by the woman. That the female produces an egg was only discovered in the 1800s. In the ancient world, and through much of time, if a couple was barren often the woman bore much of the blame even when medically the father might be the cause of the failure to conceive.

In the ancient world people needed children for a number of reasons. First, child survival rates were low so if a couple wanted several children to survive into adulthood they needed to have more children, since some of them might easily die before they reached adulthood. Also, in the ancient world children became economic assets sooner. A child could work on the farm or learn some craft at a much earlier age. Up until the twentieth century, for many people the goal was to get the children working and supporting the family as soon as possible.

In the modern world children are often still getting training into their 20s. That is a long time. Today many children are economic liabilities. It can cost a lot of money to raise a child. You might ask your parents about how much it cost to raise you. Then you might figure out how much you would be spending if you choose to raise a family. Many couples today have fewer children because they cannot afford to raise them or because they want to have a higher standard of living.

Also, in the ancient world there were no retirement plans, no IRAs, no Social Security or Medicare programs, no nursing homes, no senior citizen centers. When people got old, if their family did not take care of them, nobody would. They would be left to fend for themselves or die. So parents wanted to be fertile to have enough kids to survive to adulthood to take care of the parents when they got old.[3]

This was also one of the reasons for arranged marriages. If a father died his widowed wife and children could be quite vulnerable to poverty, death, or even slavery. However, if one of the children were in an arranged marriage, even if the child was

---

3   It is interesting to note that groups such as the Amish often do not participate in Social Security and retirement plans because it is understood that the elderly will be taken care of by relatives.

still small, the family of the future partner would be responsible for taking care of the child and his or her widowed mother.

Another reason why children were so important in the ancient world was that it was important to be buried or cremated properly. Children were required to dispose of the body and make offerings at the grave for the deceased. Often grave offerings of food and drink were believed to provide nourishment for the deceased in the underworld.

Today it is important in most cultures for children to make sure the bodies of their deceased parents are disposed of in a respectful way. But what was different in the ancient world was a common belief that if a body was not properly buried or cremated, the soul or spirit of that person would not get to the underworld. That soul or spirit could become a wandering ghost. So bodies of unrecovered drowned sailors or bodies burned in a fire, where nothing could be recovered, were considered tragic cases because the remains could not be treated properly and therefore the souls of the dead could not get to the underworld. *Antigone*, the famous Greek play by Sophocles, revolves around the duty of Antigone to ensure the proper burial of her dead brothers.

Yet a final piece to explain the importance of fertility was that many ancient cultures believed in an underworld as the place of the dead. Later religions that believed in heaven had the idea that people lived on in heaven. But for ancient people a dead person did not live on in the underworld. It was the place of the dead. So if you did not live on after death, the only way you could live on would be in your children, and especially male children to carry on your line. So the final reason for having more children was so you could live on in through your descendants.

For all these reasons, fertility, which was an essential element of religion for so much of human history and prehistory, is not part of most religions today.

D. SHAMAN

The word "shaman" is an important word to know. The word came from northern Asia. It can be pronounced with a long "a" sound for the first syllable, "shay men," or with a short "a" sound so that shaman rhymes with the word "ramen" (Ramen noodles).

A shaman in traditional tribal cultures does several things. He or she can cure illness, predict the future, and control spiritual forces. A shaman often acts as the go-between linking the natural world and the spirit world. For modern people, if someone is sick there must be something wrong with his or her physical body. In traditional tribal cultures illness is often explained as something wrong in the spirit world or a lack of harmony between the human world and the spirit world. Or illness and misfortune occur because someone has done something to offend the spirits.

Often, a shaman "travels" to the spirit world by entering a trance. He or she returns to explain what needs to be done to restore harmony between the human world and the spirit world.

It is hard for modern people influenced by science to understand this kind of thinking, but if you can imagine a world without any science, without the scientific way of looking at things, this approach starts to make more sense. How do you explain illness if you have no science?

Another term for a healer used by some Native Americans for someone who plays a role similar to a shaman is "medicine man" or "medicine woman." Here the term "medicine" refers to spiritual power or a connection to the spirit world.

Sometimes in very old movies the term "witch doctor" is used for a shaman. Often such movies are filled with inaccurate stereotypes of tribal cultures. In many of these movies the witch doctor is the villain in the story.

Finally, keep in mind that the word shaman is an outsider's word. Actual shamans or native peoples often do not use the word or even understand it as a category.

DISCUSSION QUESTIONS

1. Do you believe your life is guided by freedom or fate? Or is it guided by some combination of freedom and fate?

2. Did you listen to *Carmina Burana*? What did you think about it?

3. Are you familiar with any kinds of divination, fortune-telling, or predicting the future?

4. How important was fertility for ancient people? How important is fertility for us today?

5. Do an online image search for "shaman." You will find a wide range of images from historic black-and-white photos to modern paintings. Explore some of the images and websites. What can you find that is interesting?

Credits

CHAPTER 18

THE PLACE OF RELIGION IN CULTURE AND SOCIETY

A. THE FIRST AMENDMENT

The First Amendment of the United States Constitution is a defining statement of freedom in a democracy.

> Congress shall make no law respecting an establishment of religion, or prohibiting the free exercise thereof; or abridging the freedom of speech, or of the press; or the right of the people peaceably to assemble, and to petition the Government for a redress of grievances.

The amendment addresses five issues: religion, speech, the press, assembly, and petition of the government. Some people describe it as the "freedom of religion" amendment, which it is. But it does more. One significant part of the amendment is that in America there would be no official religion. At the time of the writing and signing of the American Constitution, most countries in Europe had an official religion, such as Roman Catholicism in Italy and Spain, and Anglicanism in England.

Before it was decided to have no official religion, what were the options? It turns out there were only a couple of possible options for an official religion, such as Episcopalian or Congregationalist. Several religious groups were not even on the table because of the prejudice against them, such as Roman Catholics, Baptists, and Jews. Hindus, Buddhists, and Muslims—except for some slaves brought from Africa—were virtually nonexistent.

The effect of the First Amendment was that no religion or religious leaders would directly influence government policies. It also meant that no religion received government support. There also would be no laws supporting religion, such as laws requiring church membership or church attendance, and no government money going to build churches and pay for ministers.

A further effect was that churches had to raise their own money and were free to compete in attracting members. Religion has flourished in America. Countless new religious groups and movements have started in America.

From the First Amendment comes the concept of "separation of church and state." Americans have struggled over the years to work out the details of this separation. For example, until the 1960s, daily prayer in public schools was common until declared unconstitutional by the Supreme Court.

Some people believe that America is a Christian nation. Many of the pilgrims who arrived in 1620 in Plymouth wanted to found a Christian theocracy. However, much later in the writing of the Constitution, which forms the American government, the words "God," "Jesus," and "Christ" were never mentioned. The religious terms used in the Declaration of Independence were "Nature's God," "Creator," and "Divine Providence." Thomas Jefferson, who wrote the Declaration of Independence, was not a traditional Christian, he was actually a deist. The religious terms he used were deist terms. Finally, the Declaration of Independence also makes it clear that governments derive their powers from the consent of the governed, not from any religious source.

It is interesting to note that the words "In God we Trust" were not put on US currency until the Civil War. Also, the original version of the Pledge of Allegiance did not include the words "under God." Both of these changes were made to promote the idea that there was a religious dimension to American identity.

B. RELIGION AND SOCIETY: THREE VIEWS

Over time different religions have had different views on the relationship between religion and society. At one extreme is the view that religion should guide society and establish society's moral values and have an influence on government. In such a society religious and moral laws should be enforced by the government. One version of this view is theocracy.

The other extreme sees society as corrupt and against religion. In this view true religion needs to withdraw from society to one degree or another. In the middle is the position that religion and state should be separate, yet religious and moral values should guide people as they vote in a democracy and should guide government officials.

1. Theocracy

In a theocracy the religious leaders are the political leaders. For example, the ancient Egyptians saw the pharaoh as a god. In ancient Mesopotamia, the priests had great influence over government, and the kings were seen as servants of the gods. Similar ideas existed among the Aztecs, Mayans, and Incas. A theocratic society has only one religion. Religious tolerance often does not exist.

"Theocracy" literally means "God rules." Religious priests either rule or have great influence on the rulers. In a theocracy the religious beliefs support the reason why the rulers have to be obeyed. If the people believe the ruler is put there by a god or is in fact a god, then people will obey the ruler. If they see the ruler as just an ordinary person sitting on the throne, then they might not obey him or her.

Rulers typically reinforced their uniqueness by living in special houses and having special ceremonies. Rulers often lived isolated from ordinary people to support the illusion of their uniqueness. If ordinary people saw rulers doing ordinary things, such as eating or relieving themselves, the idea that the rulers are special might disappear. There are not many theocracies today. But many people label Iran and Saudi Arabia as theocracies since religious authorities have significant influence on government policies. Groups such as the Taliban and ISIS want to establish theocracies.

2. The Middle Position

Many religious Americans follow this position. They believe that government and religion should be separate yet religion should have an influence on the direction of the country. Religion should work as a leaven trying to raise the moral standards of the society. Along with this goes the belief in freedom of religion. People can choose whatever religion they want.

Although a common position, among people who hold this view a great diversity of opinion and even controversy exists over what extent religion should influence government and society. For example, great disagreement exists on specific issues such as abortion.

3. Withdrawal from Society

A final view holds that true religion requires a withdrawal from society. This is the idea behind the monastic life. Monks live in separate communities disconnected from normal society. Monastic monks can be found in many traditions such as Buddhism, Christianity, Hinduism, Islam, and Taoism.

Another example of this position is the Jehovah's Witnesses. Although they hold normal jobs and participate in much of society, they do not participate in religious and cultural practices. They do not celebrate Christmas, Thanksgiving, or Easter. They see such celebrations as un-Christian and pagan. Although Christmas is supposed to be dedicated to the birth of Jesus, it includes non-Christian symbols such as the Christmas tree and mistletoe. Easter is supposed to celebrate the resurrection of Jesus but the bunny rabbit is actually a pagan fertility symbol.

Jehovah's Witnesses also do not vote. In part they see governments as corrupt and in the hands of the devil. This belief was reinforced by what the Nazis did to them. Jehovah's Witnesses were targeted along with Jews, Roma (Gypsies), and other groups. Jehovah's Witnesses were required to wear a purple triangle and were rounded up and imprisoned.

C. GOD AND NATIONS

What is the relationship between God and nations? (Long ago people would have used the word "kingdom" instead of "nation.") There are three basic views on the relationship of God and nations.

1. Chosen Nations

This view believes that God selects certain nations to be his instruments. A number of nations believe or have believed they are specially selected by God to promote God's values in the world. Today a significant number of Americans believe that America is uniquely chosen by God. Many of these ideas are influenced by the view in the Bible that the ancient Israelites were specially chosen by God.

If different nations claim they are specially chosen by God, how do you tell which one is right? Wars have been fought between countries that both saw God as on their side. The French writer Voltaire in his 1759 satire *Candide* describes such a war.

History tells of many nations that believed they were specially chosen by God yet their actions were anything but godly. Many British have believed they were chosen by God to extend their empire even though this included slave trading in the 1600s and 1700s, and going to war to protect their opium trade in the 1800s.

2. God Is Neutral

The second position is that God is neutral toward nations. Nations are judged by how they act and how they treat people. No nation is particularly chosen. God judges nations based on their actions. In this view, God is ruling over the whole world and not just one particular group of people.

3. Nations Are Not Good

A third position holds that nations are not good and that they are, in fact, evil. There are two versions of this view. In one version nations are seen as being evil or under the control of the devil. In the other version, nations are seen as idolatrous. Of course, one could see nations as both evil and idolatrous

People in this group point out all the wars between nations and all the victims who have died in those wars. Between 40 million and 60 million people died in World War II. Some people see as idolatrous the way leaders such as Hitler, Stalin, and Mao Zedong were honored by their followers.

Jehovah's Witnesses hold this position, and the history of the group has reinforced this view. They were persecuted in the Soviet Union.

A few Christians point to the three temptations of Jesus in the gospels. The Gospel of Matthew describes the third temptation: "Then the devil took him [Jesus] up to a very high mountain, and showed him all the kingdoms of the world in their magnificence, and he said to him, 'All these I shall give to you, if you will prostrate yourself and worship me.'" (Matthew 4:8–9.) The devil offers Jesus political power but the price is that Jesus has to worship the devil. Although most Christians are aware of this passage, many have not thought through what it means.

D. RELIGION AND CULTURE

Religious people live in specific times and cultures. Often cultures and religions interact. Three important points need to be understood.

1. Religions Change

Over time, religions change. For example, the original form of Buddhism (Theravada Buddhism) morphed into Mahayana Buddhism with very different ideas and beliefs. Christianity in Western Europe was limited to the Roman Catholic Church until the arrival of the Protestant reformers in the 1500s. Numerous new denominations then emerged. The Reformed tradition in Judaism developed in the 1800s in Europe with very different ideas than more traditional Judaism on how to follow Jewish law.

Some people have the view that their religion moves through time unchanged and uninfluenced by culture; however, the historical study of religion shows this is actually rare. Other people have the view that their religion has stayed the same in the essentials but has changed in nonessentials.

One current change in many—but not all—religions is an increased role for women, including in leadership. Many religious groups—but again, not all—are rethinking their teachings on homosexuality and same-sex marriage. A number of religious groups have developed teachings on ecology and the problem of climate change.

Historical study of one's own religion is important to see the developments of one's faith tradition over time. It also helps offer a sense of possibilities for future change and growth in one's tradition.

2. Cultures Influence Religions

Religions are often influenced by elements from the cultures in which the religions exist. Here are a handful of examples. From the 1500s to the late 1800s, the Plains

Indian culture developed from nomadic tribes on horseback following the buffalo herds across the vast prairies that stretched from the Mississippi to the Rockies, from Texas into Canada. Plains Indians used the buffalo for food, clothing, and skins for their tepees. One important tribe was the Lakota Sioux. The Lakota word for buffalo is "wakan," which is also the word for sacredness or sacred power. They called the Great Spirit "Wakan Tanka." Their culture based on hunting buffalo was intimately connected with their religion.

As mentioned before, many religions and denominations in the 20th century have rethought the role of women in their faith traditions and have given women an equal role in religious practice and religious leadership. For the most part, the women's movement was a cultural development that influenced religion. Although some religious people were leaders calling for equal treatment of women, for the most part the changes bringing equality for women took place in the culture. Many religions have had to play catch up.

In Islam, beyond the basics of the beliefs and practices, it is hard to make generalizations about how Muslims live out their faith because Islam is very different in different places. Islam is often influenced by the cultures where the people live. Things such as appropriate dress, the role of women, and strictness in following the Islamic law (called Sharia) are often influenced by culture.

In America, many Protestant evangelicals are heavily influenced by modern American culture. Male ministers often dress similar to successful businessmen in suits with modest haircuts. Pop music played by rock bands is common. Singing one of the thousands of traditional Methodist hymns that were very popular in their time would feel inappropriate in many of these churches.

3. Religions Influence Culture

Religions have often had great influence on the cultures in which they exist. Here are a handful of examples. In many places religion is the most visible element in the culture. In ancient Athens the Parthenon temple complex on the Acropolis dominated the skyline. The Parthenon ruins in modern Athens still impress visitors. Notre Dame Cathedral dominates the center of Paris. In numerous other French towns, such as Chartres and Rheims, the cathedrals are massive buildings that can be seen for miles around. Even the Kremlin in Moscow, which for decades was the center of an atheist government, has four cathedrals. The most famous is Saint Basil's Cathedral (Cathedral of Vasily the Blessed) in Red Square.

In monarchies, kings and queens are typically crowned by religious leaders. For example, in the year 800 Charlemagne was crowned as the Holy Roman Emperor by Pope Leo III,. In England, even today, when the next king or queen is crowned it will be done in the Westminster Abby Cathedral by the Archbishop of Canterbury.

In many Islamic countries the presence of religion is very strong and obvious, such as loudspeakers broadcasting the call to prayer. In some Islamic cities the traffic stops during prayer time. Religions have also influenced the creation of laws against what was or is seen as immoral behavior: homosexuality, use of birth control, and divorce.

In many cultures one religion is dominant and members of other religions often feel inadequate or feel they are treated unequally. Often there is a great prejudice against religious minorities. Down through history many cultures imposed legal restrictions on minority religions. For example, the Buddhist country of Myanmar is ethnic cleansing the Muslim Rohingya minority population and driving out hundreds of thousands of people.

FIGURE 18.1   Cathedral of Saint Basil in Moscow.

DISCUSSION QUESTIONS

1. What are your thoughts on the First Amendment? How does it apply today?

2. Of the three views of religion and society, which one makes the most sense to you? Do you have another view of the relationship between religion and society? Are you aware of religious groups that hold views different from your own?

3. Which view of the relationship of God and nations makes the most sense to you? Have you heard of religious groups that hold different views?

4. What examples can you give of religion influencing culture?

5. What examples can you give of culture influencing religion?

Credit

CHAPTER 19

ANGELS, THE DEVIL, AND THE END TIMES

A. ANGELS

Angels show up in many religions. They have a long history going back to ancient Mesopotamia. Belief in angels was an important part of Zoroastrianism, which later influenced Judaism, Christianity, and Islam.

In many religious traditions angels are understood as beings created by God. Angels often play the role of being heavenly messengers. Typically, angels are described as not having physical bodies. They are non-corporeal. *Corpus* is the Latin word for "body." A "corpse" is a dead body. An angel without a body would be non-corporeal. Angels are often described as having free will and an intellect, which means that they are aware, know what they are doing, and can make choices for good or bad.

A classic list of the different types of angels was created by a Christian writer called Pseudo-Dionysius the Areopagite, who probably lived in the 400s or early 500s. In his book *The Celestial Hierarchy* he listed nine ranks of angels divided into three spheres.

First Sphere
    Seraphim
    Cherubim
    Thrones

Second Sphere
    Dominions or Lordships
    Virtues or Strongholds
    Powers or Authorities

Third Sphere
    Principalities or Rulers
    Archangels
    Angels

Pseudo-Dionysius created his list by going through the Bible and organizing all the references to angels.

The three best-known angels are Gabriel, Raphael, and Michael.

FIGURE 19.1 Archangel Michael and Fallen Angels, by Luca Giordano (1666).

Interest in angels has a long history. Angels are important parts of traditional religions such as Judaism, Christianity, and Islam, and also for people outside these religions. Many people believe that angels are active in their lives, helping and guiding them. For some people, angels are the entire focus of their religious belief.

Many people believe in guardian angels. A guardian angel is an individual angel watching out for a particular person. Here is a typical image of the guardian angel who watches children.

Much more can be said about angels since there is a wide range of varying religious belief about angels. There is also a lot of religious art about angels. The angels Gabriel and Raphael show up in a number of famous paintings. Cemeteries, particularly older ones, often have many angel statues, especially marking the graves of young children who died.

FIGURE 19.2   A child and his guardian angel.

Angels are popular characters in movies such as *Angels in the Outfield* and TV shows such as *Touched by an Angel*. There are a wide variety of cultural references to angels such as the Blue Angels Navy flying team; the Hells Angels motorcycle gang; and Los Angeles, which is Spanish for "the angels."

Angels are frequent characters in all kinds of novels, movies, and animations, and angels are depicted in many ways. In fact, trying to understand the use of angel imagery becomes confusing because of the countless and varied representations of angels: good angels, bad angels, angels of light, and dark angels. People have used their imaginations to take the concept of angels in many directions.

B. THE DEVIL

The Devil is an important concept in religion with a long history. Sometimes the Devil is called Satan. The Devil is typically thought of as an immortal evil being who causes suffering to humans and often leads humans to do the wrong things.

The concept of the Devil probably first appeared in the ancient religion of Zoroastrianism. The later history of the development of the idea of the Devil is extremely complicated and confusing.

The word "Devil" shows up more than 50 times in the New Testament but not in the Hebrew Scriptures/Old Testament. The word "Satan" also shows up more than 50 times in the Bible, including 15 times in the Hebrew Scriptures/Old Testament, mostly in the book of Job. But Satan in the Bible is not a clearly defined figure. His role in the book of Job is closer to a prosecuting attorney than the source of all evil. The Devil is not mentioned in the book of Genesis. It is a snake that tempts Adam and Eve.

Religious people have very different views on the Devil. Some religious people say, "There is no Devil." In their view of a loving God who rules the universe there is no room for a Devil or demons. For some, things that are "spiritual" can only be good. There cannot be an evil spiritual being.

Many others ignore the concept in their faith life. They do not deny the existence of the Devil but see the concept as irrelevant. Evil is caused by bad choices made by humans, not by the Devil.

There are also religious people who see the Devil as active all around them. When something bad happens, they see it as the work of the Devil. The Devil is seen as the cause of everything from a flat tire to global wars. Some even believe that humans can be possessed by the Devil.

The Devil as a character has shown up in many novels, plays, and movies. An old German legend tells the story of Faust who sold his soul to the Devil in exchange for unlimited knowledge. A legend follows the great blues singer and guitar player Robert Johnson (1911–1938): that he sold his soul to the Devil at a crossroads in order to get his musical talent. In the musical *Damn Yankees!* a man trades his soul so he can become a great baseball player to help his team, the Washington Senators, defeat the New York Yankees.

The concept of demons is a very ancient one. For those who believe in the Devil, demons are seen as the Devil's helpers. In the ancient world, demons were used to explain all misfortunes and illness. Imagine a world without science to explain viruses and afflictions such as epilepsy. In such a world, believing a demon caused illness would make perfect sense. An epileptic seizure was seen as demon possession.

C. THE APOCALYPSE

The Christian New Testament ends with the Book of Revelation. The Greek word for "revelation" is *apocalypse*. The Book of Revelation is a complicated and confusing reading without a clear or obvious meaning. Christians through the centuries have argued over the meaning of the book. One wonders if even the early Christians who first read the book were confused by it.

Revelation was written by a man named John; however, most scholars have concluded that this John was not the Apostle John who was one of the 12 disciples of Jesus. Also, the Gospel of John was not named for the writer of the Book of Revelation.

The simplest meaning of the Book of Revelation is that it was written around 100 CE to give encouragement to Christians in Asia Minor (Turkey today) who were experiencing harassment and persecution from the Romans. All of the symbols in the writing can be explained by contemporary references.

The Beast in Revelation represents the Roman Empire, which the writer saw as in league with the Devil. The book describes how one cannot buy or sell without the "mark of the Beast." This probably refers to Roman coins that had an image of the emperor as a god. For devout Christians such an image would be idolatry. The number 666 is code for Emperor Nero Caesar, the first emperor to persecute Christians.

The four horsemen appear. The first, a white horseman, represents the Parthians, an enemy of the Romans that could not be defeated. The red horseman represents war and bloodshed. The black horseman represents famine. He carries a scale to weigh out food as a voice declares, "A ration of wheat costs a day's pay" (a lot of money). Finally, the pale green horseman represents sickness and death. These symbols are not some future prediction, but rather the normal things of history: enemies, war and bloodshed, famine, death and disease.

Because of its strange and weird symbolism, many have used the Book of Revelation to try to predict current or future

FIGURE 19.3 The Four Horsemen of the Apocalypse, by Albrecht Dürer.

events. Some have claimed that Revelation predicts the end of the world (the End Times) and the return of Jesus in his Second Coming. People today are making such predictions. Just browse the Internet. Try "Prophecies of Revelation" or "Prophecies of the End Times." The passages of Revelation have influenced the Jehovah's Witnesses who believe we are living in the End Times.

Down through the centuries many people have made predictions based on Revelation. So far they have all been wrong. For example, in the Münster Rebellion (1534–1535) a group believing they lived in the End Times took over the city of Münster in Germany. The rebellion came to a tragic end. The Millerites in America predicted the end in 1843. David Koresh, leader of the Branch Davidians in Waco, Texas, taught his followers that they lived in the End Times. His group came to a tragic end in 1993.

Revelation describes the lead up to a great battle. Then it jumps to the aftermath of the battle. The idea of a final battle came to Christianity from Zoroastrianism. In ancient Israel a fort called Megiddo was the site of many battles since it guarded the key trade route.[1] Any army trying to control the region had to control that trade route. Since the place became synonymous with battles, its Greek name, Har Megiddo, became the name of the final battle in the Book of Revelation: Armageddon.

Revelation contains several references to a thousand years.

> Then I saw an angel come down from heaven, holding in his hand the key to the abyss and a heavy chain. He seized the dragon, the ancient serpent, which is the Devil or Satan, and tied it up for a thousand years and threw it into the abyss, which he locked over it and sealed, so that it could no longer lead the nations astray until the thousand years are completed. After this, it is to be released for a short time. (Revelation 20: 1–3.)

People using the book as a prophecy have tried to figure out when the thousand years would occur. A thousand years is a millennium, and the plural is "millennia." Thus, speculation about the End Times and when the thousand years would take place is called "millennialism." Some disagree over whether the thousand years is yet to come or has already occurred. Thus, there are "pre-millennialists" and "post-millennialists."

One feature of apocalyptic belief is the idea of the Rapture, that holy people will be taken directly to heaven without dying while the rest of the people suffer through the End Times. The Rapture is based on Matthew 24: 40–41. "Two men

---

1   Today the site is called Tel Megiddo. A "tel" is a hill built up by many years of human occupation.

will be out in the field; one will be taken, and one will be left. Two women will be grinding at the mill; one will be taken, and one will be left." It is possible that this passage in Matthew was a prediction of the Roman destruction of Jerusalem and its environs in 70 AD and is not a prediction of the End Times.

D. THE ANTICHRIST

The Book of Revelation mentions a figure who opposes Christianity and Christians. Very likely in Revelation this figure was the Roman emperor. As stated previously, 666 is code for Nero, the first Roman emperor to persecute Christians. This figure would later be called by some the Antichrist. This term is not used in Revelation, rather it comes from the letters of John in the New Testament.

Those Christians interested in speculating about the End Times have often labeled living people as the Antichrist or made predictions about a future Antichrist. Just search online and you will see numerous examples. American presidents often get tagged as the Antichrist. In the 1500s many Protestants saw the Roman Catholic pope as the Antichrist.

Final Thoughts on the Book of Revelation

Many Christians ignore the Book of Revelation and its imagery. The image of Jesus in the Book of Revelation is very different than the image of Jesus in the gospels. Some early Christian writers suggested leaving the book out of the New Testament.

You should read the Book of Revelation and decide whether you can figure out what it means. You may find that the meaning of the book is not obvious at all. Then when you hear someone or read of someone who claims to explain what it all means, you can take what they say with a grain of salt.[2]

DISCUSSION QUESTIONS

1. What movies and TV shows have you seen with angels?
2. Are you aware of any famous paintings with angels? You could do an online image search: "Famous paintings of angels."

---

2   For a scholarly discussion of Revelation, see *Revelation and the End of All Things* by Craig R. Koester (New Haven: Yale University Press, 2014).

3. How have you seen the Devil depicted in movies and on television? Do you know any religious people who have strong beliefs about the Devil? What do you think?

4. Do online image searches for "Devil" and "Satan." What interesting images did you find?

5. What did you discover when searching online for people using the Book of Revelation to interpret current events?

Credits

- Fig. 19.1: Source: https://commons.wikimedia.org/wiki/File:GIORDANO,_Luca_fallen_angels.jpg.
- Fig. 19.2: Source: https://commons.wikimedia.org/wiki/File:Lienzo_del_altar_del_%C3%81ngel_de_la_Guarda_(Catedral_de_Sevilla).jpg.
- Fig. 19.3: Source: https://commons.wikimedia.org/wiki/File:Durer_Revelation_Four_Riders.jpg.

CHAPTER 20

QUESTIONS TO THINK ABOUT

HERE ARE SOME big questions to think about. These are central religious questions of our time, yet many are rarely discussed. And be prepared: people will have different answers to some of these questions.

A. HOW OLD IS RELIGION?

Evidence of human interest in religion is found in many prehistoric cultures. Archeologists often find religious objects such as small statues. However, the most striking evidence is that prehistoric peoples often buried their dead with grave goods such as personal possessions, tools, weapons, or food offerings. The assumption from such archaeological finds is that ancient people had beliefs about the afterlife and that one of the key practices was to bury a person with those things the person would need in the afterlife.

Cave paintings are also important and have been found around the world. Lascaux in France and Altamira in Spain are two important sites. Most of these paintings depict animals and it is assumed the paintings had some religious or ritual significance.

The oldest cave paintings on the island of Sulawesi in Indonesia are 35,000 years old.

In Africa, some carvings have been found on rocks that may be about 75,000 years old. Rock carvings are called "petroglyphs."

The problem is how to interpret all this evidence since prehistoric cultures lacked writing. In fact, the term "prehistoric" refers to the period

FIGURE 20.1 Lions painted in the Chauvet Cave in France (32,000 BCE!).

before writing. The earliest known writing is more than 5,000 years old. When archaeologists find objects buried with bodies we cannot be totally certain of the meaning of these objects. For meaning to be passed down over thousands of years it requires someone to write it down and then later someone to be able to read and understand the writing. So there is no way to know for certain the meaning and use of cave paintings. Also, we do not know whether they also did paintings outside of caves on animal skins or exposed rocks that did not survive.

Once writing appears it becomes an essential part of religion. Notice how almost all religions have special or sacred writings.

So how old is religion? We do not know. But it seems to be an essential part of human culture. Anthropologists believe that animism is the earliest form of religion. Evidence of what resembles religion goes back 75,000 years. Probably religion is older than that, but so far there is no evidence. One could speculate that religious belief and practice are two of the things that make humans human.

B. WHY DO INNOCENT PEOPLE SUFFER?

An important question in religion has been "Why do innocent people suffer?" This is a particularly important question for Christians and Jews. "Why if there is a good God in heaven who is in control does he let innocent people suffer?" When bad people suffer because of their doing bad we understand it, but when innocent people suffer we find it hard to understand.[1]

The Book of Job in the Hebrew Scriptures/Old Testament explores the question. Job was a good man who did everything right yet he experienced tremendous suffering. He lost his family, lost all of his possessions, and boils covered his body. The friends of Job try to convince him that he must have done something wrong and is being punished for his wrongdoing. Job insists on his innocence. In the end God answers Job that God's ways are beyond Job's understanding. God says, "Where were you when I laid the foundations of the earth?" (Job 38:4.) Unfortunately the Book of Job never gives a satisfying answer to the question of why the innocent suffer except to say that the answer is beyond human comprehension.

In Hinduism, the question is less intense because of the belief in karma. For many Hindus, if someone is suffering, although he or she has done no wrong in this current life, he or she must have done something wrong in a previous life. So in a certain sense in Hinduism, those who suffer are not innocent.

---

1   An important exploration of this question is Harold Kushner's book *When Bad Things Happen to Good People.* New York: Schocken Books, 1981.

C. 'GOD NEVER GIVES YOU ANYTHING YOU CAN'T HANDLE!' OR NOT.

"God never gives you anything you can't handle." Have you ever heard this saying? Sometimes it is brought up at difficult times, such as when told to survivors at a tragic funeral. So where is this passage found in the Bible? It is not. It is actually from the Roman Stoic philosopher Marcus Aurelius (121–180 AD). Interestingly, Marcus Aurelius was an emperor who persecuted Christians.

This saying provides both great insight and also great danger. For what often is the case is we find ourselves overwhelmed by a terrible difficulty that we think is impossible to get through and then it turns out we can get through it. Many of us discover we are far tougher than we thought and can bear burdens we thought were unbearable. Sometimes we face unbearable burdens yet we get through them and find ourselves better and stronger persons for the experiences.

The problem is we do not always know our limits until they get tested. How do you know how much air a balloon will hold until you blow more air into it? But you only find the limit by going too far and the balloon bursts.

The danger of this saying is that it ignores the fact that some people find themselves in unbearable situations. People have emotional and physical breakdowns from which they never recover. Some experience great trauma and for the rest of their lives are haunted by PTSD. Some people find life so unbearable they commit suicide. So the saying "God never gives you anything you can't handle" should be used cautiously.

People cannot always handle what life has thrown at them. We should always pay attention when someone says, "I can't handle this." Sometimes it's a cry for help that should not be ignored. Some have committed suicide because no one would take seriously their plea "I can't handle this."

In some cases individuals could handle the overwhelming difficulties of life with some help or someone showing understanding and compassion. Sometimes people just need someone to be with them as they deal with seemingly impossible burdens.

D. WHERE IS IDOLATRY TODAY?

The Hebrew Scriptures/Old Testament has many references to idolatry. It is perhaps the most reoccurring theme in the Bible. The most common idolatry in the Hebrew Scriptures/Old Testament was following the Canaanite religion based on the worship of Baal. The ancient kings of Israel were frequently condemned for not getting rid of the shrines to Baal, which are often referred to as "high places" with "sacred poles."

But if idolatry was such a significant issue in the Hebrew Scriptures/Old Testament, why has it seemed to many people to have disappeared? Either humans have solved the problem—they do not practice much idolatry today—or idolatry has changed forms.

If idolatry has changed forms, what are the modern versions of it? What are the false gods that humans worship today? Wealth? Possessions? Comfort? Pleasures? Celebrities? Nations? Give this some thought.

E. WHY DOES RELIGION FAIL TO TRANSFORM PEOPLE?

One problem is that sometimes religion does not seem to transform people. Many assume that religion should help believers to become better people, but not all religious people are nice people. Sometimes religious people can be mean, petty, and selfish. Sometimes they use religion as a way of protecting the needs of their egos.

So why are not people transformed by religion? If in religion people encounter God, a being of love who transcends all, then why are religious people sometimes so small and petty? After all, they worship a God of the universe. Would not that make them more broad-minded? We sometimes, however, find people who are not better people for all their religion. A few even seem worse.

F. WHAT IS THIS THING CALLED 'PROJECTION'?

Projection is a problem for human beings. Sometimes people project on other people things that are really issues for themselves. For example, an angry person might fail to see his or her own anger and instead think it is everyone else who is getting mad all the time. A person with psychological problems might think he or she is fine and it is other people who have the problems.

It is important to consider the issue of projection in religion. It can play out in two ways.

1. Projection in Religion: Part A.

It is a problem in religion that many believers project their own views onto God. This occurs all the time when people imagine that their fears and concerns are God's fears and concerns. The writer Voltaire said, "God has made us in his image, and we have returned the favor."

In the Southern states, before civil rights changes took place, many religious people believed that racial segregation and denial of equal rights to African Americans was what God wanted. In reality they were projecting their own fears and prejudices on God.

The Hebrew Scriptures/Old Testament includes the Book of Jonah, which is a profound exploration of this issue. As described in Chapter 6, in the story Jonah hates the Assyrians. He wants God to punish and destroy them. But God does not want to destroy Assyrians. God wants Jonah to preach to them so they can be forgiven. After trying to run away from his assignment, sailing in the opposite direction, being swallowed by a fish (or whale), and then being spat out exactly where he started, Jonah winds up going to the Assyrian city of Nineveh and preaching. The people repent. Jonah is furious because he really wanted God to destroy his enemies. Jonah had projected his hatred onto God. The profound message of the Jonah story is that God does not hate whom we hate.

Can you think of other examples in which such projection is occurring? Keep in mind, however, that people will disagree on what is projection and what is an accurate understanding of the values of God.

2. Projection in Religion: Part B.
Some nonbelieving thinkers have suggested that religion itself is a projection of human need. For example, the idea has been proposed that because humans often find themselves frightened they create a god who takes care of them. They call God "Father" because a good father protects his children.

The ancient Egyptians were afraid of death and the end of existence. So the Egyptians created elaborate beliefs and practices so they could hope in a life beyond death.

Others have suggested that religion was created so that moral systems would work. God or the gods enforce cultural moral values. People behave because they fear God or the gods. Could all of this be projection?

G. WHAT ABOUT PEOPLE TAKING THEIR IDENTITY FROM RELIGION?

Yet another problem in religion is that people often take their identity from it. Sometimes one's whole sense of self is tied up in one's religious faith. One's religion becomes one's identity. For some, almost every conversation comes back to religion. For others, their church or denomination is one of the most important aspects of their lives.

This can lead to the problem that when someone's faith or religion is questioned it feels like a personal attack. No wonder many people are very sensitive about religion!

H. WHY DO PEOPLE HAVE A NEED TO DEFEND RELIGION AND GOD?

Why are religious people sometimes so afraid and so needing to defend their beliefs? Many people are frightened and threatened if their religion is challenged. But if they truly trust in God and that everything is in God's hands, why are they so afraid? Most of the early American colonies had laws enforcing a specific version of Christianity. For example, it was illegal to be Baptist in several colonies.

There are many examples in the Middle Ages of popes, bishops, and kings putting extensive restrictions on Jews. Jews had to live in ghettos and wear identifying clothes. The fear was that Jews might influence Christians and draw them away from Christianity. But if the popes, bishops, and kings really believed in an all-powerful God who was supposed to take care of things, then why were they so worried?

Religious extremists see as their enemies anyone who is not as extreme as them. They are intolerant of anyone who does not see things in the same way. Why are they so afraid? Why cannot God take care of things? Cannot God defend God?

Some people are worried that some action might be offensive to God. Is that not God's problem? If God is really offended, cannot God take care of the problem without help? Sometimes people seem to feel the need to defend God and God's action in the world. But if God is really God, why would God need such help? Critics of religion might question whether people who are so insistent on defending God are not in reality defending their own views and beliefs about God.

I. WHY IS THERE SO MUCH HYPOCRISY IN RELIGION?

One problem in religion is hypocrisy. People are hypocrites when they do not live up to the moral values they say they believe in. For example, if a man speaks about the virtue of honesty yet cheats on his taxes, he is a hypocrite. A hypocrite displays "hypocrisy" and acts in a "hypocritical" way. A common example of hypocrisy is people who are very religious, yet are mean to the people around them.

But there is a spectrum of degrees of hypocrisy. At one end are sincere religious people with high moral standards who find it hard to always be completely consistent in living out their values. For example, one might believe in total honesty yet lie to a friend about the friend's new outfit so as to not hurt the friend's feelings.

At the next level are people who are not looking hard enough at their actions. This is a problem with morality in general. Many people are not aware of how their actions affect others.

Then there are people who just do not know the facts. And sadly many people do not take the time to get accurate facts. For example, there are people who harshly judge poor people without any experience of being poor or even knowledge about the facts, such as the biggest category of people in poverty in America being children.

Sometimes people do wrong because of ignorance. Scholars who have reflected on this have noted two kinds of ignorance. In the first kind there is no way a person could have known the truth. On the other hand there is some ignorance involved when one could or should have known better. A little bit of diligence would have given one the information.

The two kinds of ignorance have labels. "Vincible ignorance" is when one could or should have known the facts. "Invincible ignorance" is when one could not have known the facts. Here is a simple example. If a young man and young woman have been dating for several years and the man forgets his date's birthday, then he is guilty of vincible ignorance because he could have or should have known her birthday. If on the other hand the young man brings her roses when she is allergic to roses but she never told him of her allergy, then he has invincible ignorance. Vincible ignorance is also called "culpable ignorance." Invincible ignorance is also called "inculpable ignorance."

There are also people who are psychologically incapable of seeing how their actions are at odds with their values. There are mean people who actually think they are nice to people. In some cases these people have psychological disorders.

Finally, there are people who are knowingly and intentionally hypocritical. For example, the writer Machiavelli (1469–1527), in writing about political power, said that a prince should be willing to do immoral things to stay in power, but should always pretend to be virtuous. The prince should always pretend to be religious but be willing to do immoral and unreligious things if necessary.

J. SOMETIMES IN THE NEWS ONE HEARS ABOUT RELIGIOUS PEOPLE DOING BAD THINGS. WHY ARE SOME RELIGIOUS PEOPLE SO DYSFUNCTIONAL?

Many people are dysfunctional. People with emotional or psychological difficulties are very common. There are many dysfunctional relationships because so many people are dysfunctional. Dysfunctional people are all over the place and frequently wind up in religion. Sometimes dysfunctional people are drawn to religion.

Two things can happen. One is that religion is a healthy influence that helps people move away from their dysfunction. Many people have stories of turning to God and in the process turning their lives around. Many have found the moral teachings and the message of love within religion have helped them become more responsible and caring people who are aware of the needs of others. For example, the hope in Alcoholics Anonymous is that developing spiritual faith will help people overcome their addictions. Religion has often made people better people and healthier people.

But the opposite can also occur when people use religion to cover up their dysfunction or as an expression of their dysfunction. Mean, uncaring people often use religion as an excuse to be mean and uncaring. Religious people with big egos sometimes use religion to support their egos as they ignore the virtue of humility. Sometimes religious people are self-righteous, thinking that because they follow moral rules they are better than others who do not follow the rules. Such people use religion as an excuse to look down on others. This behavior is particularly ironic for Christians since in his public ministry Jesus avoided self-righteous religious people and spent his time with sinful people.

Most people who have spent a lot of time around religious people have encountered religious jerks who use their religion as an excuse to continue to be jerks and do not seem to be transformed by the religious message they claim to espouse. Religions are made up of flawed people. True saints are often rare.

A typical feature of dysfunctional situations is denial. Dysfunctional people deny there is a problem and try to prevent others from recognizing the problem. People who try to draw attention to dysfunctional situations will often be ostracized and blamed as if they are the problem.

Extreme examples of the problem of dysfunction can be seen in a cult leader such as David Koresh in Waco, Texas, or, perhaps the worst example, Jim Jones of the People's Temple in Guyana in South America. In 1978, 900 followers of Jim Jones committed suicide.

Sexual abuse by clergy is another extreme example of religion being misused to manipulate and abuse people, with religion misused again to cover it all up.[2] One of the reasons the sexual abuse crisis reached such a scale and went on for so long was the silence and denial of so many people. Victims who told church leaders were often ignored or told to keep silent.

We should not be surprised that dysfunction shows up in religion because religions are made of people and people are often dysfunctional. There will always be people in religion who are difficult to deal with and that should be accepted. But religious groups need to be vigilant to prevent people from hurting other people in the name of religion. One key is to insist that there always be free and open communication.

---

2   The 2015 move *Spotlight* details how *The Boston Globe* newspaper uncovered the extent of clergy sexual abuse in Boston. This led to the uncovering of similar problems in hundreds of cities around the globe. In many places this led to dramatic changes in policies to prevent future abuse.

K. MORE WARS HAVE BEEN FOUGHT OVER RELIGION THAN ANYTHING ELSE! OR NOT

Have you ever heard someone say this? It turns out to not be true. Some wars have been fought over religion, but not that many. Look at the Wikipedia article "List of wars involving the United States." Scan the long list and note that none of the wars listed was fought over religion. The main reasons for war are to conquer land, extend political control, control economic resources, and to prevent other nations or kingdoms from conquering land, extending political control, and controlling economic resources.

There are some examples of religious wars such as the Crusades (1095–1291), the Thirty Years' War in Europe (1618–1648), and the French Wars of Religion (1562–1598). Ferdinand and Isabella fought wars to conquer all of Spain and then drove out Muslims and Jews (ending in 1492). But even in these wars political issues such as conquering land, extending political control, and controlling economic resources were also important reasons for the wars.

In some places in the Middle East there has been fighting between Shia and Sunni Muslims. Although there are big religious differences between these groups, there are also ethnic, political, cultural, and economic issues that often are the bigger motivation for the fighting.

In Northern Ireland a long conflict called the "The Troubles" lasted from the late 1960s until the late 1990s. Although technically not a war, it was a clash between Catholic nationalists and Protestant unionists. The issues in the conflict, however, were not religion. There had been a long history of economic and political inequality between Catholics and Protestants. These inequalities were the real cause of The Troubles.

One last point needs to be made. The Crusades are perhaps the most dramatic example of religiously motived warfare. But keep in mind that the Crusades took place 900 years ago. They are not a very recent example.

L. WHAT ABOUT WHEN PEOPLE DO BAD THINGS IN THE NAME OF RELIGION?

Bad things happen in the name of religion such as the mass suicide at the People's Temple in Guyana, cited previously. Here are a few more examples:

Terrorist acts done in the name of religion

Sexual abuse and its cover-up

Religions failing to stand up for human rights

Missionaries going to foreign lands and destroying local cultures

Religion used to oppress people

Ethnic cleansing where religion plays a role

Military actions such as the Crusades and the Albigensian Crusade (1209–1229)

It is important to recognize that these things have occurred and to know about them. It is also important to note that when these things happen the religions are violating the religious and moral principles that they hold.

Although sometimes critics of religion see only the terrible things, these bad things are not the complete picture of religion. Through the centuries religions have done much to help the poor, support education, help people to lead more moral and healthy lives, provide emotional support for people in their struggles, set up hospitals, and other acts of charity. For example, the Catholic Church in America built an extensive school system in America with thousands of grade schools, high schools, colleges, and universities. There are hundreds of Catholic hospitals in the United States.

This chapter has looked at some important questions about religion. Some questions looked at the serious problems in religion. Keep in mind, however, that the problems in religion are only part of religion. There is much more to religion and religious people than the failures of some religious people to live up to the moral demands of their religions. Unfortunately, for some people having an awareness of these problems blocks them from seeing the good side of religion. The goal of all these questions is to get you thinking.

DISCUSSION QUESTIONS

1. Do you see examples of idolatry today where people look to false gods? What are your examples?

2. "Why do innocent people suffer?" How might you try to answer the question? Do you agree or not with this statement: "God never gives you anything you can't handle!"?

3. The French philosopher Voltaire once said, "God has made us in his image, and we have returned the favor." He is describing religious projection when

humans sometimes imagine God in their own image. Can you think of examples of religious projection?

4. Can you offer examples of hypocrisy and dysfunction in religion? Can you also provide nonreligious examples of hypocrisy and dysfunction?

5. What examples can you give of people doing bad things in the name of religion? Now, what examples can you offer of the good things that religious people do?

Credit

- Fig. 20.1: Source: Creditshttps://commons.wikimedia.org/wiki/File:Lions_painting,_Chauvet_Cave_(museum_replica).jpg.

CONCLUSION: EXPLORING OTHER RELIGIONS

THERE ARE SEVERAL easy ways to explore other religions. One way is to visit a religious service at a church, synagogue, temple, or mosque. Most religious groups are glad to have visitors and in fact at some places you may be surprised how friendly people are, often encouraging you to come back. For many religious services it is fine to just show up before the service, take a seat in the back, and watch what happens. Your instructor may have suggestions on various religious services in the area that have proved interesting places for students to visit.

Another good way to visit a religious service is to go with a friend or acquaintance who is a member of the place you want to visit. Some religious services may require some explanation to understand, and some have portions in other languages such as Hebrew in Jewish services and Greek in Greek Orthodox services. Some, such as Christian evangelical services, are not difficult to figure out. The Catholic Mass, however, is an elaborate ritual that requires some help to understand what is going on and what a visitor is supposed to do and not supposed to do.

If you do not know someone who attends the service you want to visit, call the office of the church, synagogue, or temple a few days before and tell them you want to visit. Most religious institutions have a web page with the phone number and times for services. Just tell the office that you would like to visit. Often the office will arrange for someone to meet and welcome you when you arrive.

If you are visiting the service as part of a class project and someone greets you, just introduce yourself. Have no fear of telling them "I am _____, a student at _____, and I'm here to do a class report on your service." Most religious groups are more than happy to have you there finding out about their religion.

If you do not have a Muslim acquaintance and you want to visit a mosque, call the office of the mosque before a visit. The times for prayer vary. Many mosques want to have someone available to answer questions a visitor may have and explain the requirements, such as women needing to have their heads covered and staying in the back during services.

If you have a religious background you may notice both similarities and differences between the service you are visiting and the services of your own tradition. Also, one of the things you may discover when visiting a religious service is that some congregations are very good at recognizing visitors, and saying welcoming things to them, while other religious groups often completely ignore visitors.

In attending a service, a person might think about questions such as "What am I seeing and hearing?" "What is the music like?" "Do I find the music emotionally stirring or boring?" "Do the people in the congregation seem engaged on not?" "What is the minister or leader preaching or teaching about?" "Does it make sense or not?" "Is there artwork, imagery, or symbols in this building?"

Another way to explore religions is to talk to religious leaders. Most religious ministers, priests, rabbis, and gurus got into the business because they like talking to people about religion. So typically they are more than happy to meet and share what they think and believe to a willing listener.

Another way explore religions is to read some of their primary sources such as one of the Christian gospels; selections from the Hebrew Scriptures, the *Analects* of Confucius; or the *Tao Te Ching*.[1] Also, there is much online information about religion. Sometimes it requires a little patience trying to sort out which are helpful websites and which are not. Be aware that there are also some fanatical websites out there. Be cautious with websites that are highly critical of specific religions. Such websites often do not have the correct facts.

Wikipedia is a great source of information on religion. Most of the articles on religion are informative and balanced. The only drawback is that some of the articles have too much detail. For a newcomer exploring these topics, a shorter summary might be better.

Talking to other people about their religion can sometimes be helpful and interesting. The goal is to listen to other people as they explain what they believe and why. The goal is not to argue about different beliefs. But this may not work with all people. Some people have such strong religious beliefs that it is hard to discuss religion with them.

When you travel and visit various cities or countries, check out the religious sites. Some of them are major tourist attractions such as the Cathedral of Notre Dame in Paris, but many are not so well known. A little research before your visit can help you find interesting but lesser-known religious sites that are worth a visit.

Lastly, many people find old cemeteries interesting places to visit. There are many religious cemeteries with numerous tombstones with religious symbols and markings on them. (The thing that is nice about visiting cemeteries is that when you have seen enough you can leave.)

---

1   These are very readable versions of these classics: Confucius, *The Analects of Confucius,* translated and annotated by Arthur Waley (New York: Vintage Books, 1989); and Lao Tsu, *Tao Te Ching: The Richard Wilhelm Edition* (London: Arkana, 1985).

FIGURE 21.1   Notre Dame Cathedral in Paris (before the 2019 fire).

This book, *How to Study Religion*, has led you on an investigation into the role of religion in the human experience. It is a guide for the curious. Perhaps, after completing this book, you will continue to explore the fascinating religions of the world. Stay curious!

Credits

APPENDIX: MORE INTERESTING TOPICS IN RELIGION

A. BULL WORSHIP

Cattle were important in ancient religion. In India today cows are considered sacred and many Hindus oppose killing them, even for food.

It is helpful to clarify the terminology of cattle. The word "cow" can refer to any type of cattle but more specifically it refers to an adult female, especially one that has had a calf. A heifer is a young female that has not had a calf. A calf is a baby cow. (The plural is "calves.") A bull is an adult male. A steer is a male that has been castrated. (Castration is the removal of the male testicles.) Most male cattle destined to become beef in the market are "cut," which means they are castrated because they grow bigger and because bulls are difficult to handle since they want to fight one another for dominance. The terms "bull" and "cow" are also used for many wild animals such as elephants, elk, and sea lions.

The worship of bulls has played a surprisingly large role in the history of religion, especially in ancient times. The worship of bulls and bull sacrifice have long histories. Bulls appear in ancient mythology such as the story in which Zeus becomes a bull who carries off Europa. Taurus the bull is a constellation in the zodiac. In the culture of Crete, called Minoan culture, we have artwork of gymnasts leaping off the backs of bulls. Ancient Egyptians worshipped the bull as Apis. The ancient religion of Mithraism revolved around the story of Mithras sacrificing a bull. In the Bible, when Moses came down the mountain with the Ten Commandments, he found that his people had gone astray and were worshiping a golden calf, which was probably a golden bull.

In the ancient world bulls were honored and worshiped because of their strength, their fierceness, and their sexual virility. Sexual virility is the ability to have sex often and to produce lots of offspring. It

FIGURE 22.1 Procession of the Sacred Bull of Apis.

only takes one bull to take care of an entire herd of female cows. In the ancient world, where fertility was such an important issue, virility for human males was a desired quality. The last remnant of the worship of bulls is bullfighting in Spain and Mexico, which still continues today.

In ancient times bulls were some of the most powerful things around. Today they do not seem powerful to modern people compared with autos, pickup trucks, and tractors. And bulls can be kept in a field with thin strands of barbed wire.

In the ancient world bull worship often was combined with bull sacrifice. Bull worship implies the belief that bulls have some special powers or ability. However, in the ancient world bulls were often sacrificed to honor the various gods. Since bulls were very valuable it was seen as a sign of great religious devotion to sacrifice one. In ancient Israel bulls were often offered as sacrifices to the one God of Israel, but actually worshiping a bull or a statue of a bull was considered wrong.

In general, the custom in ancient Israel was for wealthy people to sacrifice bulls, for less wealthy people to sacrifice sheep and goats, and for the poorest to offer doves as sacrificial animals. Animal sacrifice for Jews, including bull sacrifice, lasted up until 70 AD when the Temple in Jerusalem was destroyed.

One last point about animal sacrifice: typically in a sacrifice, after the animal is killed, some portion of the animal is burned as an offering. But usually most of the meat is later eaten and the animal hide is saved for later use.

B. CANON

A "canon" is an official list. (Do not get this word confused with "cannon," which is an artillery piece.) There are several common uses of the word. For example, the Hebrew Bible canon is the list of the books in the Tanakh, the Jewish Bible. The 27 books of the New Testament of the Christian Scriptures are called the New Testament Canon. Protestants and Catholics disagree over the Old Testament Canon. Protestants say there are 39 books in it; Catholics say there are 46 books.

Apocryphal books that are not in the Bible are called "deuterocanonical" books, which means they are "outside the canon."

In the Roman Catholic Church there is another use of the word canon. In the Catholic Church over the centuries certain people have been designated as "saints" because of the holy lives they led. They are put on the official list or canon of the saints. The process of becoming a saint is called "canonization." When someone becomes a saint he or she is "canonized."

C. COMFORT

This may seem a strange topic in a book on religion, but comfort is highly valued in modern society and the need for comfort has influenced religion. Many people want very comfortable lives. People live in total air conditioning, even in tropical or desert climates. Many people insist on eating tasty and desirable foods all the time regardless of the health consequences. Some people seem to want their news broadcasts in packages that are pleasant and comfortable.

We want our buildings to be comfortable. Many religious buildings have become comfortable places with cushioned seats, excellent sound systems, and climate control. Some churches even have coffee bars in the lobby, though you typically cannot take the coffee into church. (In some churches, coffee during the service might help the congregation stay awake.) But comfortable religious buildings are a new phenomenon. In the past many church buildings were not comfortable places.

If you go to Europe and see beautiful medieval cathedrals, such as Notre Dame in Paris, you will notice they are not comfortable places. Originally there were no pews. In medieval times the people stood, often for hours. The cathedrals were not heated or air conditioned—although used year-round—and there were no bathrooms!

Many church services today only last an hour because most people find a longer time to be uncomfortable. In the past, the services in many traditions were much longer.

Finally, today many believers hold to a comfortable image of a God who is loving and accepting and not demanding too much of them. This is different from many traditions in the past that depicted God in uncomfortable imagery. God was seen as judging and ready to punish sinners. God was seen as unhappy with human behavior. The goal of religious preaching was often to make people feel uncomfortable so that they would change their ways. The sermon "Sinners in the Hands of an Angry God" by Jonathan Edwards (1703–1758) is one of the most famous examples of this kind of preaching. So the question is whether the societal insistence on comfort has influenced the religious view of God.

D. CONCEPTION

The word "conception" needs to be defined for a few readers. Conception refers to the moment when a sperm and egg join together to form a new life. This usually is the result of sexual intercourse. The same thing happens for animals and humans. Due to modern science, sometimes conceptions occur without sexual intercourse. Human couples who have trouble conceiving naturally go to a doctor, who uses artificial conception. Most of the cattle we eat and that produce milk are conceived artificially. The process is called "artificial insemination." "Inseminate" means to "put a seed" into something. In this technique the male sperm of a bull is placed by a human into the female cow.

Birth control is often called "contraception" because it works against conception. "Contra" is a prefix that means "to go against."

E. ECUMENISM

Ecumenism is a movement that developed after World War II to foster understanding, toleration, and cooperation between religions. Among Christians there had been hostility, mistrust, misunderstanding, prejudice, and even hatred between different Christians. The hostility between Roman Catholics and Orthodox Christians went back to their split in 1054, called the Great Schism. "Schism" is the word for when a church splits. The hostility between Roman Catholics and Protestants, and between the various Protestant churches, went back to the 1500s in Europe. Immigrants coming to America often brought their religious intolerance with them. There also had been much hostility toward Jews by Christians, going back to the early Christian centuries.

Ecumenism is also called the ecumenical movement. Its goal is to get religious leaders to sit down and talk with one another, become more tolerant, and overcome mistrust. One goal of ecumenism is for religious people to find common ground on issues they can work on together to improve the world around them.

The movement does not require any group to give up its religion. The goal is that religious people could be true to their own religion yet have a more accepting attitude toward all religions and people from other religions. Particularly important was encouraging Christians to have better attitudes toward Jews and to get away from the stereotypes and prejudices that many people had against Jews. Much progress has been made on this front.

One result of the movement is the growth of interfaith prayer services. An "interfaith prayer service" is when people from different faiths come together to pray. The understanding about interfaith services is that the prayers offered should be more general prayers, and prayers that would separate people should be avoided. For example, an interfaith prayer service is not the place where a minister should insist that "our religion is the only way to get to heaven."

In 1948, an organization called the World Council of Churches was formed to promote understanding and cooperation among Christian churches. The Catholic Church in the 1960s held a series of meetings in Rome called Vatican II that produced 16 documents. Two of these documents called for Catholics to show tolerance and understanding toward people of other religions: *Unitatis Redintegratio* on Catholic attitudes toward other Christians, and *Nostra Aetate* on Catholic attitudes toward non-Christians.

F. ENCOURAGEMENT, EXHORTATION

To "exhort" means to encourage. An exhortation is an encouragement. In a football game, when the coach gives the locker room a pep talk the coach gives an exhortation, though nobody calls it that. (Do not confuse the word "exhortation" with the word "exorcism," which is to drive out a demon or the Devil.)

G. THE GOLDEN RULE

The Golden Rule, a very simple moral principle, states: treat others the way you want to be treated. It shows up in the ancient world about the same time in the teaching of Confucius and the Buddha. Confucius said, "Never impose on others what you would not choose for yourself." Buddha said, "Hurt not others in ways that you yourself would find hurtful."

It also shows up in the Hebrew Scriptures/Old Testament: "You shall not take vengeance or bear a grudge against your kinsfolk. Love your neighbor as yourself: I am the LORD." (Leviticus 19:18.)

The best-known version comes from Jesus: "Do to others what you want them to do to you." (Matthew 7:12. See also Luke 6:31.) A common English phrasing is, "Do unto others as you would have them do unto you." Some people make the distinction between the Golden Rule: treat others the way you want to be treated; and the Silver Rule: do not treat others the way you would not want to be treated. What do you think about the Golden Rule?

Later, the philosopher Immanuel Kant (1724–1804) would replace the Golden Rule with the moral concept of "universalizing the principle." This means that to act ethically one must "act in such a way that one's behaviors could become a universal rule." A typical thief might believe that it is acceptable for him to steal, but it is not acceptable for someone to steal from him. The thief is not willing to universalize his principle. The thief is not acting ethically. On the other hand, many people believe it is ethical to drive safely and follow traffic laws. They also want others to drive safely and follow traffic laws. Such people are willing to universalize the principle that all people should drive safely and follow traffic laws.

H. IMAGINATION

Imagination is very important in religion yet it is rarely mentioned. Reading or listening to stories such as Abraham taking Isaac up the mountain, Moses before the burning bush, Arjuna being taught by Lord Krishna, Siddhartha seeing the four sights, Jesus in the boat with his disciples, or Muhammad fleeing Mecca requires imagination. Religious stories come alive in the imagination. Heaven and hell are visualized in the imagination as no one has actual photographs of either place. Most religious artwork depends upon imagination. No one knows what Jesus or the Buddha looked like.

I. INCENSE

"What's with that smelly stuff in church?"

Incense is made up of plant materials including resin. (Resin is dried plant sap.) The plant materials are often ground up as powders, then bound together with oils, and sometimes shaped into sticks. Incense is used in many traditions, usually as a sign of offering one's prayers: the smoke of the incense rises to heaven just as prayer rises to heaven.

FIGURE 22.2 Burning incense sticks

For many modern people incense is hard to understand. Many people today live in very clean societies with clean air, an environment in which most people bathe, wear clean clothes, and use deodorant. The modern world has great plumbing and there are no livestock around. In many places throughout the world, strict environmental laws have eliminated air pollution.

Now imagine more primitive times when people did not bathe and did not use deodorant. Imagine a time where everyone's cook fire and any sort of forge or blacksmith shop filled the air with smoke. Imagine a time where horses, cows, pigs, and chickens were everywhere and there was no plumbing. Everything smelled pretty awful! (If you ever visit a Third World country you may discover a whole host of unfamiliar smells.) In such a smelly world incense was a relief. It was a good smell. But it had to be powerful to overcome all the competing smells.

J. LEGALISM

Another word a student of religion should know—but should use cautiously—is the word "legalism." This is not a factual category, but rather a judgment word. Legalism is an over-insistence on strictly following laws that often ignore the original intent of the law. Legalism, as with any judgment, depends on whom you ask.

There are some people who see the Orthodox Jewish dedication to the Jewish laws as legalism. For example, Orthodox Jews often will not work, shop, or drive cars on Saturdays (called the Sabbath). They can only eat fish if it has fins and scales. So they will not eat shrimp, or lobster, or even catfish. To some people outside the Orthodox Jewish tradition this seems like legalism.

But Orthodox Jews do not see it that way. They see the law as God's gift, and following the law as a sign of their love for God. Also, in following the law they would rather make the mistake of being too careful, rather than not being careful enough.

Some older Roman Catholics see legalism as part of their history. For example, into the 1960s Catholics were not supposed to eat meat on Fridays. A good Catholic might feel guilty even if he or she forgot it was Friday and had a hamburger for lunch.

K. MYSTICISM

"Mysticism" is an important word in studying religion, but it is not an easy word to define since many things are called "mysticism" and what happens in "mystical experiences" is often very hard to describe. Mysticism is an important part of monotheistic religions.

For monotheists, mysticism is a broad term for any attempt to directly experience God. Many people regularly go to religious services and are devout believers yet do not have powerful religious emotional experiences. They do not have the experience of an encounter with God. They do not experience mysticism. In mysticism, "mystics" want to directly experience God. All monotheistic traditions have mystics.

Two famous Roman Catholic mystics are Saint Francis of Assisi (1181–1226) and Saint Teresa of Ávila (1515–1582). In Islam, Al-Ghazali (1058–1111) was a famous mystic. Also, in Islam there are small groups called Sufi Muslims who spend their lives devoted to prayer and use dance as part of their mystical experience. (Examples of Sufi dance, called a dervish, can be found on YouTube.) Judaism has a mystical tradition called the Kabbalah. Mysticism is also an important part of the Hasidic Jewish tradition and the Sikh tradition.

Mysticism is also a part of the major Eastern religions: Hinduism, Jainism, Buddhism, and Taoism. There are many forms of mysticism between these religions and even within the various religions. For example, there are many forms of mysticism in Buddhism. Attempting to sort out and explain the many forms of mysticism in the Eastern traditions is beyond the scope of this book.

Also, the terms "mysticism" and "mystical experience" are used to describe elements of Native American traditions, African tribal traditions, other traditional religions, and New Age Religion.

L. 'OPIUM OF THE MASSES'

FIGURE 22.3   Karl Marx

Karl Marx (1818–1883) was an economic philosopher. He was also an atheist. He saw great injustices around him in the capitalist world where a few people at the top got immensely wealthy while all the workers remained in great poverty. Although the workers created the good things that created the wealth, only the owners of the factories benefited. In that unjust situation Marx saw religion as blessing the whole social structure and never questioning it.

Marx saw religion as telling the working class to hold on for a future in heaven and not try to change the conditions around them. Marx saw religion is being like opium for the many working people. Opium was used as a pain killer. Marx saw religion as dulling the pain of the working class so they could accept the unjust conditions and not fight for change. He called religion the "opium of the masses." Marx also saw religion as a man-made creation that promised happiness in the afterlife, distracting workers from seeking happiness in this life.

M. PENTECOSTALISM

According to Christian tradition, 40 days after Jesus rose from the dead he ascended into heaven. The New Testament's Acts of the Apostles describes what happened next to the followers of Jesus:

> When the time for Pentecost was fulfilled, they were all in one place together. And suddenly there came from the sky a noise like a strong driving wind, and it filled the entire house in which they were. Then there appeared to them tongues as of fire, which parted and came to rest on each one of them. And they were all filled with the Holy Spirit and began to speak in different tongues, as the Spirit enabled them to proclaim. (Acts 2: 1–4.)

Most Christians see "speaking in tongues" as a miracle of the early church or as a symbol that the early Christians were to preach the gospel to all nations. However, some Christians believe that speaking in tongues is an ordinary Christian experience that should be repeated in the present. These Christians call themselves "Pentecostals" because the story described in the Bible took place on the Jewish Pentecost.

Speaking in tongues—also called glossolalia—is not speaking an actual language. The sounds are not actual words and they have no language structure. People who speak in tongues often describe it as a powerful religious experience.

Some Pentecostal groups have the word "Pentecostal" in their title such as the United Pentecostal Church. Other churches that speak in tongues include the Assembly of God churches and the Church of God in Christ, also known as the COGIC church. Sometimes those interested in the Pentecostal experience call themselves Charismatic Christians.

Services at Pentecostal churches often include prophecy and prayers for healing. These are called the "Gifts of the Holy Spirit." Pentecostal services can be very lively with people praying aloud, waving their hands, and jumping up and down. Sometimes people are so overwhelmed by their religious experience that they fall to the floor. This is called being "slain in the spirit." This practice has led to Pentecostals being called "holy rollers" (for being seen as rolling on the floor).

Should you get a chance to visit a Pentecostal-style church you may find it a very interesting experience. It might be helpful to go with someone who is a member to explain what is going on. You can also see examples of speaking in tongues on YouTube. But you have to choose carefully among the videos; some videos are posted by those who do not believe in speaking in tongues.

N. SCIENTOLOGY

Scientology is based on the teachings of L. Ron Hubbard (1911–1986) as developed in his book *Dianetics: The Modern Science of Mental Health*. (Scientology is often confused with the Christian Science movement, but they are very different. Christian Science is described in Chapter 10.) The Church of Scientology was organized in the 1950s. Actors Tom Cruise and John Travolta are prominent members. The Wikipedia articles on Scientology explain the concepts of Scientology and describe the many controversies surrounding it.

O. SNAKE HANDLERS

There is a small and unusual group of Christians known as "snake handlers." They exist in several small independent churches, mostly in the Appalachian region. They often follow typical Pentecostal practices such as speaking in tongues, but they go further.

FIGURE 22.4 Handling of serpents.

Inspired by a verse in the Gospel of Mark, "They will pick up serpents, and if they drink any deadly thing, it will not harm them" (Mark 16:18), this group handles poisonous snakes during its church services. Most Christians ignore this passage, but not these churches. They see snake handling as a witness of their faith and a way to demonstrate their trust in God. From time to time snake handlers get bit, sometimes they die. (A bite from a snake will not always kill you. It depends on what kind of snake bites you, how much venom is injected, and your overall health.)

The vast majority of Christians and the vast majority of Pentecostals see the practice of handling snakes as wrong and not consistent with the true spirit of the gospels. If you are interested in exploring this topic there are several videos on YouTube. But keep in mind the general advice: "Do not try this at home!"

P. SYNCRETISM

Syncretism is a mixing of different traditions. Syncretism occurs when a religion picks up elements of other religions or elements from other cultures. It is common in religious history and is common today. Sometimes the effects are minor, sometimes more dramatic. For example, when Buddhism came to the Kingdom of Tibet in the Himalayas it mixed with the local polytheistic religion. The mixing of these traditions produced the unique form of Tibetan Buddhism.

Sometimes the effects of syncretism are more subtle. Just visit a Christian church preaching about Jesus. Jesus spoke the ancient language of Aramaic. Very likely he wore a beard and some sort of tunic. The music of his time would have been ancient Mediterranean music. Jesus called himself "The Good Shepherd," an image that made sense since he lived in a world of sheep and goats and Jesus mentioned sheep and goats in his teachings.

Today, in many Christian churches the minister is beardless and wears a modern business suit. He preaches in English and is projected on a video screen. The music is American-style pop. And church members would have to make a special trip to a petting zoo to see live sheep and goats. Thus, the 2,000-year-old teaching of Jesus is preached in a very modern setting.

According to some people, Messianic Judaism is another example of syncretism. Christians believe that Jesus is the Messiah and that he is the Son of God. Jews typically reject these Christian claims about Jesus. In the eyes of many Jews, if a Jew accepts Christian beliefs then that person is no longer a Jew in the religious sense. There is a small group of Messianic Jews, however, who do identify themselves as Jews and yet embrace the beliefs that Jesus is the Messiah and the Son of God.

What examples can you find of the mixing of traditions in religion?

Q. VOCATION

The word "vocation" comes from the Latin word *vocare*, which means "to call." The word can be used in two ways. The simplest way is when one's job choice is called a vocation, especially if one believes a particular job or occupation is the right choice for oneself.

But the word can also be used for the belief that one receives an actual calling from God to choose a specific career and lifestyle. In the Roman Catholic Church the choice to become a priest, monk, or brother and live a celibate life is seen as a vocation. Becoming a priest includes a long process of discernment to ensure that the call is an authentic one. The call to become a religious sister is also called a vocation. For Catholics, marriage is also seen as a vocation.

R. ZOROASTRIANISM[1]

An ancient religion that is very important is Zoroastrianism, although most people do not know about it. There are fewer than 200,000 Zoroastrians in the world, with the largest number in India. The religion developed in ancient Persia, which today is Iran. The religion of Islam began in the 600s and quickly swept over Persia. Over the ensuing centuries Zoroastrianism would be overwhelmed. Only a few Zoroastrians live in Iran.

Zoroastrianism, however, is very important for its influence on Judaism, Christianity, and Islam, and for many cultural ideas about religion. In Zoroastrianism a number of important religious concepts were worked out that many religions today take for granted: angels, demons, heaven, hell, judgment of the dead, resurrection of the dead, and a final battle in which evil will be destroyed.

These elements worked their way into the Jewish world and then the Christian world, and finally the Islamic world. In fact, the Christian gospels reflect the influence of Zoroastrian ideas and the debate in the Jewish world over whether to accept these ideas. At the time of Jesus the Jewish Pharisees were open to these new ideas, including resurrection of the dead. The Jewish Sadducees were traditionalists and were not open to new ideas. They held to the older idea that all dead people went to the underworld called Sheol. In the New Testament's Acts of the Apostles, Paul is on trial before the Jewish Council, the Sanhedrin. He starts an argument between the Sadducees and Pharisees on the council by claiming that he believes in the resurrection of the dead.

---

1 For more background on Zoroastrianism, see Fisher, *Living Religions* (9th ed.), "Special Section: Zoroastrianism."

The Zoroastrian religion was founded by Zoroaster, also known a Zarathustra, who lived sometime between 1700 and 500 BC. Zoroastrians believe in a supreme being, Ahura Mazda. They also believe in a spirit of evil named Angra Mainyu or Ahriman. The sacred texts of Zoroastrianism are called the Avesta. Sometimes the Zoroastrianism religion is labeled as "dualism" since it sees two divine beings, a good one and a bad one, struggling against each other.

Credits

- Fig. 22.1: Source: https://commons.wikimedia.org/wiki/File:Bridgman_F_The_Procession_of_the_Sacred_Bull_Anubis.jpg.
- Fig. 22.2: Copyright © Davis Wilmot (CC BY-SA 2.0) at https://commons.wikimedia.org/wiki/File:Burning_incense_sticks_at_Wutai_Shan.jpg.
- Fig. 22.3: Source: https://commons.wikimedia.org/wiki/File:Karl_Marx.jpg.
- Fig. 22.4: Source: https://commons.wikimedia.org/wiki/File:Handling_of_serpents,_a_part_of_the_ceremony_at_the_Pentecostal_Church_of_God._This_coal_camp_offers_none_of_the..._-_NARA_-_541340.jpg.

HOW TO STUDY RELIGION: BIBLIOGRAPHY

Adair, James R. 2007. *Introducing Christianity*. New York: Routledge.

Cross, F. L., and E. A. Livingstone, eds. 1984. *Oxford Dictionary of the Christian Church*. Oxford: Oxford University Press.

Cunningham, Lawrence S., and John J. Reich. 2006. *Culture and Values: A Survey of the Humanities*. Alternate Volume, 6th ed. Belmont, CA: Thompson Wadsworth.

Kohn, Livia. 2008. *Introducing Daoism*. New York: Routledge.

Lawrence S. Cunningham, and John Kelsay. 2010. *The Sacred Quest: An Invitation to the Study of Religion*. Boston: Prentice Hall.

Fisher, Mary Pat. 2005. *Living Religions*. 6th ed. Upper Saddle River, NJ: Prentice-Hall.

Frankl, Viktor E. 2006. *Man's Search for Meaning*. Forward by Harold S. Kushner. Boston: Beacon Press.

Hamilton, Edith. *Mythology*. 1969. New York: Bay Back Books/Little, Brown and Co.

Mathews, Warren. 2008. *World Religions*. 6th ed. Belmont, CA: Wadsworth Publishing.

Mueller, J. J. ed. 2011. *Theological Foundation: Concepts and Methods for Understanding Christian Faith*. Winona, MN: Anselm Academic.

Poceski, Mario. 2009. *Introducing Chinese Religion*. New York: Routledge.

Prebish, Charles S., and Damian Keown. 2009. *Introducing Buddhism*. New York: Routledge.

Prince, Jennifer R. 2014. *The Handy Bible Answer Book*. Canton, MI: Visible Ink Press.

Renard, John. 2015. *The Handy Islam Answer Book*. Canton, MI: Visible Ink Press.

_____. 2012. *The Handy Religion Answer Book*, 2nd Ed. Canton, MI: Visible Ink Press.

_____. 1999. *Responses to 101 Questions on Hinduism*. Mahwah, NJ: Paulist Press.

Rodrigues, Hillary P. 2016. *Introducing Hinduism*. 2nd ed. New York: Routledge.

Segal, Eliezer. 2008. *Introducing Judaism*. New York: Routledge.

Shepard, William E. 2014. *Introducing Islam*. New York: Routledge.

Smith, Huston. 2009. *The World's Religions.* Anniversary Edition. New York: HarperOne.

Westrheim, Margo. 1999. *Celebrate! A Look at Calendars and the Ways We Celebrate*. Oxford: One World.

Werner, Stephen. 2018. *The Handy Christianity Answer Book*. Canton, MI: Visible Ink Press.

Wylen, Stephen M. 2014. *Settings of Silver: An Introduction to Judaism*. Mahwah, NJ: Paulist Press.

INDEX

CPSIA information can be obtained
at www.ICGtesting.com
Printed in the USA
LVHW100911151220
674161LV00003B/7